In a time when teachers are feeling more constrained than ever, this book serves as a path forward to breaking free from the biases and social norms that hold us back. Ebarvia has created a comprehensive tool kit that marries necessary theory to practical classroom application, which is nothing short of amazing and will be one of the most frequently pulled books from your professional library.

—Susan G. Barber
Teacher, Author, and Consultant
MuchAdoAboutTeaching.com

Get Free: Antibias Literacy Instruction for Stronger Readers, Writers, and Thinkers hits that beautiful sweet spot between inspirational and practical. Through stories, real examples of student work, and artfully synthesized theory, this book provides reflections, tools, and tangible strategies for educators who seek to help us all get free.

—Sarah-SoonLing Blackburn
Educator, Author, Speaker

What does it mean to be free? And how can we, as educators, create conditions for students to answer that for themselves? Ebarvia asks the most important questions of the moment and guides readers on a journey to help them answer the questions for themselves. With every word, it is clear Ebarvia has a deep belief in educators to rise to the occasion and support students to become the critical changemakers we need for a more just society.

—Val Brown
Educator Activist and Organizer

Ebarvia has written for us a guide for how to use education the right way: how to invite students into freedom through literacy and classwork. This is genius and I'm so excited for it to be out in the world.

—Lorena Germán
Author of *Textured Teaching: A Framework for a Culturally Sustaining Practice*
Co-Founder of #DisruptTexts

Get Free is a powerful resource for teachers striving to improve literacy instruction while creating a just and inclusive classroom. It blends academic research with real-world experiences to provide practical strategies for nurturing stronger readers. The book shows teachers how to create classrooms that embrace every student's unique identities and experiences, making it a must-have for transformative educators.

—Britt Hawthorne
New York Times bestselling author
Raising Antiracist Children: A Practical Parenting Guide

Ebarvia's book *Get Free: Antibias Literacy Instruction for Stronger Readers* highlights the often overlooked and necessary aspects of the literacy classroom that truly centers students. Supporting educators to create bold, honest, and brave spaces for ALL students, this book is the one I'll be giving to all the educators I know. Freedom is the goal and Ebarvia will help us to get there!

—Tiffany Jewell
New York Times bestselling author
This Book Is Anti-Racist

This is the book I needed my teachers to have when I was a student, the book I needed as a teacher, and the book I need now as a teacher-educator. It is a gift and offering for educators interested in equity and social justice—one that centers the humanity of everyone on this journey.

—Jung Kim
Professor of Literacy, Co-Department
Chair of Education, Lewis University

This beautifully crafted, research based, practically minded book will help you to solve a whole host of problems in your classroom. Students not finding the work of literacy class relevant? This book will help. Are you only able to reach a group of students while somehow others don't click into your teaching? This book will help. Concerned (or not sure) about the ways in which power and privilege affect your school community? This book will help. By uncovering the subtle biases we hold that have dramatic effects on students, outlining ways to build real community in our classrooms, and then setting the table for some deep, vibrant teaching that develops both antibiased schools and relevant reading, writing, and discourse work, Ebarvia masterfully plots a journey we can and must all begin—today.

—Kate Roberts
Author and Consultant

What a gift Tricia Ebarvia has given us in the form of this brilliant book. Weaving together thoughtful scholarship and practical pedagogical tools, Ebarvia has constructed a must-read for educators. I can't wait to share this book broadly with my networks!

—Karen Scher
English Language Arts Lead, Facing History and Ourselves

Get Free: Antibias Literacy Instruction for Stronger Readers, Writers, and Thinkers guides literacy educators through the self-work required to effectively teach against historical and current inequities within literacy education. By providing practical examples and relevant lesson plans, the book empowers the reader to create inclusive, equitable, and transformative literacy learning experiences for students—*and teachers*.

—Yolanda Sealey-Ruiz
Professor of English Education, Teachers College,
Columbia University
Co-Author of *Advancing Racial Literacies in Teacher Education:
Activism for Equity in Digital Spaces*

Get Free is a must-read for every teacher of literacy. In the book, Ebarvia reminds us that our personal identities cannot be separated from the work we do as teachers and that unpacking our experiences and biases is critical. Then she serves as mentor and guide on a journey to help us understand what it can look like in a classroom to be free as a teacher and learner.

—Franki Sibberson
Literacy educator, Past President of the
National Council of Teachers of English (NCTE)
Co-Author of *Still Learning to Read: Teaching Students in Grades 3–6*

Built on decades of teaching and leading, *Get Free* provides key activities and concrete examples for how to create and sustain an antibias practice of literacy. These chapters, strategies, and key questions give educators the tools to see how identity shows up in our teaching and learning, and how to support deep learning to get free through literacy.

—Liza A. Talusan
Author, *The Identity-Conscious Educator:
Building Habits and Skills for a More Inclusive School*

For Brian, Matthew, Toby, and Colin —
you make me a better human. I love you.

Get Free

Antibias Literacy Instruction for Stronger Readers, Writers, and Thinkers

Tricia Ebarvia

Foreword by

Sonja Cherry-Paul, Aeriale Johnson,
Anna Osborn, Kimberly N. Parker, and Tiana Silvas

CORWIN Literacy

FOR INFORMATION:

Corwin

A SAGE Company

2455 Teller Road

Thousand Oaks, California 91320

(800) 233-9936

www.corwin.com

SAGE Publications Ltd.

1 Oliver's Yard

55 City Road

London EC1Y 1SP

United Kingdom

SAGE Publications India Pvt. Ltd.

Unit No 323-333, Third Floor, F-Block

International Trade Tower Nehru Place

New Delhi 110 019

India

SAGE Publications Asia-Pacific Pte. Ltd.

18 Cross Street #10-10/11/12

China Square Central

Singapore 048423

Vice President and
  Editorial Director: Monica Eckman

Executive Editor: Tori Mello Bachman

Content Development Editor: Sharon Wu

Production Editor: Amy Schroller

Copy Editor: Lynne Curry

Typesetter: C&M Digitals (P) Ltd.

Proofreader: Dennis Webb

Indexer: Integra

Graphic Designer: Scott Van Atta

Marketing Manager: Margaret O'Connor

Printed in the United States of America

Library of Congress Cataloging-in-Publication Data

Names: Ebarvia, Tricia, author.

Title: Get free : anti-bias literacy instruction for stronger readers, writers, and thinkers / Tricia Ebarvia; foreword by Sonja Cherry-Paul, Aeriale Johnson, Anna Osborn, Kimberly N. Parker, and Tiana Silvas.

Description: Thousand Oaks, California : Corwin, 2024. | Series: Corwin literacy | Includes bibliographical references and index.

Identifiers: LCCN 2023028299 | ISBN 9781071918364 (paperback) | ISBN 9781071925393 (epub) | ISBN 9781071925409 (epub) | ISBN 9781071925416 (pdf)

Subjects: LCSH: Language arts (Secondary) | Reflective learning. | Critical thinking—Study and teaching (Secondary) | Anti-racism—Study and teaching (Secondary)

Classification: LCC LB1631 .E327 2024 | DDC 428.0071/2—dc23/eng/20230721
LC record available at https://lccn.loc.gov/2023028299

This book is printed on acid-free paper.

23 24 25 26 27 10 9 8 7 6 5 4 3 2 1

CONTENTS

Visit the companion website at
http://www.resources.corwin.com/GetFree
for downloadable resources.

A NOTE ON ARTWORK

Writing is putting one word after another to make meaning—but the words on these pages are made more meaningful by the beautiful artwork of Gian Wong.

When I began to imagine how *Get Free* might look and feel in readers' hands, I knew I wanted the visual elements to reflect who I am just as much as my words did. I first encountered Gian's work on Instagram and then on his website (gianwong.com). While I loved the creative ways he brought colors and shapes together, it was the way he integrated Filipino culture throughout his art that resonated with me. Growing up, I didn't always feel like school was a place where I could share my Filipino heritage. To have that part of my identity reflected in these pages *means* something, everything.

Philippine history may be marked by colonization, but it is also one that has inspired resilience and liberation. On the cover, the ribbon element bearing the subtitle symbolizes freedom, the "ability to let loose and be liberated" (Wong) as does the bursting, contrasting typography of the title. Indeed, every element on the cover is a nod to Filipino culture: the red, blue, and yellow colors of the Philippine flag; three stars representing the three major island regions of Luzon, Visayas, and Mindanao; the waves evoking Philippine beaches; the modern rendering of the sampaguita, national flower of the Philippines; and, of course, Maya birds, indigenous birds to the Philippines, breaking free in flight.

Likewise, interwoven throughout the book are patterns and imagery inspired by traditional ethnic textiles and Filipino culture, and the central theme of each chapter is mirrored in Gian's corresponding artwork. I am so grateful for Gian's time, talents, and understanding. May the words and images that come together in these pages remind us of the beauty that is possible whenever we come together in community.

FOREWORD

The Sampaguita, the national flower of the Philippines: symbolizes how, like a flower, we can be abundant and bloom through others

INTRODUCTION

The Philippine sun ("araw"): symbolizes the spark and light in each individual that makes them unique

CHAPTER 1: OURSELVES

A scene of the Mayon Volcano: symbolizes reflection and the self through a reflected image of the famous volcano

CHAPTER 2: COMMUNITY

The Maya bird ("mayang pula"), a common bird in the Philippines: symbolizes how a bird takes that first step to bravery that inspires others to take action

CHAPTER 3: IDENTITY

The Philippine Mango ("mangga"): symbolizes how we can open our different sides to people, similar to a mango having different sides that reveal what's inside

CHAPTER 4: CONVERSATION

Coconut trees: symbolizes different trees bent as if they are talking to one another

CHAPTER 5: READING

Philippine kalesa; symbolizes how literature transports and opens us up to different places, ideas, and perspectives

CHAPTER 6: PERSPECTIVES

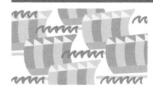

Vinta boats, traditional outrigger boat from Mindanao: symbolizes how we can all be in different boats with different ideas

EPILOGUE

The Chocolate Hills, a geological formation in Bohol: symbolizes multiple small things can make up a whole wonder, like the Chocolate Hills

ACKNOWLEDGMENTS

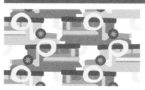

A Philippine Jeepney road scene: symbolizes how everyone from different backgrounds can come together in one place, like in a Jeepney ride

FOREWORD

By Sonja Cherry-Paul, Aeriale Johnson, Anna Osborn,
Kimberly N. Parker, and Tiana Silvas

The great storyteller Virginia Hamilton described herself as a writer of "liberation literature" which widens readers and their worlds, making it possible for them to see beyond their circumstances. In *Get Free,* Tricia extends a vision of educational liberation that is grounded in scholarship and rooted in love, challenging and changing the world before her by making it possible for educators to liberate themselves and their students.

The world is on fire. In this moment, we're all being asked to think about what we value, which struggles we are willing to lend our voices, time, and energy to, and where we can find community to keep going. This was not unlike when we first met Tricia. We were experienced educators working in different schools across the country, trying to figure out how to uphold what we knew was excellent literacy instruction for often the most marginalized children, how to navigate our complex practitioner identities, and, perhaps most importantly, how to find others who would walk beside us, and even carry us, on the days when we were exhausted, disillusioned, and troubled.

Tricia has guided us forward, putting into action the words of Toni Morrison: "The function of freedom is to free someone else."

Tricia has taught us that liberation is a complex mixture of reflection and action, of internal work and communal work. *Get Free* provides research and strategies that teachers can explore on their own and in their communities with students and colleagues. And in inviting us into the work she has done with her students, Tricia challenges us to be a part of a larger, global community of educators doing the work necessary to create the liberatory world we want and need.

From Tricia, we have learned to (re)examine not only the curriculum, but our instructional practices. She has taught us that a willingness to ask *why* opens up possibilities for identifying inequities, confronting them, and radically (re)imagining how things can be otherwise. We've learned to put these reimaginings into action and to hold ourselves accountable for evaluating the effectiveness of our work. We accomplish this by building relationships with children where power dynamics are fluid, by humbling ourselves to listen, being accountable for our mistakes, and addressing harm. We achieve this by working in community with one another—even and especially during times of tension.

To be in community with Tricia is to be deeply loved, continuously challenged, and called into a lifetime of deliberate action.

Tricia calls us to reckon with ourselves, asking us to interrogate our role in the perpetuation of injustice. She does not ask us to do it alone, though. Every time she challenges us to experience discomfort, Tricia invites us into her own journey with the vulnerability getting free requires of us. Most importantly, Tricia demands we do this work in community; otherwise, we cannot hope to dismantle broader systems of inequity.

As we have walked hand-in-hand with her toward freedom for all of us over the years, Tricia has often quoted Gwendolyn Brooks from her poem, "Paul Robeson," as her aspirations for our relationship as colleagues and sister friends:

> that we are each other's
>
> harvest:
>
> We are each other's
>
> business:
>
> We are each other's
>
> magnitude and bond.

Certainly, we are responsible for each other and for our world. *Get Free* is an urgent opportunity for us to realize liberatory educational spaces where all children thrive. May we accept this generous invitation that Tricia has provided and do the work for justice and liberation.

ABOUT THE AUTHOR

Tricia Ebarvia is a lifelong educator, author, speaker, and literacy consultant. She is an expert in curriculum design, culturally responsive and sustaining pedagogy, and social justice education, as well as a teacher, consultant, and member of the National Writing Project. For more than two decades, Tricia taught high school English, including courses in American literature, world literature, and Advanced Placement English. In addition to teaching, Tricia designed and facilitated racial literacy leadership programs for students as well as district-wide equity initiatives for faculty and staff. Since 2021, Tricia has served as the director of Diversity, Equity, and Inclusion at a Pre-K to 8 independent Quaker school in Philadelphia, where she continues to teach, coach teachers, and partners with families to support positive identity development and academic growth of students.

Tricia's deep belief in education as a vehicle for social change and justice undergirds and informs all her practice. Tricia is a cofounder of #DisruptTexts, an antibias, anti-racist effort to advocate for equitable and diverse language arts curricula and pedagogy. She is the codirector of the Institute for Racial Equity in Literacy, a professional development institute attended by hundreds of educators worldwide. Tricia is also the coeditor of the blog series, 31DaysIBPOC, which amplifies the voices and experiences of educators of color each May.

Tricia is the recipient of several awards, including a National Education Association Leadership Grant, the 2021 Divergent Award for Excellence in Literacy Advocacy from the Initiative for Literacy in a Digital Age, the Pennsylvania High School Teacher of Excellence Award from the National Council of Teachers of English. Tricia has also been recognized as an Outstanding Asian Pacific American Educator by former Pennsylvania Governor Tom Wolf. Tricia's work has been published and featured in *The New York Times*, *Literacy Today*, *Education Update*, *The Council Chronicle*, *Research in the Teaching of English*, *Education Week*, and in the *Journal of Adolescent & Adult Literacy*.

A NOTE ON CONTEXT
Who You Are Is Where You Are

Context matters.

Who we are is where we are. Place matters. The land matters.

I was reminded of this when I attended the 2020 Wisconsin State Reading Association's annual conference. Monique Gray Smith, an Indigenous author of mixed Cree, Lakota, and Scottish descent, called on teachers to know whose land they stand on, to express gratitude, and to develop a literacy of the land and water.

For most of my life, I have lived on Lenapehoking, the occupied and ancestral lands of the Lenni Lenape Nation, who have been caretakers of this land for more than ten thousand years. I honor and thank them for their stewardship: past, present, and future.

But acknowledgment is not enough.

As David Truer, an Ojibwe author and historian, writes, "That Native American cultures are imperiled is important and not just to Indians. It is important to everyone, or should be. When we lose cultures, we lose American plurality—the productive and lovely discomfort that true difference brings." As an educator, I am committed to making sure the truths of Native and Indigenous peoples and nations are affirmed, that stories are taught responsibly and in solidarity with Native and Indigenous scholars and communities.

And I call on readers of this book—and all educators—to join me in doing the same.

INTRODUCTION

GET FREE...
GET FREE...
GET FREE...

A liberatory consciousness requires every individual to not only notice what is going on in the world around her or him, but to think about it and theorize about it—that is, to get information and develop his or her own explanation for what is happening, why it is happening, and what needs to be done about it.

—Barbara Love

To the extent that people reflect upon their lives and become more conscious of themselves as actors in the world, conscious, too, of the vast range of alternatives that can be imagined and expressed in any given situation, capable of joining in community and asserting themselves as subjects in history, constructors of the human world, they recreate themselves as free human beings.

—William Ayers

In high school, I read Charlotte Brontë's *Jane Eyre*—and I *loved* it. More specifically, I loved the romance between the bookish, humble Jane and the dashing, inscrutable Rochester. If social media was around when I first read the novel, I would have used #janechester in all my Tweets and Instas.

What I loved about *Jane Eyre* so much the first time I read it was that it was deeply *comforting*. Like Jane, I was bookish and quiet and insecure, and I could see myself reflected in Jane's character. And since I'm confessing things, I'll also admit that all of my first romantic crushes were reflections of Rochester—boys who were aloof, mysterious, and yes, "bad boys."

But when I reread *Jane Eyre* in college, my reaction was different.

I was taking a course on "Literary History." Instead of reading texts from various literary movements throughout time, my professor organized the course around key texts and counternarratives that "took issue" with them. For example, we read *The Heart of Darkness* and then analyzed *Apocalypse Now*. We read *Romeo and Juliet* and then studied *Shakespeare in Love*. And yes, we studied *Jane Eyre* and then a book that would forever change my feelings toward #janechester— *Wide Sargasso Sea* by Jean Rhys.

ENGAGING A COUNTERNARRATIVE

Jean Rhys's novel reimagines the character of Rochester in this prequel to *Jane Eyre*. Why was Rochester so mysterious and melancholy? Who was he before he met Jane? Rhys's answer is that as "romantic" as Rochester seemed to be in *Jane Eyre*, that he was likely not the hero Brontë—and readers like me—imagined him to be. Instead, he was a British colonizer who would ultimately imprison his first wife, a Creole heiress from Jamaica, in the attic of his English manor.

After reading *Wide Sargasso Sea*, I could no longer take comfort in the false belief that being like Jane would result in a happy ending with my own Rochester. In my first readings, I willfully ignored the fact that Rochester already had a wife, a wife that he had locked up in the attic of an English manor and treated like a prisoner, even an animal. Bertha, the name used in *Jane Eyre* for Rochester's wife (Rhys gives her the name Antoinette in *Wide Sargasso Sea*), was simply an obstacle to be overcome so that Jane could get her happy ending. I had relegated Bertha to the role of "obstacle" and like Rochester (and Brontë herself), I did not see Bertha as a full person. In contrast, Rhys *humanizes* and *centers* Antoinette's experiences. Her character is more developed, layered, complex. Her voice is the **counternarrative** I needed.

A counternarrative is a story that stands in contrast to and challenges the values, beliefs, and an established dominant narrative. Often, counternarratives do this by focusing on the perspectives that are missing, marginalized, or actively erased from the dominant narrative.

Of course, when I reread *Jane Eyre* in college, I was a different person than I was in high school. In college, I took classes in multicultural American literature, I took Asian Studies courses, and I became an officer in an Asian American student organization. One of my mentors in college worked in the Office for Academic Multicultural Initiatives. I met Grace Lee Boggs who was a guest of honor at a naming ceremony of a student lounge in honor of Yuri Kochiyama. I learned what the word *diaspora* meant. Each of these experiences transformed me and in turn, transformed and *informed* my response to the books I read, including the ones I had once loved, like *Jane*.

To attribute the change in my reaction to *Jane* to maturity, however, is only half the story. Yes, I was a different person, but the more important question was not how I had changed—*but who was I before?*

As I look back, I realize that my initial response to *Jane Eyre* was tied to my upbringing. Jane was headstrong and practical, much like my Filipina immigrant mother, and despite the expected mother-and-teenage-daughter conflicts we often endured, I admired my mother's strength (still do). The ending of the novel, in which Jane gets her man, also fit neatly and securely in the traditional view of marriage and success that my Catholic and Filipino family subscribed to. The novel, then, affirmed many of the beliefs and ideals I'd grown up with.

As readers of Brontë know, a common interpretation of Jane's character is that she represents the dueling tensions between reason and passion—and resolving that tension with independence and grace and dignity was important and necessary. Putting reason above passion—otherwise known as "being practical"—was a core value for my first-generation immigrant parents, and yes, for me.

So the thought never occurred to me to think about the novel from anyone else's point of view, especially that of Bertha's/Antoinette's/the "other."

I was too invested in only seeing her through my own.

The more years that I spend in the classroom and the more teachers that I meet, the more I become convinced that my experience is not unique. As English teachers, we all have complicated relationships with texts. But we also have a responsibility to our students to consider how our own reading of a text might be problematic, maybe even harmful. Consider your own relationship with texts you read and loved. How might you open yourself up to seeing this text from another perspective?

WHO IS THE *I* WHO READS?

We know that reading is a complex and complicated process: there's so much that happens from the moment our eyes see marks on a page to the ideas and questions that take shape in our minds. And much research exists on these cognitive processes of reading. But this book isn't about that. This book is about examining—indeed, interrogating—the *I* who reads.

Who was the I who read *Jane Eyre* for the first time? When I think back to my experience reading *Jane*—and countless other texts—I was engaged in my reading, but I never stopped to think about *why* a particular text resonated with me.

Because human beings are social animals, **we cannot separate who we are from who we were socialized to be.** And for our students, this also means who they are socialized into *becoming*. How might this affect how they read?

When we read texts—a novel, film, advertisement, conversation, or, really, anything from which we can draw meaning—we bring the sum of what makes us who we are into that reading experience. As many teachers can attest, students can respond to texts with emotional, gut-driven reactions like "I love that book!" or "I hate that book!" While these reactions might be common, we often don't ask students to interrogate these reactions to reflect on what may have shaped them. If reading is a transactional, creative experience in which a reader and text meet, as Rosenblatt (1995) observed, then **how can we help students dig deeper and ask themselves,** *why* **am I responding this way?**

On social media, in the news, and around dinner tables, our reactions to current events and social issues are often just as emotional—and as critically unexamined—as the responses students have to the books they've loved or hated. But underneath these knee-jerk reactions are complex identities informed by a range of experiences and biases. Race, gender, and class are just a few of the identities that affect how I see and react to the world—but so are my passions, interests, fears, anxieties, family life, among others. Unpacking *who is the I who reads*—discovering the ways in which our identities can both clarify and limit our responses—is thus critical to our understanding of ourselves as readers, our understanding of the texts we encounter in English class, and our understanding of the world.

Because when we are better able to understand what informs our responses—when we can better understand who we are and why—we can start to *get free.*

What does it mean to *get free?*

I believe that through intentional, critical self-reflection, we can begin to free ourselves from the ways in which our socialization causes or maintains harm to ourselves and others.

In my own journey in learning, unlearning, and relearning about the legacy of activism in our country—especially the activism of women of color, and of Black women in particular—I came across the powerful work of the Combahee River Collective, a group of Black women activists who saw "Black feminism as the logical political movement to combat the manifold and simultaneous oppressions that all women of color face" (Taylor, 2017).

Indeed, historically and currently, it has been Black women who have led the fight for justice and equity and provided the blueprint for all activist movements. When I read about the Combahee River Collective's work in *How We Get Free*, edited by Keeanga-Yamahtta Taylor, I could not stop thinking about the urgent need for all of us—especially those of us working in classrooms with students, day in and day out—to *get free*. Then, in 2019, I read a social media post by author Matthew Salesses, who is Asian American and was adopted by a White family. In his post, he shared how his White mother became defensive when he asked her to read books with people of color to his children, her grandchildren. Salesses attributed his mother's defensiveness to the racial bias she couldn't admit to herself, and he ended his post imploring his mother—and other White people—to "get free get free get free."

> *Those words—get free, get free, get free—kept pulling and tugging at me and would not let me go, especially as I interrogated my role as an educator.*

Over the years, I've asked students to define what being free means to them. Among their responses: to be able to do what you want, to be able to make your own decisions, to be who you want without others telling you what to do, to be your own person, to not have anyone or anything holding you back.

When I've asked students what holds them back from being free, their answers are expected: school, teachers, parents, sometimes themselves, sometimes their friends. But almost always, students share that what often holds them back are unspoken rules, norms, and expectations that others—and *society*—have for them. When we dig even deeper, students almost always point to the ways that they've been socialized, often unconsciously.

What would it mean to "get free" as an educator?

Although I still struggle to define and redefine what being free could look, sound, and feel like in the classroom, my working definition looks something like this:

> To *get free* means that we are no longer burdened by the unexamined biases that get in the way of seeing ourselves and others more clearly.
>
> To *get free* means moving beyond our socialization to be able to think and act as more fully independent, critical thinkers, and compassionate, empathetic human beings.
>
> To *get free* means to develop a "liberatory consciousness."

In her essay, "Developing a Liberatory Consciousness," Dr. Love (2018) reminds us that "humans are products of their socialization and follow the habits of mind and thought that have been instilled in them." Thus, Dr. Love calls for "a liberatory consciousness [which] enables humans to live 'outside' the patterns of thought and behavior learned through the socialization process that helps to perpetuate oppressive systems."

Schools are active instruments of socialization; every pedagogical choice we make as teachers advances the social norms and values of the school and larger society. Schools can actively or passively perpetuate oppressive systems (and can be such systems themselves). For example, as teachers, our curricular decisions make clear whose voices and what issues are valued enough to be worthy of study. As Alexander (2016) wrote for the *New York Times*, "The mind of an adult begins in the imagination of a child." I think about the stories I've read, stories like *Jane Eyre*, and I feel a sense of shame—shame for the way I dismissed Bertha, how I refused to see her as less than fully human, not worth my attention as I instead centered Jane and Rochester's love story.

I can't help wonder—how often are we lulled into ignoring the "other" in texts like *Jane Eyre*? How often does our socialization—and the identities that emerge from this socialization—*limit rather than expand* our understanding of the texts we read, the issues we care (or don't care) about, and the people we become? I don't want to be the type of person who can ignore someone's suffering—even if that someone is a fictional character. After all, if reading literature provides us with what Kenneth Burke called "imaginative rehearsals" (Gallagher, 2009) what exactly was I rehearsing when I read *Jane Eyre* uncritically for the first time? What—and *whose*—ways of seeing the world was I absorbing?

Of course, it's not just traditionally canonical texts like *Jane Eyre* that can lull us into ignoring the perspectives of historical marginalized groups. In 2018, Slate magazine's Represent podcast produced a brief series called "Pre-Work Watching," in which Slate writers and editors revisited some of the media they'd grown up watching and discussed how problematic much of that media was. In an episode titled, "The Unexamined Privilege of Gilmore Girls," one writer admits, "Rory Gilmore was my teen idol. That sort of horrifies me now" (Matthews & Chan, 2018). In another episode titled "Friends From India," another writer shares, "I grew up watching the show in Mumbai. I worry about the damage its gender stereotypes still do there" (Soni, 2018). Consider your own media diet and a recent or favorite television series or film you've watched: What work is that media doing to challenge or perpetuate stereotypes and other harmful thinking? How?

As a. brown (2017) reminds us in *Emergent Strategy*, "We are in an imagination battle . . . and I must engage my own imagination in order to break free."

I believe that if we can *get free* . . .

> we can look beyond the rigid confines of our experiences and examine those intersections where our socialization meets our relationships to texts, others, and ourselves.

> we can get closer to living and acting in the world outside the racist, sexist, homophobic, transphobic, classist, ableist, and other bigoted ways in which we've been socialized.

> we can challenge the norms that threaten the most vulnerable fellow members of our society and interrupt the role we play in participating in that harm.

As Dr. Love writes, many of us "want to work for social change to reduce inequity and bring about greater justice yet continue to behave in ways that preserve and perpetuate the existing system." But if we can *get free*, we can individually and collectively take steps to ensure more equitable academic and *human* outcomes for all students.

To *get free* means turning the lens on ourselves as readers, writers, thinkers, and social beings and examining all the ways in which we are *not* free, all the ways in which we are bound by what society tells us who we are, who others are, and who we are to each other. To get free means being identity-conscious, socially aware educators, guiding identity-conscious, socially aware readers and writers. To get free means engaging in active and expansive perspective-taking. I hope that this book can serve as a starting point for readers to journey toward freedom so that we may serve all our students well.

Although we can never truly be free of the biases that we hold as social beings, by examining the *who is the I who reads (and writes)*, we can surface the ways in which our biases have worked and continue to work for and against us daily. To be *anti*bias, then, is not about completely eliminating our biases—a lofty and impossible goal. As Stanford psychology professor Dr. Jennifer Eberhardt reminds us, "bias is not something we cure, it's something we manage. There's no magical moment where bias just ends and we never have to deal with it again" (Chang, 2019). Instead, being antibias—to *get free*—is to act in a way that doesn't allow those biases to have power over who we are, what and how we teach our students, and how we respond to others and the world.

THE FIERCE URGENCY OF NOW

▶ "We have also come to this hallowed spot to remind America of the fierce urgency of now. This is no time to engage in the luxury of cooling off or to take the tranquilizing drug of gradualism. Now is the time to make real the promises of democracy." —Dr. Martin Luther King, Jr.

Recent and ongoing events continue to convince me of our complicated and dynamic relationships to the texts we read in school and how we read the world. More and more, it feels like fear—as manifested through overt and systemic racism and xenophobia, along with all other forms of bigotry—has infected every part of our society and placed a stranglehold on our ability to communicate with one another honestly and responsibly. Political polarization combined with the echo-chamber effects of social media have made it almost impossible for us to hear each other. Worse, it's made it hard to hear—and understand—ourselves.

Unfortunately, schools have not done enough to address these issues. Teachers, fearing backlash, stay away from issues that "feel" too political (and yet what isn't political when it comes to schooling?). Meanwhile, our government continues to under-resource too many of our schools—a *political* decision—especially schools that serve primarily Black and Brown children (Black & Crolley, 2022). "Don't Say Gay" laws and book bans and challenges dominate school board meetings across the country (again, another political decision) (Meehan & Friedman, 2023). Students of color are suspended or expelled at disproportionately high rates, perpetuating a school-to-prison trajectory that devastates lives and communities (Chen, 2022). School curricula too often fail to reflect the diverse, rich, and complex experiences of marginalized communities (Armstrong, 2021), and this lack of "mirrors and windows" (Bishop, 1990) prevents all students from developing an understanding and empathy of others different from themselves.

Furthermore, as I write this, families and children in Flint, Michigan, a predominantly Black American community, continue their fight for clean drinking water after decades of neglect from the city government (Hudson, 2023). Twenty-nine percent of American Indian/Alaska Native children experience poverty, compared to 9 percent of White children (Azalia et al., 2021). Statistics show that Black boys and men are at least three times more likely to be shot by police than White men (Bunn, 2022). The number of hate crimes in the US has risen in recent years and hate crimes specifically against Asian Americans and Pacific Islanders, Sikhs, and bisexual people have more than doubled (Li & Lartey, 2023). According to government released data, in June 2019, an estimated thirteen thousand migrant and refugee children were separated from their families at the Mexico-US border, and many of these families remain separated. Hate crimes against LGBTQ+ communities rose another 70 percent from 2021 to 2022 (Li & Lartey, 2023).

As I reflect, I cannot help wondering how the stories we read in school—and the ways we interact with those stories—have led us to this moment in time. **Are we—through our reading and nonreading, through our actions and inactions—socialized into people who care about others or who care only about ourselves?**

IN THIS BOOK

As teachers, we know that we do more than teach texts, plays like *A Raisin in the Sun,* and books like *The Great Gatsby, The Woman Warrior.* And while this book *is* about how we teach skills—deep thinking, informed perspective-taking, authentic writing, and critical self-reflection—this book is for teachers who know that we teach more than skills, too.

We teach kids.

We teach video game players, app designers, sports fanatics, Netflix binge watchers, Instagram photographers, sisters, brothers, oldest children, middle children, youngest children, dancers, critics, musicians, Native Indigenous children, Chinese American girls, Mexican American boys, cisgender and transgender kids, queer students, immigrants, citizens, undocumented citizens, activists, future CEOS, filmmakers, comedians, writers, readers, humanitarians. We teach young people—human beings who are complex and messy and brilliant.

Whether you are a new or veteran teacher, in this book, I invite you to come with me as we see our students in all their complexities, messiness, and brilliance; as we examine our practices through a critical, liberatory lens; and as we shine a light on the places we know our literacy instruction might fall short. And while we teach content and skills, we know we can always do more.

Let me be clear: the work I share in this book is based on the premise that the work of examining our experiences, identities, and biases is and never has been separate from the content and skills we teach; in fact, I argue that this study of *who is the I who reads* (and writes) is essential to the type of academic rigor we strive for in our classrooms. When we help our students apply a critical literacy lens to their learning, we prepare them for the type of analysis that is necessary to be responsible and engaged members of their communities. This is not an either-or (a fallacy I address in Chapter 6): **the work of critical literacy—and developing a critical consciousness—is inseparable from the work of rigorous academic study.** When we make important, intentional shifts in our pedagogy, we can get closer to the informed citizenry we need to imagine and effect a more just society. What I share are not lessons in isolation or units of study, but a window into a larger approach rooted in critical pedagogy. There is no meaningful literacy without a literacy of who we are as meaning makers.

▶ "We do not have to choose between rigorous lesson and a culturally responsive one. Our current political moment, and indeed our nation's history, demands both." —Clint Smith

In the following chapters, I welcome you into my classroom. And although I have been teaching for many years, in writing this book, I do not want to position myself as the expert. My teaching has always been in a constant state of revision as the students in my classroom change each year, and as I continue to reflect on and unpack my own practices.

In the spirit of transparency, I also think it's important for readers to know that while I have more than twenty years of classroom experience, teaching several courses at varying academic levels, most of the years were spent in a single school district. The suburban district where I taught for the majority of my career would be considered by many—based on traditional measures of success such as test scores, AP classes, and graduation rates—to be successful, competitive, and high achieving. The student population has changed over the years, but it is predominantly White and upper-middle class. According to the Office of Civil Rights, in 2017, enrolled students were: 73 percent White, 19 percent Asian, 3.9 percent Black, 1.3 percent multiracial, 2.5 percent Latinx, and .2 percent American Indian or Alaskan Native, and .1 percent Pacific Islander or Native Hawaiian. The teaching staff and administration, too, is predominantly White. In 2021, I transitioned to a new role in school administration, and I am currently the director of Diversity, Equity, and Inclusion for an independent Friends school that serves students from Grades Pre-K to 8 in Philadelphia. In my new role, I am thankful that I still get to teach, including classes with our very youngest four-year-olds and our fourteen-year-old eighth graders. The students I work with and learn from daily are a diverse group that is 25 percent Black/African American, 14 percent multiracial, 4 percent Latinx, 3 percent Asian, and 50 percent White. The school has a long history of a commitment to racial and social justice, and 40 percent of students at this school also receive financial aid.

I share all this because context matters. The ideas I share in the book are borne from my day-to-day work with kids, and teaching in any context comes with its share of advantages and challenges. While one could argue that both of the schools I've worked in are financially resourced, neither students nor staff are necessarily better equipped to navigate issues of identity and bias—and in some ways, it can be more challenging. Racial bias and prejudice can show up in school as active resistance to more equitable practices, but it can also show up in the actions of well-meaning progressives. The same general measures—test scores, AP classes, and graduation rates—that label a school successful can also hide many inequities. Whatever context you teach in, whether you are a White teacher in a predominantly White district, a Black teacher in a rural school, or a Latina teacher in a bilingual education program, I hope you will find some strategies that can help you work with the kids sitting in your individual classrooms.

With that in mind, I start this book with a chapter on reflecting on who we are as teachers. It is one of my fundamental beliefs that *we teach who we are*. If we are not reflective and critical about the identities we as teachers bring into the classroom, we are ignorant of the ways in which these identities may impact our students (perhaps in some harmful ways). *Although you may be tempted to skip this chapter and get right to the lessons in the rest of the book, I urge you to resist this temptation.* Because so much of the work I suggest in this book focuses on students' sense of identity and socialization, as teachers, we too must be willing to engage with our own identities, to wrestle with the ways in which these identities have been socialized, to be the types of models for vulnerable, critical thinking our students need today.

The remaining chapters of the book include strategies and other practical ideas. As we all know, the key to any powerful learning depends on a classroom culture built on trust and risk-taking, which is the subject of chapter 2. Because I believe that any meaningful reading and writing is borne out of students' experiences, in chapter 3, I ask students to interrogate their own personal identities through powerful reflective writing and rich mentor texts. From there, students learn to listen to, consider, and unpack the perspectives of others through conversation strategies in chapter 4 and in their reading and writing experiences in chapters 5 and 6. I end the book with some final thoughts about how we can bring all this work together in service of our students.

In simple terms, the book breaks down like this:

- Self
- Others
- Together

Or, put another way:

- Understanding ourselves
- Appreciating the diverse perspectives of others
- Synthesizing reading and writing in ways that help us *get free*

While you may browse the table of contents and choose to zoom in on a specific strategy, I've organized the book in "chronological" order as the school year unfolds, with lesson suggestions and classroom experiences that build on each other. For example, the self-reflective critical thinking skills that students will need as they engage in discussion in chapters 5 and 6 are made possible by the reading, writing, and conversational experiences they encounter in chapter 4. While some of the strategies I share might be applied at several different points throughout the year, I encourage you to consider the scaffolding that will be necessary to make these strategies successful.

And while you'll find plenty of lessons and practical ideas, what you won't find are detailed unit plans, scopes, or sequences. None of this work is meant to be prescriptive; I hope to inspire teachers to think beyond what I offer. With each idea, I'll share my thinking process and rationale behind the moves I'm making and what I hope students might take away. I invite you to think about the purpose of these lessons and strategies, and then adapt them as needed for your context and students.

So let's get to work.

Let us, one page, one step, at a time—*get free*.

CHAPTER 1

. . . .

STARTING WITH OURSELVES

We Teach Who We Are

The task of resisting our own oppression does not relieve us of the responsibility of acknowledging our complicity in the oppression of others. Our ongoing examination of who we are in our full humanity, embracing all of our identities, creates the possibility of building alliances that may ultimately free us all.

—Beverly Daniel Tatum

[Identity is] an evolving nexus where all the forces that constitute my life converge in the mystery of self: my genetic make-up, the nature of the man and woman who gave me life, the culture in which I was raised, people who have sustained me and people who have done me harm, the good and ill I have done to others

> *and to myself, the experience of love and suffering—and much, much more. In the midst of that complex field, identity is a moving intersection of the inner and outer forces that make me who I am, converging in the irreducible mystery of being human.*
>
> —Parker J. Palmer

As teachers, we wield tremendous power in our classrooms. Our interactions with students, day after day, pieced together over time, can build community in small and significant ways—or undermine it. Our decisions about curriculum, and whose experiences are represented in the literature we teach and how, send messages to our students about the human experiences that we need to pay attention to—and which we can ignore. Our instructional choices signal to our students whether we value compliance or engagement. Our assessments can guide students to better learning or reduce them to numbers on a test.

Conversations about how we wield this power happen every day. In planning meetings, department rooms, in the brief exchanges we have in the hallways with colleagues—every day, teachers discuss the best ways to reach our students, to make learning truly engaging for all the kids in the room.

Yet underneath all these conversations about what we're teaching and why, there's something deeper that often goes overlooked and unsaid.

It's us.

Teaching is an intensely human activity. The best teachers are those who know that teaching—and students—cannot be standardized. Giving two teachers the same curriculum and asking them to follow it "with fidelity" is an impossible task. Not only are the teachers different individuals, but they're also charged with the care of dozens of individual children. Although I read Palmer's (1997) *The Courage to Teach* as a pre-service teacher many years ago, his words hold true: "Good teaching cannot be reduced to technique; good teaching comes from the identity and integrity of the teacher." *We teach who we are.* This is what can make our practice so powerful—even transformative—but also potentially dangerous.

We bring all our identities—and the experiences that informed them—into our teaching. So, we must interrogate the ways in which these experiences have shaped our practices and our relationships with kids. As Dr. Talusan (2022) writes in *The Identity Conscious Educator,*

"The work of an educator—teaching, reading, advising, coaching, and collaborating—is not identity neutral. In fact, identity informs and impacts how you act, how you interact with others, and how you see the world around you" (p. 13). We have our *professional* experiences, such as our formal schooling, professional development, and our time in the classroom, our years of kid-watching and theory-making. We draw upon all these when we make decisions.

But I would argue that it's often our *personal and social* identities and experiences that have the most profound effects on our teaching and that which most often—and most dangerously—go unexamined.

In her essay, "Dangerous Discussions: Voice and Power in My Classroom," educator Wolfe-Rocca (2018) shared what happened in her classroom when she led her class through a discussion about racist graffiti in the boys' bathroom at school. She did not want to avoid the issue, but in her eagerness to discuss the incident with the class, the discussion took a turn for the worse when (predominantly White) students in the class downplayed the racism faced by African American students in the school, including one student in her class. Wolfe-Rocca writes,

> I should have known better. In my desire to make sure this terrifying incident wasn't swept under the rug—as has been the case with too many instances of racism at my school—I am mortified to admit that I dove headlong into this discussion without the care and planning it required. Doubtless, this reckless urgency was a manifestation of my whiteness and it did real harm to Cory and others.

As Wolfe-Rocca reflects, it was the privilege afforded to her as a White woman that caused her to engage in this discussion without first considering how students of color—and here, an African American student—would react to having to navigate a conversation about racism in a room full of White students.

Stop to think about an experience you've had in the classroom that might be similar to the one described here. In what ways do you think your own identities might have affected your interactions with students?

Just as students bring their whole selves into our classrooms, so do we. If we don't take the time to do the hard work of understanding our personal identities with regards to gender, race, social class, ability, and other life experiences, then we fail to truly understand the dynamics at work in our classrooms. Because that's when bias—borne from our identities and experiences—can do real and lasting harm to our students.

UNDERSTANDING HOW BIAS WORKS

Although the word *bias* often carries negative connotations, the truth is that biases are natural, even necessary, and they are neither inherently good nor bad. From a cognitive perspective, biases are simply mental shortcuts that our brain uses to process information. After all, consider how much information we are bombarded with at any given moment. For example, as I sit here and write this sentence, my fingers feel each pat-pat-pat of the keyboard. Through my window, I can hear cars driving down the street, punctuated by birds chirping in the distance. An old episode of *The Good Place* is playing on the TV in the background, and I can hear my twelve-year-old practicing piano downstairs. My foot is starting to fall asleep, and I feel a faint ache in my neck from staring at my laptop. If I gave equal attention to all these stimuli, I wouldn't be able to focus.

But the amazing human brain can process multiple pieces of information at once by prioritizing some information and sending other information to the background. Then my brain regulates all the things I'm doing automatically, like breathing and maintaining my balance so I can sit upright to type. I don't have to think about doing these things, just like I no longer have to think about which route to take when I drive to work each morning. This allows me to focus my attention on whatever podcast or audiobook I'm listening to. And that's how bias works in our brains.

Biases are the automated processes in our brains that inform our decision-making. Instead of having to give equal attention to every single possible choice when making a decision (which would be exhausting), biases help our brains prioritize what factors we should use to make that decision. The problem is that these biases have been shaped by our experiences, and our experiences have been socialized by racism, sexism, homophobia, transphobia, classism, ableism, and so on. That's why slowing down and taking a step back to understand how biases impact our behavior. In other words, instead of taking the same route to work because it's what I've always done, I might make a conscious decision to try a different route. Again, biases are neither inherently good nor bad; we can be biased *for* or *against* anything, just as there are many ways of getting from point A to point B. I can have a bias *for* the underdog in a story, just as I can have a bias *against* romance novels. Instead of abdicating my decisions to these biases, however, I can stop to think more carefully about which decisions are better aligned to my values as someone who seeks to create a more just world.

COMMON TEACHER BIASES

Educating ourselves—asking hard, uncomfortable questions that we might not like the answers to—can be the first step towards self-awareness and uncovering the biases that affect, and *infect*, our teaching.

Before we continue, I want to pause here and just talk a little bit about how biases impact our thinking processes. As teachers, we know that when we think—especially when we process new information—we construct our understanding based on previous knowledge. That's one reason we might use anticipation guides which ask students to reflect on their experiences. In calling up relevant personal experiences, students might be better able to relate to the literature they are reading. We absorb new information and try to make it "fit" with what we already know—and into our existing schema—even as we build new understanding.

The problem, of course, is that **our existing schema is often limited**. As I wrote earlier, because I was well-versed in a literary diet primarily made up of the Western canon, when I encountered texts that did not fit the schema I had constructed of what "literary" meant, I could more easily dismiss such texts. On the other hand, I think of all the books by Asian and Asian American authors I'd read over the years and shared with White colleagues, whose response to those texts was far less positive than my own as a reader. Was it because these texts lacked literary merit or was it because White readers lacked the schema to read and appreciate these texts?

I will never forget a session I attended at the National Council of Teachers of English (NCTE) in 2017 where the importance of limited schema was made clear. Jessica Lifshitz, a fifth-grade teacher and Heinemann Fellow, shared an experience she had when she and her wife were on their honeymoon. At breakfast one morning, another female guest stopped to introduce herself and her husband and mistook Jessica and her wife as mother and son rather than a married couple. Why? Here's Lifshitz's explanation:

> I believe that when she saw us, she knew, somehow we were family. Maybe it was the way we stood or the way we spoke or the way we looked at each other. But the kind of family that we were, didn't match any of the schemas she carried with her about family. We didn't look like any of the images of family that she had ever been exposed to and had stored in her mind. So she tried, without realizing it, to match us to the closest schema that she could find. And the closest thing that she could come up with was mother and son.
>
> Perhaps, this woman, who probably meant no ill intent, had such a narrow understanding of family and we just did not fit into it. So in a desperate attempt to match us to what she already knew, she ended up erasing who we really were. And

she tried to shove us into her existing schema so that she felt comfortable, so that she experienced what Piaget referred to as equilibrium.

Consider your own existing schema and the ways in which your experiences, like all of ours, have been limited. What impact might this have on your work with students?

All human beings have biases. I am not immune, and neither are experts. In her book *Biased: The Hidden Prejudice That Shapes What We See, Think, and Do*, MacArthur Grant recipient and Stanford University professor Dr. Eberhardt (2019) points out, "We all have ideas about race, even the most open-minded among us. Those ideas have the power to bias our perception, our attention, our memory, and our actions—all despite our conscious awareness or or deliberate intentions." Likewise, Daniel Kahneman, a renowned cognitive scientist in this field, writes about his own biases in his book *Thinking, Fast and Slow*. As teachers, we need to be mindful of the ways in which these affect our own thinking if we are to have any hope of helping our students read and write beyond their own biases.

In the next few pages, I've chosen five cognitive biases and will unpack how these might show up every day in our teaching practices. In my experience, these five biases are those that have the potential to do the greatest harm if unexamined—and on the flip side, addressing these biases can have the greatest benefit for our students, particularly as our practices relate to inclusion and equity. As you read about each of these biases, pause to think about how these biases have manifested themselves in your own practices. Reflect on why and how you might take steps to make instructional decisions more informed of these biases.

Although our focus is on our own individual biases in this chapter, the truth is that any serious efforts to dismantle systemic oppression must actually address the *system* in systemic. No doubt that we must do the hard work of interrogating our own individual biases, but this will not be enough if we fail to recognize the larger system in which those biases are formed. At the end of this chapter, I share some self-reflection exercises that ask you to think about individual identities in the context of a larger systemic framework, as well as how systemic biases play a role in reading and writing curricula, instruction, and schools.

Bias 1: Curse of Knowledge

When I first started teaching, I was assigned five world literature classes, all ninth grade. At the time, the course was focused on reading literature from different parts of the non-Western world with the purpose of learning about other cultures through their literature. Of the texts in the curriculum, I had read only one title. Everything else in the curriculum was new to me.

Despite not knowing very much, not having much prior knowledge of the material, I had a terrific first year. I still remember many of my students from that year, and although the experience has receded in my memory as a kind of haze, it's a golden-tinted haze, warm and bright. What *is* crystal clear to me, however, is just how smart my students seemed to be. Every day, I walked away from class impressed with all the rich insights students brought to the texts we read. Maybe I was lucky and just had a really great group of kids, or maybe I actually did know more than I thought I did. Either way, I still feel grateful for having had such a positive first-year teaching experience—and for the grace and patience I'm sure my students gifted me on many occasions.

Over the years, however, things changed. I noticed that my students didn't seem to have the same insight into the literature. At the same time, I was becoming a better teacher—or at least a more experienced one—having practiced teaching the same novels over and over again. But my students seemed to know less and less.

Did my students really know less? Maybe—but probably not. This is where the curse of knowledge bias comes in. The **curse of knowledge** is "the tendency to be biased by one's own current knowledge state when trying to appreciate a more naive perspective, [even when] that more naive perspective is one's own earlier perspective" (Birch & Bloom, 2006, p. 382). In other words, as teachers gain more knowledge, as we increase our own expertise over material, we have a harder time seeing the material from the points of view of our students. Our expertise starts to feel like common knowledge that everyone should have and we forget that the information was once new to us, too. Instead, we might feel discouraged as teachers, we might give in to "my students don't know anything!" thinking and blame students for not knowing what we, as teachers, have spent years learning.

The **curse of knowledge** bias occurs when we understand something so well that it becomes hard for us to understand how others can't. This then makes it difficult for us to explain or teach others. Consider a text you've taught for years: Are there any particular texts that individual students struggle with? Or a text particular groups of students struggle with? Why? In what ways has your expertise on this text actually been a barrier to your ability to teach it?

Also, let's remember that knowledge is subjective. While we build expertise in texts—I'm sure there are many American literature teachers

who can probably recite lines from *The Great Gatsby* in their sleep—this knowledge is reinforced by our years teaching. As our knowledge about a certain text becomes more fixed, our goals for student learning may become more prescribed as we decide that students must learn X, Y, or Z when reading a certain text. We design activities and assessments around *our* knowledge, so the cost of time and effort to change our approach to teaching these texts becomes greater if we have to create new materials (this is known as the sunk cost fallacy bias, see page 34). Yet, when students encounter a text for the first time, the full range of possibility, of literary interpretation, is open to them. Instead of honoring this, we find ourselves continually corralling them toward the same ideas and the same perspectives.

As teachers, being mindful of the curse of knowledge is critical to equitable practices. Because we think of ourselves as the "experts" in the room, we might overvalue our expertise. Instead, however, we should think beyond the binaries of teachers and students, beyond expert and novice. As early childhood educator Aeriale Johnson reminds us:

▶ Something to try out: Read a text "cold" with your students. Choose a text you've never read before and read, respond, and analyze it side by side with your students. Several years ago, a colleague in another state and I did a brief "mentor text exchange." We mailed each other copies of poems that neither one of us had read before and read them with our students. While I don't recommend not pre-reading material as a regular practice, every once in a while, and with a text suggested by a colleague, it can be a useful way to appreciate the reading process as an experience of shared discovery and meaning-making with the learners in our classroom.

> [W]hen we put ourselves in the position of learner in a dynamic where we ultimate possess power, we surrender that power to our students in order to learn from them. In the midst of this yielding, we may begin to see brilliance in children we may have previously been unaware of as we allow them to inform what we teach, how we teach it, and in what ways they will demonstrate their understanding (Johnson, 2018, pp. 19–20).

Bias 2: Nostalgia

If you have ever heard your family, your friends, or our colleagues wax poetic about "the good old days," or if you've found yourself longing for the past, you might be experiencing the **nostalgia bias**, also known as "rosy retrospection." According to Dr. Burton (2014), nostalgia is "sentimentality for the past, typically for a particular period or place with positive associations, but sometimes also for the past in general."

Feeling sentimental about the past is normal, and some psychologists argue that nostalgia can be a useful way to allow human beings to cope with our past traumas, allowing negative feelings to wash away in retrospect rather than become consumed by them. But how might nostalgia negatively impact our teaching?

Similar to the effects of the curse of knowledge, nostalgia can lead us to make incomplete and inaccurate assessments of the past. Who hasn't complained themselves or heard fellow teachers complain that when they first started teaching, students were different, better? When we're feeling nostalgic, we might engage in distorted and idealized versions of the past, and "[i]f overindulged, nostalgia can give rise to a utopia that never existed and can never exist" (Burton, 2014). As educator Gonzales (2016) puts it, "[W]hen we settle for a 'kids today' diagnosis, romanticizing the past and blaming our teaching problems on the collective inferiority of a generation, we only make things worse." Giving in to nostalgia makes our work counterproductive. When we spend too much time comparing our students to the past, we fail to appreciate the students sitting in our classrooms now, who may bring some challenges but who also have tremendous promise and potential. How many times have we been guilty of thinking, *Well, when I was in school, we never did X, Y, or Z?* Maybe not. Or maybe you did back then and don't remember. But what does it matter to the kids sitting in front of you right *now?*

While it's tempting to romanticize the past, consider the ways in which the **nostalgia bias** might prevent us from fully appreciating the strengths that our students today bring to the classroom.

Nostalgia also reinforces a deficit-model of evaluating our students; instead of focusing on what they can do, we spend time and waste energy focusing on what we perceive students lack. Indeed, our own "rosy retrospection" can get in the way of seeing what's in front of our eyes. Furthermore, the potentially harmful effects of nostalgia can be intensified when comparing the present to a past that is significantly different from our personal experience. Consider what might happen if a teacher has students who are demographically different from those they taught earlier in their career or even in their own schooling. **If nostalgia tempts us to idealize the past, what might that mean for us as educators as our student population becomes increasingly diverse?**

In "Culturally Sustaining Pedagogy: A Needed Change in Stance, Terminology, and Practice," scholar Django Paris warns of the historic and present danger of such deficit thinking:

> Deficit approaches to teaching and learning, firmly in place prior to and during the 1960s and 1970s, viewed the languages, literacies, and cultural ways of being of many students and communities of color as deficiencies to be overcome in learning the demanded and legitimized dominant language, literacy, and cultural ways of schooling.

Furthermore, Paris notes:

> The dominant language, literacy, and cultural practices demanded by school fell in line with White, middle-class norms and positioned languages and literacies that fell outside those norms as less-than and unworthy of a place in U.S. schools and society (Paris, 2012, p. 93).

Indeed, our own "rosy retrospection" can get in the way of seeing what's in front of our eyes.

We cannot ignore that our tendency toward nostalgia may also have particularly harmful implications for students of color and other marginalized groups. We can see the nostalgia bias clearly when thinking about text selection. No doubt that the stories that we're exposed to during childhood can leave an indelible mark on our hearts and minds. From fairy tales to picture books, these stories tend to stick with us.

However, what happens when our favorite childhood stories turn out to be more complicated than what we remember? For example, racism in beloved childhood favorites like the Dr. Seuss books and Curious George series have been researched and well-documented (Campbell, 2019; G. Smith, 2019). For many educators, novels like *To Kill a Mockingbird* or *Little House on the Prairie* still elicit feelings of nostalgia for their childhoods. A public example of this happened in 2022 when author Kate DiCamillo pointed out her affection for the novel *Island of the Blue Dolphins,* which her teacher read to her class as a child, even though scholar Reese (2018b, 2022) a tribally enrolled member of Nambé Pueblo, has pointed out the clear inaccuracies and harmful portrayals of the Aleut people in the novel. Many teachers and authors still defend using these texts because of their own nostalgia.

Bias 3: Anchoring

Even though I've taught for many years, the beginning of the school year is still one of my favorite times of year. True, I might be a bit sad for the end of the summer, but there are few other times that are filled with such anticipation and promise. Any negative energy from the previous year has receded with the warm summer air and sunshine as the clean slate of each September beckons.

And yet can we really say the same for all our students? Does a brand new school year offer each student the same clean slate we wish for ourselves as teachers?

In my first few years of teaching, one of the first things I would do when I got my class lists was show them to other teachers. As a relatively inexperienced teacher, I admit I wanted to know if I was going to have any students who might be "problems." Sometimes the information I sought was about potential behavior—these problems were the ones that I had least confidence in handling. Other times, the information was about what "level" a student had been recommended for by the previous teacher. I would then make a mental note to myself to keep a closer eye on students who were not recommended for the honors level I taught (in my district, students may override any teacher recommendation with parent permission). In my mind, I was doing my due diligence as a teacher.

Notice the language I used here as a younger teacher: framing students as "problems" to be "handled." How much more effective could I have been as a teacher if I framed situations with new students differently? What if I instead asked myself, *How can I best reach this student or meet their needs? What skill do I need to work on so I can best teach this student*?

Then one day at a district committee meeting, I had a conversation with an eighth grade teacher that challenged me to think differently. It was at least a few weeks, if not months, into the school year, so I already had some sense of the students by then. Still, extra information could be helpful. I showed them my ninth grade class roster as it was likely they had taught many of the students the year before. As their eyes scanned through the names, they commented on the students they knew. To be fair, the vast majority of their comments were positive, but every now and then, the teacher let out their surprise at seeing the name of a student they did not recommend for the honors course. Sometimes it was because the student lacked motivation ("he never turned in his homework") or lacked skills ("she had a hard time writing a thesis statement").

But as I listened to their comments, it was my turn to show surprise. Of the names the teacher pointed out, I had honestly not seen the issues that they shared. In fact, in some cases, it felt like they were describing a completely different student than the one who was sitting in my classroom.

Why does this matter?

In *Thinking, Fast and Slow*, Kahneman (2013) describes experiments he conducted with his colleague, Amos Tversky, and found that people were often disproportionately and unknowingly influenced by a single piece of information (often the first piece of information) given to them in solving a problem, even if that information was unrelated to the problem itself (p. 119). For example, participants were asked Einstein's age when he died. In one scenario, participants were asked

if Einstein was older or younger than 142 years old when he died. In another scenario, they were asked if Einstein was older or younger than thirty-five years old when he died. In the two scenarios, participants were "anchored" to a high number (142) and to a lower number (35). Participants who were anchored to the higher number made guesses that were substantially higher than those who were anchored to the lower number. Thus, this **anchoring bias** occurs when we rely too heavily on one piece of information when processing information or making decisions—and often, unknowingly. (This is also why we tend to be swayed by "sale" prices when we are shown and "anchored" to higher, suggested retail prices.)

How many times, I wonder, have I allowed one piece of information to inform my judgments of students? If a colleague tells me that a student was recommended for the lower level English class, consider how this information might affect my expectations about that student's ability, even before meeting them? How might the data that follows a student from teacher to teacher—whether that data is comprised of test scores or anecdotes—affect our first impressions of a student?

We know first impressions matter, but when we **anchor** our expectations of students based on these first impressions, we may inadvertently limit our understanding of what students can and can't do. Reflect on a student you've had where your first impressions might have been wrong: how did you come to recognize this, and what did you do?

Of course, some information about students is necessary to know ahead of time, especially information related to a student's IEP and all information that is needed to keep a student physically and emotionally safe. But if we're not careful, we may inadvertently be swayed by nonessential (and biased) information that simply isn't fair to use in judging students. We might allow one positive or negative incident with a student to affect how we treat them in class or assess their work.

Bias 4: In-group Bias

I have a confession. It's hard not to have favorite types of students. I've always had a special place in my heart for students who are engaged, on the quiet side, thoughtful writers, and avid readers. These are students who are like me—or at the very least, students who are *most similar to* the type of student *I* was in school.

Psychologists have long documented the **in-group bias** we show for those who are similar to us. This preference for those we see as in our own group likely had some evolutionary purpose by making us more wary of those who might be unfamiliar and pose a threat. And of course, showing a favorable bias toward one's own family would no doubt help a group to care for one another and survive. But in a classroom, what are the potential dangers of such a bias?

Reflect on the students you have had over the years. Are there some students who stand out more favorably to you than others? In what ways were these students similar to you, either to the person you are now or as the student you were in school? How might this **in-group bias** have affected your relationships with students who were different from you?

When I look back on my own teaching career as well as my current practices, I know I have been guilty of having more positive feelings toward students who mirrored what I saw as ideal classroom behavior—on-task, obedient, polite, willing to engage, responsible, and nonthreatening—and I'm sure I'm not the only teacher, either.

As I look at this list, however, I can't help noticing that the list is ultimately about compliance more than anything else. And because I was a student who was always more than willing to comply, reinforced by my own cultural upbringing in which deference to adults was valued—*and because I credited that compliance with my own success*—I rewarded similar behaviors explicitly and implicitly in my classroom. As education researcher and writer Shalaby (2017) argues in *Troublemakers*, teachers often label students unwilling to comply as "troublemakers," with results that can be harmful, if not traumatic, for young people:

> In one study, researchers found that as many as 46 percent of kindergarten teachers report that more than half their class has trouble following directions; 34 percent report that children struggle to work independently; 20 percent report that kindergartners have poor social skills and are "immature." These figures lead us to question whether the demands of early schooling are reasonable; after all, it seems we should expect immaturity from a five-year-old.

> Instead, we turn a gaze of pathology on children. At the age of five, if you cannot follow directions and work independently, you are likely to be given a long series of interactions with the school's various mechanisms for identifying, labeling, and remediating deficits. Suddenly and swiftly, children become problems.

▶ How many "troublemakers" are simply students who are least like us?

Although Shalaby's research focuses on early childhood education, let's be clear: The middle school and high school students sitting in our

secondary classrooms are equally affected. In fact, we should remember that every student sitting in our classrooms brings with them a lifetime of experiences with previous teachers, positive and negative. I don't think I have ever explicitly disregarded other students or showed bias *against* them, but because intent is not the same as impact, I must ask myself—how might I have favored students who are similar to me *at the expense of other students*? On his Hidden Brain podcast, psychologist Shankar Vedantam synthesized research on in-group bias, noting the findings scientists Nancy DiTomaso, Mahzarin Banaji, and Anthony Greenwald discovered:

> Discrimination today is less about treating people from other groups badly, DiTomaso writes, and more about giving preferential treatment to people who are part of our "in-groups."
>
> The insidious thing about favoritism is that it doesn't feel icky in any way, Banaji says. We feel like a great friend when we give a buddy a foot in the door to a job interview at our workplace. We feel like good parents when we arrange a class trip for our daughter's class to our place of work. We feel like generous people when we give our neighbors extra tickets to a sports game or a show.
>
> In each case, however, Banaji, Greenwald and DiTomaso might argue, we strengthen existing patterns of advantage and disadvantage because our friends, neighbors and children's classmates are overwhelmingly likely to share our own racial, religious and socioeconomic backgrounds. When we help someone from one of these in-groups, we don't stop to ask: Whom are we not helping? (Vedantam, 2013)

This bears repeating: When we help someone from one of our in-groups, *we don't stop to ask: Whom are we not helping?* According to research published in *Education Week*, the current teaching force in the United States is 80 percent White and non-Hispanic. Meanwhile, students of color make-up 54.8 percent of K-12 students in our schools. Additionally, 77 percent of teachers in the United States are women, while our student population is much more gender diverse (Riser-Kositsky, 2023). The potential for in-group bias based on racial and gender difference alone, especially where equity programs or inclusive practices aren't prioritized, is worrisome. After all, research has shown negative outcomes for Black students, especially when taught by White teachers.

For example, in an extensive longitudinal study of more than eight thousand tenth grade public school students, researchers found that

White teachers had consistently lower expectations for Black school children, particularly Black boys. Among the findings:

- White and other non-Black teachers were twelve percentage points more likely than Black teachers to predict Black students wouldn't finish high school.

- Non-Black teachers were 5 percent more likely to predict their Black male students wouldn't graduate high school than their Black female students.

- White male teachers are 10 to 20 percent more likely to have low expectations for Black female students.

- For Black students, particularly Black boys, having a non-Black teacher in a tenth grade subject made them much less likely to pursue that subject by enrolling in similar classes (Rosen, 2016).

Additional research has also shown that Black students are disciplined at disproportionately higher rates than White students. For example, according to the US Department of Education Office for Civil Rights (2014), Black boys are nearly four times more likely to be suspended than White boys (p. 1). According to another study, "Black students as young as age five are routinely suspended and expelled from schools for minor infractions like talking back to teachers or writing on their desks" despite the fact that Black students did not actually "act out" any more than their White peers (Rudd, 2014, p. 1). Consider how this over-disciplining of Black students not only leads to lost learning time in the classroom, but also has a devastating social and emotional cost for students and their relationships with their teachers and peers, a cost that is also shared by students' families. In a painful and necessary blog post, educator Parker (2018) shared the challenges she faced as a Black mother when her son's school system failed to meet his needs. She writes:

> What happened to my sun happens to Black boys in preschool every single day.
>
> There is such stigma and shame I experienced as I was so quick to think I was the problem. Instead, we are in a system that, if we do not intervene, will continue to push Black boys out of preschool, denying them experiences, teachers, schools, that have the potential to ground them in powerful educational beginnings. (Parker, 2018)

While most teachers believe themselves to be well-meaning and work hard to reach all students, research studies continue to confirm that implicit biases have a very real and devastating impact on our students. To pretend otherwise is to be complicit in these continued inequities.

Part of the reason I became a teacher was because of the way my parents raised me. They instilled in me and my brother a deep respect for education. My parents' own education—they both hold degrees from a top university in the Philippines—no doubt played a role in their ability to emigrate to the United States in the 1970s. Together they scrimped and saved, spending nothing more than what was necessary and only buying things if they were on sale (and if my mom had a coupon). My parents moved from one modest home to another, from one school district to a better one. From their experiences, my parents knew that working hard would pay off.

This, of course, is the American Dream—America is the land of opportunity, a place where anyone who is willing to work hard can make it. Although my parents weren't exactly the "tired, hungry, and poor" described in Emma Lazarus's poem, they did arrive in America each with one suitcase in hand. In an alternate universe where I become a politician, this would be the story I would tell—the narrative that you'd hear as a montage of faded childhood pictures plays to an Aaron-Sorkin-inspired soundtrack.

So what does my family story have to do with bias?

As first-generation immigrants who came to the United States for more opportunities, my parents knew that you couldn't take anything for granted, that it was through consistent effort that we could be successful. They believed in my abilities but reminded me that I had an obligation to use them wisely and well. If you work hard, they insisted, you can do anything.

Like many Americans, I grew up believing in the just world hypothesis.

The **just world hypothesis** describes people's tendency to believe that life is inherently fair—that individuals get what they deserve. In the US, it's easy to see how this bias might be particularly strong with the country's "pick yourself by your bootstraps" mentality. While this bias might *feel* like the truth, the problem is that the bias not only downplays the role that luck or chance might play, *but it also ignores the powerful, negative effects of systemic, historic, and contemporary discrimination*. In simple terms, if you're not successful, it's your fault. Because if you worked hard, you'd be successful *because we live in a just world*.

Take, for example, the experiments that Michael Lerner conducted in the 1960s when he discovered this bias.

In one, he showed people what appeared to be live footage of a woman receiving painful electric shocks for making errors in a memory test. (She was actually his accomplice.) Some groups of viewers had the option of ending her ordeal; others didn't. The latter – forced to watch suffering with no chance of relieving it – formed far lower opinions of the woman, seemingly to "bring about a more appropriate fit between her fate and her character". Those opinions were worst when they were told the woman got no financial reward for her pains. The greater the injustice, the more people appeared to need to believe the victim brought it on herself (Burkeman, 2015).

In Lerner's experiment, note that when participants were forced to watch the woman suffer, even when she was helpless and could not reasonably be held responsible for her suffering, the participants resorted to blaming the victim, that somehow she *must* be at fault. As journalist Nicholas Hune-Brown notes:

> When presented with an obvious injustice, we try to resolve it: we end the cruel experiment, cure the patient, free the innocent man from jail. When we are helpless to change things, however, rather than give up our belief in the essential rightness of the universe, we begin to rationalize away the unfairness. The sight of a woman suffering without any hope of compensation was simply incompatible with a just world; in order to reconcile those two facts, observers irrationally decided she must have done something to justify her punishment (Hune-Brown, 2015).

It's not hard to see how the just world hypothesis might play out in education—and also actively *perpetuated* through our actions as educators.

Consider how many times we reinforce this bias in our classrooms: We might tell students to behave well so that they can get extra recess. We might withhold recess from another student who misbehaves. We often tell students that if they study and work hard that they will do well on the test, get a good grade in class, get into a good college, find a good job, and make a good living. Is this not the driving ethos of schooling in the United States?

And yet we know that *injustice exists*. Teaching and learning cannot be reduced to a matter of karma—that what goes around comes around. While it may be true that a student who prepares for a test may get a higher grade, what about the student who might be dealing with issues at home and cannot concentrate enough to study? Or what about the student who has carried a label of "troublemaker" from one teacher to the next and not received the support and skills to even know how to study? Or what about the student who studies and *does* know the material but does not perform well on tests? We end up reinforcing a

kind of victim-blaming with our students, rationalizing that because *we've* done our job as teachers that it must be the *student's* fault if they're not doing well.

Because of the **just world hypothesis**, we tend to assume that justice exists, that "what goes around comes around." Reflect on your own experiences growing up, both in and out of school. In what ways was this message conveyed to you? And what are the potential drawbacks in thinking this way?

Or we might believe in *earned individual success* when the real story is much more complicated. Take my family story, for example. Yes, my parents worked hard and earned much of their success. But they also had several advantages that many immigrants—and especially refugees—do not. They hold *engineering* degrees which were particularly valued at a time when the US began to prioritize the sciences. The Immigration and Nationality Act, passed in 1965, opened up the borders to countries that had been banned for decades. Had my parents been born just ten years earlier and tried to immigrate then, they simply couldn't. My parents were also multilingual, and in addition to their native Filipino dialects, they were fluent in English because English was taught in the Philippine schools. Furthermore, while my mom came with just one suitcase, waiting for her were family members who had emigrated years before and supported her with a place to live as she got started.

So while I may have worked hard and found some success, my success is not mine alone. None of our successes or failures are. I think about refugees today, and throughout history, forced from their home, in search of a better life, and about the obstacles they face that I, with my privilege, cannot even fathom. Where is the "just world" for them?

With so many countless factors affecting a student's learning—and too often *beyond a single student's individual control*—can we really say that all students get what they "deserve"?

What makes disabusing ourselves of the just world hypothesis so difficult is that it also forces us to confront the concept of privilege. The advantages my parents had, the ones they've passed on to me—these are the source of my privilege. In *So You Want to Talk About Race*, author Oluo (2018) unpacks the concept of privilege, which works hand-in-hand with the just world hypothesis:

> [W]e do not want to believe that we do not deserve
> everything we have, and we do not want to think of ourselves
> as ignorant of how the world works. The concept of privilege

violates everything we've been told about the American Dream of hard work paying off and good things happening to good people. We want to know that if we "a" we can expect "b," and that those who never get "b" have never done "a." The concept of privilege makes the world seem less safe. We want to protect our vision of a world that is fair and kind and predictable. That reaction is natural, but it doesn't make the harmful effects of unexamined privilege less real. (p. 63)

In what ways have our own privileges contributed to our belief in the just world hypothesis? As teachers, how do we perpetuate this bias in the ways we talk about the world with our students? How many times does a belief in a just world permeate our analysis of characters and conflict when we read literature?

Related to the just world hypothesis is a logical fallacy known as the **fundamental attribution error**. This fallacy causes us to *attribute* a person's mistake to something *fundamental* about that person's abilities or character *rather than examine the context in which that mistake was made*. For example, if a student turns in a hastily and poorly written essay, the fundamental attribution error might lead a teacher to believe that the student isn't a good writer. However, there could be many reasons why a student turned in a poorly written essay. They might have had three other tests that day, or misunderstood the assignment, or had extenuating circumstances at home, or might be disengaged from the teacher's class—and none of these reasons may have anything to do with the student's actual ability. Just as the just world hypothesis assumes that individuals get what they deserve, the fundamental attribution error assumes that individuals' mistakes are due to their individual abilities versus their circumstances.

TOWARD AN ANTIBIAS STANCE

We've reviewed a few biases, but having knowledge is only the first step. Research has shown that aside from awareness of our implicit biases, we must also be concerned about the effects that these biases have (Devine et al., 2012). And of course, because we are teachers, this concern is a given. No one goes into teaching with the intent to do harm to our students, and if we come to the realization that we might be unintentionally harming our students, the words of Dr. Maya Angelou can guide us: "Do the best you can until you can do better. Then when you know better, do better" (Winfrey, 2011).

Below you'll find some opportunities for self-reflection, which can serve as important steps in acting to reduce the impact that these and other biases might have on our teaching practices. Later in the book, we'll use an antibias approach to our reading and writing practices. But

in the meantime, take the time now to invest in the self-reflection below that is necessary for us as teachers before we turn our lens on students.

Self-Reflection 1: Bias Checkup

Human beings are complicated and full of contradictions—and the human brain processes information in sophisticated ways. Our human intellect has allowed us to put men in space and find cures for once deadly diseases.

Yet we are all susceptible to flaws in our thinking that can have profound effects on the students in our classrooms. While it may be uncomfortable, we need to move from a stance of humility: we must recognize our discomfort, name, and own it. Understanding our biases can help us do that. And in doing so we will be better able to resist them and help our students.

Invitation to Reflect

Take a moment to consider the five biases discussed here and summarized in Figure 1.1, and reflect on the following:

- Which of the biases most resonates with your own experiences when you were a student in school? Why? *In-group bias*

- Which of the biases most resonates with your teaching experiences? In what ways? *Curse of knowledge (maybe? idk)*

- Now that you're aware of these biases, what small and concrete steps might you take tomorrow, next week, and over the next several months to help you reduce the negative impact of these biases on your practices and your students? *Reconsider my own experiences, weaknesses, etc.*

FIGURE 1.1 SUMMARY OF COMMON TEACHER BIASES

BIAS	WHAT IT IS	HOW IT MIGHT AFFECT CLASSROOM PRACTICES	WHAT YOU CAN DO ABOUT IT
Curse of Knowledge	• Occurs when our expertise prevents us from being able to appreciate a more naive or beginning learner perspective	• Unrealistic expectations about what students should know at the beginning of a lesson • Lack of scaffolding or appropriate background instruction	• Change the texts you teach with students so that you cannot compare what your current students bring to the text to prior students' insights. • Position yourself as a learner when reading new texts together.

BIAS	WHAT IT IS	HOW IT MIGHT AFFECT CLASSROOM PRACTICES	WHAT YOU CAN DO ABOUT IT
Nostalgia	• Occurs when we romanticize the past • Belief that the past was inherently better than the present	• Incomplete and inaccurate assessments of prior students' knowledge or ability when compared to today • Failure to appreciate current students' abilities and talents • Deficit-based approach to teaching rather than asset-based	• Keep a sample of student work from year to year that represents the full range of ability of students as a measurable, objective record of the past.
Anchoring	• Occurs when we allow initial information to disproportionately affect our judgment	• Judgment of students that too heavily relies on our first impressions • Fixed belief about students' abilities based on initial performance or interactions	• Limit the amount of information you have about students from previous teachers to what is absolutely essential only. • Create learning experiences early in the year that allow students to showcase their strengths (versus assessments that spotlight their weaknesses).
In-Group Bias	• Occurs when we show a preference for those who are similar to us	• Favoritism toward or benefit of the doubt afforded to students who may be similar to us (intentional or not)	• Create and maintain a list of each student's strengths and revisit and update throughout the year. • Reflect on your own weaknesses as a person and identify students who exhibit that weakness as a strength. For example, if you are not artistic, identify and honor students who have this as a strength.
Just World Hypothesis	• Occurs when we believe that world is inherently just and fair; a belief in "what goes around comes around"	• Holding students responsible for factors that are beyond their control	• Reconsider your own personal experiences by taking into account the advantages that you have had. • Reflect on experiences in your own life that you felt were not fair or where the outcome did not seem justified by the circumstances. • Learn more about your students' background to create a more complete picture of their own advantages and disadvantages.

In addition to the five biases discussed in detail in these pages, here are a few more that are worth thinking about and how they might affect our work:

- *Sunk Cost Fallacy*. You might experience the **sunk cost fallacy** when you're watching a terrible movie but refuse to stop watching because you've already invested so much time that you might as well finish. Likewise, even though we know a lesson or unit isn't going well, we might continue anyway because we've already spent too much time on it. Or consider when we invest a lot of our time and energy into creating lessons over the years: it can be hard to let go of those lessons, regardless of how effective or ineffective the lessons have become.

- *Ikea Effect*. According to the **Ikea effect**, we tend to value those things that we build and create ourselves. This, in part, explains the success of companies like Ikea (and the entire Do-It-Yourself industry, for that matter). How might this bias affect the way that we judge (or misjudge) the lesson plans and instructional materials that we design and build ourselves?

- *Confirmation Bias*. Entire books could be written the way that this single bias operates in schools. In short, **confirmation bias** occurs when we only seek evidence that confirms a preexisting opinion or belief we have rather than seek the best evidence, regardless of whether or not it supports that preexisting opinion or belief. In Chapters 5 and 6, we'll spend more time on this bias as it relates to supporting students in reading and analyzing texts. Here, however, consider how confirmation bias may impact the way you look at student data, what student data you collect in the first place, the texts you choose, the way you interpret those texts and then teach their themes to students.

UNPACKING OUR EXPERIENCES

As we've seen, examining our biases can go far in illuminating those places where our practices fall short. But becoming a self-reflective, critical thinker—and a teacher who can model this disposition for our students—goes beyond a checklist of biases. Instead, we must build **a habit of persistent wondering**, digging beneath the surface of our own knee-jerk or gut reactions to discover what in our experiences has shaped our responses to others and the world.

Our experiences and identities exist in a state of mutual reinforcement. The experiences we have shape how we see ourselves, how we identify with and to others and the world. In turn, the identities we present to others also shape our experiences and how the world and others treat us, fairly or unfairly. In unpacking our own identities and experiences, we can see more clearly the ways that they affect our teaching.

In the spring of 2018, my colleagues Lorena Germán, Julia Torres, Dr. Kim Parker, and I launched the Twitter chat, #DisruptTexts. Our goal was to inspire conversation about disrupting the traditionally White, male, and Eurocentric canon of literature by approaching these texts through the lens of critical pedagogy and critical race theory, and by suggesting alternative titles as counternarratives or even replacements. Since then, we've been humbled by the tremendous success of the #DisruptTexts movement, with many teachers responding favorably to shifting the conversation about the canon into more diverse territory.

Of course, there's also been pushback.

Often those who defend the canon base their pushback on quality and tradition. The argument goes like this: There are certain literary works considered essential for cultural capital (although we should ask: whose culture?). To be considered "educated," students must read these books. Thus, to *not* teach these books is doing a disservice to our students.

But here's the thing: Most teachers, especially secondary English teachers, were educated in a *system*—a "canon" of texts that included some voices but excluded many more others. I was raised in this "canon" of literature, and I won't pretend that I didn't take pride in mastering these texts. To call into question the validity of the "canon" means that we have to acknowledge our complicity in this exclusion. We defend our own perceived expertise. And when that expertise is challenged, it feels personal.

I speak from my own experience. As an Asian American, Filipina American woman who has always felt the pressure to "fit in" and "prove" myself in many spaces, I saw my expertise in the "canon" as evidence of my intellect—and perhaps as a way to be accepted and respected in a White dominated field. Knowledge about a specific set of texts was a way to have academic power, but I never stopped to question who made up these rules about power in the first place. (Perhaps this was another reason why I also loved canonical texts such as *Jane Eyre* so much.)

Ironically, when my students and I read Achebe's *Things Fall Apart*, we discussed how schools were often used as one of the most effective tools of colonizer nations. Control what people think, I reminded them, and you can control what they do—and what they can't. What I didn't recognize was my own complicity in such a system. After all, one could argue that the Western Canon is as much a tool of colonization as it is a representation of the greatest thinkers and writers of the Western world. To what extent do our curricular choices today perpetuate this

colonial legacy? To be clear, is it wrong to read the work of White, Western authors? Of course not. Is it wrong if those are the *only* books our students read? Yes.

Invitation to Reflect

In the words of anti-apartheid leader Steve Biko, "the most potent weapon of the oppressor is the mind of the oppressed." Consider your own school experiences:

- What messages about being a "good student" did you receive in school, implicitly and explicitly? Who gave you these messages and how?

- What books and authors did you study in school? What patterns regarding race, gender, culture, ethnicity, and so forth do you notice among these books and authors?

- How was your learning assessed when you were a student? What did these assessments teach you about what "counts" as learning and as knowledge?

- What did your own teachers emphasize when reading books? What types of meaning-making and reader-response were valued? Which were not valued?

Self-Reflection 3: Privilege Checklist

Another example of the way my identities have affected my teaching is through my privilege.

I grew up and live in an affluent, predominantly White, somewhat progressive suburb. I live and work in two of the most "high performing" districts in the state as indicated by many local and national school rankings (for whatever those are worth). At first glance, my community seems like a great place to live: lots of public parks, low rates of violent crime, access to multiple grocery stores and shops. But one reason for this is because of the racial segregation—carefully and explicitly orchestrated through our legal system—that has shaped many metropolitan areas.

I have to acknowledge that. I can say I live where I live because I want what's best for my kids, because my parents live close by and family is important. This is all true—but it is *also* true that I'm complicit in an ongoing system of structural racism. This structural racism has limited the diversity of people around me and my ability to empathize with others. Like my #DisruptTexts colleague and author Lorena Germán, most of my teachers were White women. As Germán makes clear, "Is it bad to have a white woman teacher? No. Is it bad to have all white women teachers over x many years? Yes." Like Germán, I experienced significant and "tangible cultural gaps" in school that informed my education (V. Brown & Keels, 2021). School and home make up nearly the entirety of a child's world and how these worlds look, feel, and sound—who's part of those worlds and who is not, who has power and who does not—create worldviews that children internalize about themselves and how the world works.

Across all parts of the country, our neighborhoods and schools are more segregated by race now than they were during legal segregation. When I reflect on my own racial literacy in recent years, it's been my relationships with other people of color that have transformed my understanding of racism, especially anti-Black racism.

Why does this matter in my teaching? Because if I don't fully comprehend what impedes my own ability to understand racism as it exists in my own life, how can I teach students about racism with the complexity and knowledge required? How can I teach *To Kill a Mockingbird? Huck Finn? Gatsby?* Or really—any American literature? How can I teach students about holidays like Thanksgiving or figures like Martin Luther King, Jr. responsibly? How can I offer students "diverse" narratives in my classroom library if I haven't unpacked what I mean or assume about what counts as "diverse"? Or if I don't understand that using the term "diverse" can also reinforce Whiteness as a norm and all books written by non-White authors as *not* the norm, and therefore, "diverse"? As educator Everett (2017) writes, "one must ask diverse for whom or diverse from what? The word diverse as it is currently used centers heteronormative whiteness as the default."

It's the privilege that my personal experiences afford me that also partially explains my shock and grief at the racial slurs that have been hurled at and attacks on elderly Asian people on public transportation, the police that have been called on Black Americans going to the pool or watching birds in a public park, and the "family detention centers" that have been erected to imprison refugees. The truth is that none of the injustices we're seeing today are new, just the latest iterations; everything present has its precedent.

Although I am privileged—or perhaps because I am—and went to traditionally excellent schools, never in my schooling were the full atrocities of racism and other forms of discrimination ever really explained. And of course, racism and more specifically, White Supremacy, doesn't have to make the news or be as explicitly visible as the examples listed above. As Germán also says, "When a lot of people think of white supremacy, they connote white men in hoods on corners screaming racial slurs and doing extreme things, but white supremacy could be used interchangeably for racism" (V. Brown & Keels, 2021).

This lack of knowledge limits my ability to teach fully and truthfully. Instead, I might combat racism with platitudes like "be kind" or simply

encourage kids to "not see color," which only further erases the experiences of people of color. If we refuse to see race, how can we even begin to talk productively about racism? School-aged children in the United States are becoming increasingly diverse, making up more than half of the student population. How can we as teachers address race and racism if we do not first turn the lens on ourselves? If we do not examine our own racial socialization, then how can we fully understand ourselves, much less our students?

Invitation to Reflect

Consider, as I did above, how your own specific privileges may inform your experiences. Privilege can be difficult to wrestle with—we often do not want to see the ways in which we are advantaged. Because of the **negativity bias,** we tend to focus on negative experiences first. Consider, for example, when someone asks you how your day has been. Many of us might recall negative experiences first: the missed call, the traffic on the way home, the line at the store, or any number of things.

Likewise, it may be easier to think of all the ways in which we are disadvantaged first before considering the many more ways we might be advantaged. Privileges, especially when you have always had them, can be hard to see. But acknowledging the way our privilege has worked to our advantage *and to our disadvantage* is critical in understanding our relative positionality to others.

For this self-reflection exercise, I follow educator and author Sara Ahmed's advice to take an inventory of my own privileges as a way to surface the complexities of how I might navigate the world. Drawing from a chapter in Oluo's (2018) *So You Want to Talk About Race,* Sara suggests making a list of all the ways in which you have privilege. For example, my own privileges include the following:

- Upper middle class
- Well-resourced neighborhood
- Married
- Partner works full time
- Cisgender
- Straight
- Fluent English-speaker
- Able-bodied
- Family close-by who often can care for my children (no childcare costs)

- US citizen and passport ✭
- Health insurance and access to good and convenient health care ✭
- Driver's license and own a car ✭
- Reliable internet ✭
- Homeowner
- College educated (Master's degree) —

Additionally:
- white
- Received a good education

Oluo then argues that because we enjoy those privileges that it is our responsibility to advocate for others to have the same opportunities that these privileges afford. Our privilege, in other words, does not need to come at another person's expense. For example, because I do not have to worry about childcare when I go to educational conferences, I should petition organizations to have affordable childcare options available or to provide greater flexibility in their professional development offerings.

After making your own list, revisit it periodically. As Ahmed has pointed out, it's in our privileges that our biases may be hiding.

Self-Reflection 4: Personal and Social Identities and Connecting with Students

As much as this is a book designed to help our students be more reflective and responsible thinkers, our effectiveness in helping them do so is limited by our own ability to understand *who we are* as teachers and as human beings. As much as this is a book designed to help our students, it's also about helping ourselves. I posit that the better we understand ourselves, the better position we will be in to help our students. If we can model reflective thinking in our classrooms, we can help our students navigate the question *who am I?* As Dr. Lyiscott (2017) reminds us:

> Some of the most deeply problematic issues of inequity within the field of education are sustained by well-meaning people embracing progressive politics without intentional frameworks of self-reflection to guide their praxis in a healthy direction.

Invitation to Reflect

Take a moment to consider your own personal identities and the backgrounds and experiences that inform them. Of these, which have had the most impact on the way you navigate the world? Which are the most significant to your identity as a teacher and your relationship with students? Use the graphic in Figure 1.2 as a guide.

FIGURE 1.2 PERSONAL AND SOCIAL IDENTITIES AND IMPACT ON TEACHING STUDENTS

REFLECTING ON MYSELF . . .	CONSIDERING MY STUDENTS . . .	
WHO I AM PERSONALLY WITH REGARDS TO . . .	HOW THIS BACKGROUND MAY BE A BENEFIT TO MY TEACHING PRACTICES	HOW THIS BACKGROUND MAY BE A DRAWBACK IN MY TEACHING PRACTICES
Race		
Gender		
Sexuality		
Socioeconomics		
Religion		
Family Life or Structure		
Ability		
Education		
Geography		
Friend or peer group		
Political affiliation		
Media consumption		

To share from my personal reflection, consider what I have already shared about my own experiences regarding school, race, and socio-economics and their effect on my teaching. Or consider the influence of my friends and peers. For example, my friends and I have always prioritized academic achievement, both as students and now as parents with our own school-aged children. While we understand that getting good grades isn't everything there is in life—after all, what good are grades if we are not good people?—we made it a priority to study, even at the expense of other hobbies and interests. Our parents were also the type to call up grandparents and aunties about our report cards. While my friends and I don't go this far as parents, I know that we communicate the message to our own kids that academic achievement is a priority. Because many of my close friends are also Asian American and, like me, second-generation children of Asian immigrants, this emphasis on academics is both rooted in cultural beliefs and a response to White dominant culture. As Dr. Sealey-Ruiz (2020) writes, "Individuals who develop racial literacy are able to engage in the necessary personal reflection about their racial beliefs and practices and teach their students to do the same."

Thus, my personal experience may benefit my students in that I can empathize with families and kids who might prioritize grades over other interests. I know what it is like to navigate the pressure of academic achievement as a student, to feel the anxiety over getting high grades to get into a good college. Over my career, many students, also Asian American and children of immigrant parents, shared these struggles with me. I can empathize with the difficulties and negative impact of that pressure; it's this understanding that I hope I can use to help my students and their families.

On the other hand, because my experience among my friends has been limited, I have less experience with students and families for whom academic achievement may not be as high a priority, for any number of valid reasons. Even though I played sports in school and took piano lessons for many years, I don't know, for example, what it's like to be such a talented athlete or musician that I would dedicate extended time and energy to either endeavor. As a teacher whose personal experiences have always prioritized academics, I might discount—or even dismiss—the investment my students and their families have in other areas. Furthermore, if the proverb is correct and it "takes a village," my village of friends has reinforced the importance of academic achievement among my own children. This may make it harder for me to see how such villages of support are not necessarily in place for all students.

To continue reflecting on your own identities and their impact on your teaching, see Dr. Talusan's (2022) research and the reflection tools she offers in her book, *The Identity Conscious Educator: Building Habits and Skills for a More Inclusive School*.

Self-Reflection 5: Inclusive Literacy Classroom Audit

While it is human to have biases, the problem with biases—especially when unexamined—is that they can prevent us from reaching *all* of our students. If we want our literacy practices to be truly inclusive, we need to regularly "check in" with ourselves and perhaps invite a colleague or your department into this process.

Invitation to Reflect

Consider, for example, using the questions in Figure 1.3 to check in with yourself. The questions build upon the ideas in this chapter and take them a little bit further. As you answer these questions, pay attention to how you feel as you respond. Set aside some quiet time to reflect on your responses—or, better yet, consider inviting a trusted colleague

to respond and discuss together. You might also work in small groups at a department or faculty meeting to discuss as well. Making self-reflection a regular part of your work as a professional can be difficult but necessary.

FIGURE 1.3   HOW INCLUSIVE IS YOUR LITERACY CLASSROOM, REALLY?

ANCHOR QUESTION	CONSIDER . . .
How inclusive is the media you consume, personally and professionally?	• What do you read by people of color, LGBTQ+ authors, and writers with disabilities? What books, news articles, publications? • What television programs, films, podcasts, and other multimedia do you consume and who creates that media? Whose voices are privileged? • What professional literature do you read? How often and in what ways do you extend your professional reading to include all voices? • How diverse is your professional learning community?
How inclusive is your curriculum?	• In what ways is your curriculum shaped by your own educational experiences? • Whose voices are centered in the texts you teach? Whose voices are marginalized or missing? • How do you recognize and celebrate the backgrounds of diverse authors already included in your curriculum? • In what ways do you integrate cultural and racial literacy in your instruction? • How often do you conduct an audit of your curriculum? In what ways has your curriculum changed to meet the needs of today's students? To what extent do you regularly examine and revise your curriculum to search for problems or gaps?
How inclusive is your classroom library?	• How does your classroom library mirror your own reading preferences versus those of your students? • Do you know which voices are represented on your bookshelves? Which voices are missing? • In what ways do you include—and how do you find—#ownvoices titles to add to your library? How are these voices integrated versus othered in the way you organize or share titles?
How inclusive are your mentor texts for writing?	• What writing—and whose voices—do you hold up as mentors of excellent writing and for what purpose? • What is your definition of good writing? In what ways does that definition include or exclude particular voices or linguistic varieties?
How inclusive is your language?	• How often do you use gendered versus non-gendered language? • How do you model respectful and asset-based language (versus deficit language) to describe others, both with students and colleagues? • How does your language affirm the identities of others in ways that demonstrate respect for their cultures, identities, and experiences?

ANCHOR QUESTION	CONSIDER . . .
How inclusive are your class discussions?	• How equitable are your class discussions? In what ways do you ensure that all student voices are heard? • How do you scaffold class discussion to encourage "courageous conversations"?
How do you model inclusive thinking for your students?	• How often do you show (think aloud) inclusive thinking when discussing your decisions and responses to texts? • In what ways do you demonstrate intellectual and cultural humility in front of students?
How often do you discuss inclusive practices with your colleagues?	• In what ways—and how often—do you and your colleagues reflect on your practices to ensure that all voices are recognized and respected? • How do you ensure that the voices of educators of color are heard and appreciated? • In what ways do you advocate for inclusive practices beyond your classroom?

Self-Reflection 6: Learning From the Experiences of Educators of Color

Coming face-to-face with our own biases, especially as we realize that these biases may have led us to unintentionally harm students, can be a painful process. This process can be even more painful for teachers who feel unsupported or isolated in doing antibias work in their schools. And if you are an educator who is from a marginalized community—and perhaps from *multiple* marginalized communities—then this process can feel overwhelming.

▶ "Social justice is humanizing our classroom environments so that all students not only see themselves but also really see others. It is when we see others we are able to not only express empathy but also assertively pursue justice alongside those experiencing oppression. Social justice is a serious pursuit of equity and expressing empathy for others in their paths to seek justice. It's NOT a trivial unit or lesson or checkbox. It's how you conduct your classroom daily. It is also how you live your life. Do you humanize and democratize your classroom space? Do you truly value diversity, equity, and justice in your daily life?" —Shana V. White

In May 2019, Dr. Kim Parker and I organized #31DaysIBPOC. For each day during that month, we featured a personal essay of a

different educator at the website, 31daysIBPOC.wordpress.com. It was our hope that we could "write in solidarity about the many ways we define ourselves, our practices, and our lives."

Invitation to Reflect

Scan the QR to read the #31DaysIBPOC blog

For this reflection, scan the QR code to go to the #31DaysIBPOC website and read the stories these educators share. If you are a White teacher, the essays may provide an important perspective or counternarrative that you might not have immediately available to you. To process these essays (individually or in a group), consider using the following questions:

- What information resonated with your own experiences?

- What surprised you? Why did this surprise you? What assumptions did you previously hold that made this surprising?

- What information challenged your perspectives or beliefs? Why, and in what ways?

- How did you feel as you were reading? Can you name those emotions? Where might these emotions be coming from?

Many of the essays included in the #31DaysIBPOC series are written by educators of color who share their own racial identity development stories and how their journeys impact their work with students. These stories should serve as reminders that antibias work must be as much personal as it is professional. We do not leave who we are in our personal lives at the door when we enter our classrooms.

CHALLENGING SOCIETAL BIAS

Up to this point, we've looked at bias starting at the perspective of our individual experiences. Before I close this chapter, it's important to name the ways that bias on a societal bias—*particularly bias that is rooted in White Supremacy culture*—impacts us as people and educators.

Any time any group of people comes together—whether they form informal organizations, institutions, religious congregations, art classes, school communities, clubs, study groups, or sports teams, and many others—they create a *culture*. Culture can be defined as a "social system of meaning and custom that is developed by a group of people to assure its adaptation and survival. These groups are distinguished by a set of unspoken rules that shape values, beliefs, habits, patterns of thinking, behaviors and styles of communication" (Institute for

Democratic Renewal and Project Change Anti-Racism Initiative, 2000, p. 32). Although cultures created in different groups vary, a larger *shared* culture (or imposed, depending on your point-of-view) exists on a societal level—"values, beliefs, habits, patterns of thinking, behaviors and styles of communication" that are characteristic of *society as a whole*. In the United States, that culture can be described as White dominant or White Supremacy culture.

Self-Reflection 7: White Supremacy Culture

In the late 1990s, scholar Tema Okun, in collaboration with Kenneth Jones, drafted a list of White Supremacy culture characteristics. In a 2023 interview with The Intercept (Grim, 2023), Okun reveals that the original paper was never meant to be posted or shared as widely online and out of context, as it has since the murder of George Floyd in 2016. In this widespread use, the characteristics of White Supremacy culture have been used in productive ways to challenge the harmful impacts of White Supremacy, but it has also been misused and weaponized.

For example, although the characteristics are presented as a list, they are not meant to be used as "a checklist to assess or target someone." As Okun explains, the characteristics are "linked together," and that nobody "uses one characteristic." When used well and as intended, Okun argues, understanding the characteristics of White Supremacy culture can be transformative and liberating: When we can identify the ways that White Supremacy limits and restricts our thinking, we can disrupt that pattern and expand our ability to consider multiple perspectives, possibilities, and solutions. As Okun (2021a) concludes, "The good news is that while white supremacy culture informs us, it does not define us. It is a construct, and anything constructed can be deconstructed and replaced" (p. 5).

In other words, by identifying and disrupting societal biases caused by White Supremacy culture, we can *get free*.

In 2021, Okun revised and updated her work on White Supremacy Culture Characteristics, which can be found on a centralized website (WhiteSupremacyCulture.info) created by Okun. In the update, Okun expounds on central elements not previously developed or named explicitly. Okun explains, "fear is an essential characteristic, as is the assumption of 'qualified' attached to whiteness. Defensiveness [is] broadened to include denial [and] a class lens and issues of intersectionality are important to address" (Okun, 2021b, p. 1). Another key feature of Okun's revised version are the antidotes she shares, practical ways to challenge these characteristics. The Racial Equity Principles outlined on the website are also useful and can support the work throughout this book.

Invitation to Reflect

Okun (2021a) identifies the following characteristics of White Supremacy Culture (pp. 6–28):

- Fear

- Perfectionism

- Qualified

- Either/Or Binary

- Progress is Bigger/More and Quantity over Quality

- Worship of the Written Word

- Individualism and I'm the Only One

- Defensiveness and Denial

- Right to Comfort, Fear of Open Conflict, and Power Hoarding

- Urgency

As Okun reminds us, it's not that any of these characteristics are inherently bad by themselves, but when they operate to control our behavior, when they become the driving force behind our decision-making, and when they prevent us from considering other ways of being, that's where the *supremacy* part of White Supremacy culture harms us.

Read Tema Okun's work, White Supremacy Culture Characteristics

Even if you have already encountered Okun's work, for this reflection, take some time to review her revised and updated paper, which provides expanded context and discussions about the nuances of each characteristic.

And while the characteristics are about Whiteness specifically, people of all racial identities are vulnerable to the harmful effects of White Supremacy culture. As I have already shared, my own racial and cultural identities do not immunize me from internalizing White Supremacy culture, but they do inform the way I respond and why.

After reading and reflecting on Okun's update, perhaps with a colleague or friend, consider the following questions:

- Which characteristics feel most familiar to you? In what ways?

- How do you see multiple characteristics working together in your life?

- Which characteristics do you see most often in school?

Self-Reflection 8: Biases in Our Literacy Practices

Schools often reflect the values and beliefs of the communities they serve. Unfortunately, no community in the United States is immune to White Supremacy culture, and neither are schools. In fact, much of what we consider acceptable school rules, policies, and practices are informed by many of the characteristics of White Supremacy culture. For example, the emphasis on standardized testing and data-driven decision-making often minimizes or completely eclipses other ways of assessing learning. Again, it's not that there isn't a role for quantitative data, even standardized tests, but the problem arises when these tests effectively reign supreme in school decision-making and state and federal law.

Invitation to Reflect

In my experience as an English teacher, I've observed many biases in how we teach reading and writing: what counts as "reading," what counts as "writing," what counts as "academic," how we define rigor, how we measure learning, how we define literacy, what types of narratives we teach and how we teach them. But if we are to take an *antibias approach* to literacy, we must

1. Identify biases in our literacy practices
2. Teach *against* those biases

Figure 1.4 lists some of the biases I have observed across my teaching career. Some of these may resonate with your own experiences as a teacher or as a student. You may have observed other biases as well. Recall that biases are neither inherently good nor bad, but they do inform the critical decisions we make as teachers about whose stories are worth telling, how we respond as readers, and how we encourage students to make sense of their world in their writing. In other words, these biases undergird all of our literacy practices. By identifying and noticing when they inform our decisions, we can then ask ourselves questions such as: *Am I doing what's best for students or what's easiest or most convenient? Does this bias perpetuate one way of learning or being in the world at the exclusion of other equally valuable ways of learning or being in the world?*

As you look at Figure 1.4, what feels familiar? What other "counter practices" would you suggest to interrupt these dominant practices? How do the biases in our literacy practices overlap or relate to Okun's characteristics of White Supremacy culture?

FIGURE 1.4   BIASES IN OUR LITERACY PRACTICES

BIAS (DOMINANT PRACTICE)	EXAMPLE	WHAT TEACHERS CAN DO (COUNTER PRACTICE)
Teaching stories of individual heroism over stories of collective action and community	Text selections focus on "hero" stories such as *The Odyssey*. Literary analysis may emphasize a protagonist's individual actions and conflicts.	Teach more stories that focus on communities and the interactions between and among characters v. a single character.
Focusing on individual effort and responsibility over social contexts and circumstances	Literary analysis may prioritize an individual character's actions with less analysis on setting and social-political context.	Ask students to consider how a character's environment (cultural norms, historical context, and systems of oppression) may impact their choices.
Prioritizing content recall over skill application	Assessments may prioritize being able to memorize and recall factual information from texts rather than applying novel reading skills to new texts and contexts.	Ask students to apply the skills they have practiced in one text to a new text.
Prioritizing product over process	Assessments are largely summative rather than formative. Students' grades do not reward progress and improvement, only final products.	Consider other forms of data collection that are ongoing and include qualitative assessment, such as portfolios that reveal growth over time.
Valuing quantity over quality	Writing assignments measured by word or page count versus informed by purpose of task.	Focus on meeting a task versus a minimum number of words, sentences, or paragraphs.
Favoring traditional print media over audio-visual media	Most curricula center the written and print texts such as novels, short stories, poetry.	Teach students how to read and analyze film, podcast, video, graphic novel, art—expand the definition of "text."
Favoring traditional writing forms over other genres and modes	Most writing is focused on literary analysis or formal argument.	Expand students' writing tasks to include more real-world writing application and genres.
Engaging in monologue over dialogue	Most talk in class is one-directional, from teacher to students, or from one student to another mediated by the teacher.	Practice more authentic forms of conversation and provide multiple opportunities for unstructured dialogue.
Valuing certainty over open-endedness	Essays center on thesis statements that point to a single conclusion and all evidence supports that single conclusion.	Provide students more opportunities to read, study, and write essays that entertain multiple perspectives and are rooted in inquiry.
Teaching one way versus many ways	Essay writing may focus on a single form as "correct" (i.e., five-paragraph essays).	Use a diversity of mentor texts to expand students' understanding of writing possibilities.

Self-Reflection 9: From the Individual to the Systemic

As you've read throughout this chapter, you've noticed the theme *our beliefs matter*. What we believe about ourselves and others—and what we believe constitutes a "just" society—matters. Our beliefs (and biases) drive our behaviors. Our behaviors drive our practices. Our practices drive our pedagogy. Our pedagogy drives the curriculum, which becomes policy. Policies drive impact, and our impact determines outcomes. The outcomes we see—academic *and* socio-emotional—are neither accidental nor inevitable, but rather the indirect and direct result of all the beliefs we hold about children and learning.

During the Institute for Racial Equity (IREL) that I co-facilitate with Dr. Sonja Cherry-Paul, we ask participants to consider their individual beliefs and actions in the context of various systems of oppression (see Figure 1.5). We draw from Garcia and Van Soest's (2003) work on systems of oppression to help participants think about interconnectedness of four different levels of oppression: the individual, interpersonal, institutional, and the cultural.

FIGURE 1.5 SYSTEMS OF OPPRESSION

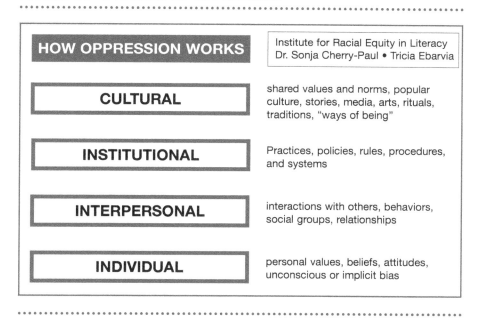

Adapted from Garcia and Van Soest (2003)

Invitation to Reflect

Review the model of systemic oppression in Figure 1.5 and consider how one or many of the beliefs you have as an individual informs—or is a result of—your experiences at an interpersonal, institutional, or

cultural level. For example, when I think about my experiences at each level:

- My *individual* belief that hard work pays off (just world hypothesis) may affect
- My *interpersonal* relationships if I judge others who are less "successful" as simply not working "hard enough," which may be reflected in
- My classroom (*institutional*) practices when I interpret students' lack of homework completion as a lack of effort, rather than as another deeper issue, which feeds into
- A larger *cultural* belief that some types of people may simply lack the work ethic to be successful.

Another way to use this model for self-reflection is to move in the other direction. For example:

- Because of the *cultural* stereotypes that "Asians are good at math" . . .
- At the *institutional* level in schools, Asian American students may be encouraged to take higher level STEM-related subjects, which leads to
- Racially segregated classrooms that are with disproportionate representation of Asian American students in honors science classes, which means that students' *interpersonal* relationships may also be racially segregated, which informs
- My *individual* belief as a teacher (and person) that all Asians are "good" at only certain subjects.

Try this exercise for yourself, starting at any point, to help you to surface the relationship between our individual and cultural beliefs.

Self-Reflection 10: Breaking the Cycle

Learn more about Harro's Cycle of Socialization

Learn more about Harro's Cycle of Liberation

Other useful models for thinking about how our socialization impacts our beliefs and behaviors are Dr. Bobbie Harro's Cycles of Socialization and Liberation. Dr. Harro's research (Figure 1.6) outlines the cycle in which we are socialized into certain beliefs and behaviors based on our experiences throughout life—and how these beliefs and behaviors are then reinforced. Dr. Harro's Cycles of Socialization and Liberation consists of various stages, outlined in Figure 1.6, which offers an abbreviated description of the varying stages of each cycle. You can read more about both models by scanning the QR codes on this page as well.

Invitation to Reflect

As you study Dr. Harro's model of socialization, consider the ways in which this applies to you: where do you see your personal experiences reflected in this cycle? Then take a look at the second model that Dr. Harro offers to us to consider: the Cycle of Liberation. In this latter model, we can thus try to imagine what it might look like to "get free" and to develop the "liberatory consciousness" (Love) we need to act outside the more damaging effects of our socialization.

FIGURE 1.6 CYCLES OF SOCIALIZATION AND LIBERATION

CYCLE OF SOCIALIZATION (ADAPTED FROM HARRO, 2018)		
STAGE	**DESCRIPTION**	**REFLECTION QUESTIONS**
The Beginning	Although individuals are born without preexisting "biases, stereotypes, prejudices" and so on, the world that we're born into already has such "mechanics in place."	What harmful patterns of thought (biases and prejudices) and systemic injustices (discrimination) existed before you were even born?
First Socialization	We then begin to learn "values, roles, rules" and how to be in the world from our caregivers, the "people we love and trust" (who have themselves already been socialized into certain values, roles, and rules).	What potentially harmful patterns of thought (biases and prejudices) and systemic injustices (discrimination) were you first exposed to as a child? What "values, rules, and roles" did you learn about yourself and others from your earliest caregivers?
Institutional and Cultural Reinforcement	As we experience more of the world, institutions (schools, churches, legal system) and culture (social practices, language, media) "bombard" us with messages. Sometimes direct and sometimes indirect, these messages tell us what to value and believe and how to behave.	What messages did you learn about your own role(s) and responsibility(ies) in the world from schools, churches, and other organizations? What messages did you learn about others? What messages were direct? What messages were indirect?
Enforcements	Throughout our lives, the "values, roles, and rules" we learn from our first caregivers, as well as through our interactions with institutions and cultures, are enforced and reinforced continuously.	How were the dominant messages about yourself and others enforced and reinforced as you grew older? How did the totality of these messages impact you?
Results	As a result of being inundated with messages about how to be in the world, both direct and indirect, we respond in any numbers of ways, including but not limited to "dissonance, silence, anger, dehumanization, guilt, collusion, ignorance" and the "internalization of patterns of power."	As you have embarked on your own journey to be more aware of the potentially harmful ways you have been socialized, how have you responded? What beliefs, feelings, thoughts, or behaviors have surfaced?
Direction for Change	In facing how we are impacted by our socialization, individuals come to a point where they can choose to change, raise their consciousness, interrupt harmful patterns, etc.	Reflect on a moment, encounter, or opportunity that you have had your own consciousness raised around your identity, socialization, and issues of justice. What happened? How?
Action	Given this choice, individuals may change, at least in some ways, or may choose not to change, thus reinforcing the status quo and restarting the cycle with the next generation.	In what ways have you identified and interrupted harmful patterns of thought or behavior? In what ways have you not? Why? What work do you still need to do?

(Continued)

From a young age I was encouraged to ⟩

(Continued)

CYCLE OF LIBERATION (ADAPTED FROM HARRO, 2018)		
STAGE	**DESCRIPTION**	**REFLECTION QUESTIONS**
Waking Up and Getting Ready	As individuals learn more about how systems of oppression work, they can begin to identify and notice where and when these harmful patterns of thought and behavior appear in their own lives.	What harmful patterns of thought and behavior have you recognized in your own experiences and socialization? What made you notice these patterns? What did you have to unlearn and relearn?
Reaching Out	During this intrapersonal stage, individuals begin to raise their consciousness, and they seek out more and new information and learn about how systems of oppression work. They may explore tools for support.	How have you reached out to seek new information and learning? How have you begun to speak out in order to learn more?
Building Community	During this interpersonal shift, individuals begin to reach out to other people, both people similar to themselves, as well as people with different identities or experiences.	How have you formed relationships and connections with those who share similar identities and those who are different? Where did you go, who did you seek, and what was this experience like? What have you learned?
Coalescing	During this stage, and working with others, individuals begin to prepare, plan, and organize to dismantle systems of oppression.	How have you taken what you've learned on your own and with others and channeled that into positive change for greater social and racial justice? Examples may include educating others, lobbying, fundraising, refusal to participate in harmful systems, etc.
Creating Change	During this stage, focus is turned toward the larger systems of power that are responsible for perpetuating oppression. This may include advocating and influencing policy changes, disrupting assumptions, definitions, taking on leadership roles, etc.	In what ways have you advocated, initiated, and effected change at a larger systems level in the communities, organizations, and institutions you participate in? What challenges have you faced and how are you overcoming them?
Maintaining	Because the status quo in society often reverts back to systems based in oppression, during this stage, individuals intentionally reflect on, model, and maintain their commitment to fighting against injustice.	What actions or habits have you changed in your life to make your commitment to dismantling systems of oppression something that is both sustainable and long-term? How do you help others engage in this work?

FINAL THOUGHTS, NEXT STEPS

While much of the book has so far focused on teachers, the remaining chapters will bring you into my classroom where I'll share reading, writing, listening, and thinking strategies that can help our students build habits of critical self-reflection and nuanced thinking. As you read, I invite you to learn alongside your students, doing the same reading and writing that you ask them to do. Not only will this enable you to be a more effective model for your students as a co-learner, you will likely discover some things about yourself along the way. Figures 1.7 and 1.8 offer suggested resources to help you dig deeper into the topics I've presented so far.

FIGURE 1.7 A BEGINNER'S GUIDE TO LEARNING ABOUT BIASES

LEARN MORE

- Learning for Justice, "Test Yourself for Hidden Bias" and Critical Practices for Antibias Education Framework

  In this professional development module online on the Learning for Justice website, learn about how stereotypes, prejudice, discrimination, and bias can function in classrooms. Follow up this module by examining Learning for Justice's suggestions for classroom practices to combat bias using their framework for antibias education.

- Hidden Brain, "Think Fast with Daniel Kahneman"

  In this weekly podcast, psychologist Shankar Vendantam discusses the intersections of psychology, society, and culture. In this episode, he discusses the brain's two response systems that are at the root of cognitive biases with Nobel Prize winning cognitive scientist, Daniel Kahneman.

- Implicit Association Test (IAT), Harvard University

  The Implicit Association Test (IAT) is a tool developed by Project Implicit researchers at Harvard University. There are several different IATs that measure a variety of types of biases. The tests are free for anyone to take, but require a log-in, which can be obtained directly on the website.

- Awareness of Implicit Biases, Yale University

  Yale University's Center for Teaching and Learning has compiled an extensive set of resources online to identify bias in instruction and offers strategies to combat such biases.

FIGURE 1.8 A BEGINNING READING LIST TO UNLEARN AND RELEARN OURSELVES, OTHERS, AND OUR HISTORY

- *The 1619 Project* by Nikole Hannah Jones

- *America for Americans: A History of Xenophobia in the United States* by Erika Lee

- *An African American and Latinx History of the United States* by Paul Ortiz

- *An Afro-Indigenous History of the United States* by Kyle T. Mays

- *Biased* by Jennifer L. Eberhardt

- *A Black Women's History of the United States* by Daina Ramey Berry, Kali Nicole Gross

- *A Different Mirror: A History of Multicultural America* by Ronald Takaki

(Continued)

(Continued)

- *A Disability History of the United States* by Kim E. Nielsen
- *Disability Visibility* edited by Alice Wong
- *Dreams from Many Rivers* by Margarita Engle
- *Everything You Wanted to Know about Indians But Were Afraid to Ask* by Anton Treuer
- *History Teaches Us to Resist* by Mary Frances Berry
- *How to be an Antiracist* by Ibram X. Kendi
- *An Indigenous People's History of the United States* by Roxanne Dunbar-Ortiz and *An Indigenous People's History of the United States for Young People* adapted by Debbie Reese and Jean Mendoza
- *Is Everyone Really Equal? An Introduction to Key Concepts in Social Justice Education* by Oslem Sensoy and Robin DiAngelo
- *Love and Resistance: Out of the Closet Into the Stonewall Era* and *The Stonewall Reader* edited by Jason Baumann
- *A More Beautiful and Terrible History* by Jeanine Theoharis
- *The Myth of the Model Minority* by Rosalind S. Chou and Joe R. Feagin
- *The Next American Revolution* by Grace Lee Boggs
- *Our America: A Hispanic History of the United States* by Felipe Fernández-Armesto
- *Pushout* by Monique Morris
- *A Queer History of the United States* by Michael Bronski
- *Race for Profit* by Keeanga-Yamahtta Taylor
- *Racial Healing Handbook* by Annaliese Singh
- *Stamped: Racism, Antiracism, and You* by Ibram X. Kendi and Jason Reynolds
- *Strangers from a Different Shore: A History of Asian Americans* by Ronald Takaki
- *Teaching to Transgress* by bell hooks
- *The Warmth of Other Suns* and *Caste* by Isabel Wilkerson
- *Waking Up White* by Debby Irving
- *Where Do We Go From Here: Chaos or Community?* by Martin Luther King, Jr.
- *White Rage* by Carol Anderson

How can we *get free* through **community?**

Our young people's social media feeds are filled with examples of individual excellence: professional athletes, music artists, Hollywood actors, YouTubers, politicians, tech giants, and countless others. Our national myth-making and narratives are filled with stories of individuals who overcame hardship through the sheer strength of their will and determination.

And yet.

I wonder how we might be better off focusing less on *individual* achievement and more on *community* and *connection*, less *competition* and more *cooperation*, less *me* and more *we*.

Schools are powerful, but not just because of the academic content and skills that students learn, though these are critical. Schools are powerful because every time students walk down our hallways and into our classrooms, students have opportunity after opportunity to experience infinite possible ways of being in the world. They can, for example, experience what it's like to be and be treated as a worker-producer in a capitalist society. They can experience what it's like to compete against peers in the pursuit of excellence, to see their value celebrated and defined by their accomplishments.

But they can also experience what it's like to be valued because they are part of a community, that their presence makes the community better, where dignity and respect are treated as a given and not commodities or privileges to be earned. They can experience what it's like to be seen and cared for by others, not because of what they do but for who they are.

In this chapter, we turn our lens on how *intentional community building* is critical in creating an antibias classroom and more just world. Every time we invite students to feel part of a community, where they feel seen and valued, we protect students against the loneliness and fear that can leave them vulnerable to those who would gladly take advantage. Every time we teach *against* the societal bias that favors rugged individualism at the expense of community, we are not only engaged in *imagining* a better world but actively *creating* one with our students.

CHAPTER 2

....

CREATING BRAVE SPACES

Community First

> *"We urgently need to bring to our communities the limitless capacity to love, serve, and create for and with each other."*
>
> —Grace Lee Boggs and Scott Kurashige

> *"If you have come here to help me, you are wasting your time. But if you have come because your liberation is bound up with mine, then let us work together."*
>
> —Lilla Watson

The minute I walked into Dr. DeVita Jones's classroom, I could feel joy, palpable and bursting. Dr. Jones's scholars were a bright and energetic group of second graders, and I felt fortunate to have the opportunity to observe her students explore the power of words during their daily writing workshop. I watched the way her students knew where to go, what to do, and how to read and write with agency and independence beyond what many might expect of most eight-year-olds.

My visit to Dr. Jones' classroom was one of several opportunities I had to observe my elementary colleagues and their young scholars at work and play. I learned a lot during my visits, but I was most impressed by their fearlessness—the way so many children approached their reading and writing with boundless joy: the way they called out and shared, crisscross-applesauce-seated, from the class carpet, the way they were willing to ask questions and guess answers, the way they listened and cheered for one another.

I had to wonder: did the teenagers sitting in my classroom feel this joy? I wasn't sure.

As a high school teacher, I spent many years focused on content, feeling the pressure of covering all the material, moving from text to text, checking off all the literary devices and themes along the way. But what I came to realize—and what my elementary colleagues beautifully reminded me—is that transformative learning doesn't happen via content. It happens through the relationships we build, on the first day and every day—relationships that encourage risk-taking and inspire joy, like the joy I saw on so many of Dr. Jones's young scholars.

Strong relationships don't just inspire joy in learning, either. Strong relationships are critical to creating a sense of belonging for each student in our classrooms. This sense of belonging is perhaps more critical now than ever. In April 2023, Vivek H. Murth, the Surgeon General of the United States, wrote in *The New York Times:*

> Loneliness and isolation hurt whole communities. Social disconnection is associated with reduced productivity in the workplace, worse performance in school, and diminished civic engagement. When we are less invested in one another, we are more susceptible to polarization and less able to pull together to face the challenges that we cannot solve alone—from climate change and gun violence to economic inequality and future pandemics. As it has built for decades, the epidemic of loneliness and isolation has fueled other problems that are killing us and threaten to rip our country apart.

When students feel a sense of belonging, they not only feel more connected to each other but also to the conversations we're having in class, to the issues that matter to them. There's a shared understanding that they belong to the world, that the learning they're doing *matters* and has *purpose*.

THE THIRD TEACHER

One thing that elementary teachers know all too well is how much the physical space of the classroom matters. Every elementary classroom I've walked into—during my observations as a teacher and in visits to my own children's classrooms—make intentional use of the physical space. Thoughtful nooks for reading, bulletin boards that celebrate students' work, and classroom libraries filled with books that provide mirrors and windows into rich human experiences can make all the difference.

In their Critical Practices for Antibias Education, Learning for Justice reminds us that "when asking students to explore issues of personal and social identity, teachers must provide safe spaces where students are seen, valued, cared for and respected." Furthermore, teachers need to also pay attention to the way the physical space can be powerful: "Without saying a word, classrooms send messages about diversity, relationship building, communication and the roles of teachers and students."

Several years ago, when I was researching classroom design, I came across a wonderful book titled *The Third Teacher*, a collaborative work by OWP/P architects, VS Furniture, and Bruce Mau Design (2010). The authors—from three different global design firms—believe, as Montessorians and proponents of the Reggio Emilia approach do, that in any classroom there are three teachers. First, there is the teacher. Then other students. The environment is "the third teacher." Combining design principles with research in education, psychology, and cognitive science, the authors make an argument for the importance of the physical learning environment. What messages about teaching and learning do our students see when they walk into our classrooms? Desks arranged in separate rows tell students that working individually is what's valued. Desks arranged in groups tell students that working together is valued instead. And desks, whether in rows or groups that all face the teacher tell them who the most important person is in the room.

Or consider the one-size-fits-all message that identical desks and seats send—that even though some students may be bigger or smaller than others, or that some students learn better standing versus sitting—that everyone needs to learn the same way. We differentiate our instruction, but imagine how powerful differentiation could be if we differentiated our learning environment.

Try this. Enter your classroom as if you were a student. Even before students enter your room, what do they see? I wanted students to know that my classroom could be a safe place for each of them to learn, which is why I have had a sign on my door for more than a decade that read: "This classroom is a safe learning environment for all students regardless of ability, gender, ethnicity, race, religion, and sexual orientation." Now, I know that what matters more than any sign is what happens inside the classroom, but we know that words can be powerful. A sign like this not only tells students what they can expect, but I read that sign every day, too. It's a reminder to me that the first responsibility I have as a teacher is to provide a learning environment for my students where they know their identities will be respected. Related, several years ago, I visited Tampa Preparatory School and saw this sign outside a classroom window. I think it's important that kids

TEACHER PLEDGE

I WILL NOT BE PARTISAN BUT I REFUSE TO BE NEUTRAL.

I WILL SPEAK OUT FOR UNDERSTANDING, INCLUSION, AND EQUITY.

I WILL FIGHT HATRED AND INJUSTICE WHEREEVER I SEE IT.

know what they can hold their teachers to and what I, as a teacher, need to remember in my role.

For almost twenty years, I had two questions posted on my classroom door that sent important messages about expectations: What are you reading? What are you working on? I also kept a dry-erase sign with "Mrs. Ebarvia is currently reading . . ." that I update during the year. My hope is that as students walk in and out of the classroom, or linger by the door before class starts, that they'll see these signs and begin to internalize their implicit messages of lifelong learning. Even though I no longer have this classroom, I still have a "What I'm Reading" sign outside my office. (Figure 2.1 shows photos of my classroom space.)

Once you enter your classroom, pause a moment to look around. When your students walk into your room, what is the first thing they notice? What's the big message? When students walked into my class, the first thing they noticed were books, books, and more books. Students knew that reading would be a priority in this classroom. My colleague next door had large block letters that spell out the word L-O-V-E. He wanted his space to be one that fosters a shared love of learning and community of people who care about each other. What do students see first or most prominently when they walk into your room?

FIGURE 2.1 MY CLASSROOM SPACE

The pictures here of my classroom reveal a space twenty years in the making. While I was fortunate to be in a district that recently invested in flexible seating, building a classroom community is more than the physical space. Over the years, I built my classroom library by shopping used bookstores, scrounging through library thrift sales, and applying for grants, adding a few books at a time. My hope is that when students walk into my room that this is a space in which we will read and learn from one another. The way the desks are arranged, the messages on the wall—these are *first* steps in creating a community space, but as you can see in the rest of this chapter, it's what we *do* in that space that ultimately matters.

VULNERABLE AND BRAVE SPACES

No meaningful learning can happen if students don't feel welcome, safe, and seen in our classrooms. And because exploring our personal identities and biases is incredibly vulnerable work, building a sense of community is not just critical but *required*. As educator Silvas (2017) has pointed out:

> A classroom is an intricate web of delicate strands woven together. We've all experienced the highs and lows of students' emotions; for students to grow academically, their emotions have to fit just right to form a supportive and safe environment. All students have social, political, and cultural differences. As a teacher, this makes creating safe spaces even more challenging.

If for any reason you cannot make a commitment to being intentional about building community and taking the time to do so, I caution against proceeding with some of the ideas I share in this book, *especially those related to deep, personal identity work*. Asking students to engage in self-reflection related to any one of their identities— particularly regarding race, gender, social class, among others— *without* the safety net of a supportive community can do more harm than good. For some students, it can even be traumatic. Furthermore, students should never be asked to write or share anything personal that they are not comfortable writing or sharing. We must respect students as the narrators of their own stories. Their stories belong to them, not us, even if we might be a necessary audience. As Silvas (2018) also points out:

> As we read their writing, we must remain open and grounded. If students decide to share a traumatic or adverse experience, they are showing trust, and we must continue to develop that trust. There will be times their writing will remain private. On the other hand, students' safety and well-being are the top priorities. Teachers have a responsibility to take action and follow reporting protocols if students reveal something that puts their safety in jeopardy.

Notebooks as Sacred Spaces

Just as we scaffold our reading and writing instruction to meet students where they are, we can take the same approach with students regarding speaking and sharing in community. My students use writer's notebooks regularly, and many years ago, I made a rule to never collect or read these notebooks unless students voluntarily shared or I asked them first (which I have yet to ever do).

I have always preferred that when my students are in class that we have physical notebooks. We also start each class writing in our notebook, and it doesn't take long before students get into the habit of pulling out their notebooks and favorite pen when they get to class. I am not opposed to using digital notebooks, and I regularly used digital notebooks with students for taking notes specific to the content we were studying in class. However, for personal notebook writing that we use to start class, build community, and explore our identities, my students have always used physical notebooks. In this way, their physical notebooks offer a refuge from the distractions of the digital world. I've had many students over the years express gratitude for this small respite from technology. All that said, if a student has an accommodation or specific learning need that requires a digital notebook, I would never force that student to use pen and paper.

When we begin our writer's notebook work early in the year, I tell students that the purpose of their writer's notebook is to explore their own ideas in a safe and uninhibited way. "The writing you do in your notebook is a conversation you have with yourself," I tell them. "It is not my position to intrude on that conversation unless you invite me into it." I never grade their notebooks. I understand that this isn't the practice of all teachers, and teachers need to do what works best for their students. Some teachers might wonder how I know students are "on task" if I don't check their notebooks: I often write when they write, modeling and sharing my own notebook work as well. But, when I'm not writing with them, I'm walking around the room as they write, my eyes skimming lightly over the pages. There is no mistaking students who are engaged in writing, heads bent over in thought, pencils scratching the page.

I start the year with frequent, low-stakes writing and sharing, such as asking students to choose one word or one sentence to share. I offer students opportunities to share their writing in small groups. Although I hope I can push them to share what they've written, I let students know they can also give a summary instead. I often let students choose their seats, so that the possibility of students sitting with peers they might trust to listen is, while not guaranteed, a little more likely. I encourage students to share not just what they are comfortable sharing, but "just beyond." When we push ourselves just slightly over our comfort zone, sharing gets a little easier each time. See specific prompts for notebook work in Chapter 3.

If you are a teacher who collects students' notebooks with their personal writing, take a moment to reflect on your motivation for doing so. What is your purpose for having students write personally in their notebooks in the first place? Does collecting it from them (for "points," for example) undermine this purpose? What message does this send? What are your assumptions about student learning and accountability?

Respecting Students' Personal Stories (and Boundaries)

That said, only students know what's "just beyond" their comfort zone, and it will be different each time depending on what we're writing. It's a delicate balance, encouraging students to share but also respecting their boundaries, yet if there is ever a choice to be made between one or the other, it is always the latter. We have tremendous power as educators, which is complicated not just by the power we have over a student's grades, but also by factors that may include gender, class, and race. As educator Flecha (2018) reminds us,

> a teacher's role as their students' primary audience is complicated by their systemic and often, racialized power over a student's life. We work in a profession dominated by white women teaching black and brown children. Believing that this does not impact what students choose to tell their teachers, how teachers hear students, and how teachers respond to students' words is intensely, insultingly, dangerously naive.

What makes this work particularly difficult is that we may never fully know the full impact of our power as teachers on students. Even though I argue that our students need to feel welcome, safe, and seen, the truth is that I'm not sure that I, or any teacher, can guarantee our students' emotional safety. Even the most seemingly innocuous topic might be a sensitive one. While we might then be tempted to stay away from bringing the personal into the classroom and stick to "content only," we know that this would be futile; after all, any discussion of literature or current events can be fraught with the personal.

Instead, what we can and must do is build habits of writing and self-reflection that our students can use to help them grapple with and clarify their thinking, especially during times they might feel most vulnerable. It's when our students feel vulnerable that we can help them lean into that vulnerability and be brave—in their reading, writing, and thinking.

In 2018, the day after the Parkland High School mass shooting, the first and most important thing my students did in class that day was write in their notebooks. It was not a day to stick to the content; it was a day to write through their confusion, grief, and fear. And because students knew that their notebook pages could be the safe and brave space they needed, that's just what they did.

Read my reflection following the Parkland shooting tragedy.

Unfortunately, in the many tragedies and injustices students have witnessed—including the murder of George Floyd and the January 6 insurrection—our notebooks became the place where students could turn. In many ways, writing in our notebooks regularly became a type of preventative self-care routine that we could draw from when we needed it most.

For more guidance on teaching with a trauma-informed approach, consider Silvas's suggestions, summarized here:

1. **Class Declarations of Trust:** Create routines for listening and speaking that allow for a judgment-free community that allows students to be vulnerable on their own terms.

2. **Privacy and Security:** Respect student privacy while maintaining our role as professional, trusted, and mandated reporters.

3. **Choice:** Return power to students by allowing them as much choice as possible regarding how and when to write, respond, and share.

In addition, Figure 2.2 includes more considerations for trauma-informed practices as developed by Flecha.

FIGURE 2.2   TRAUMA-INFORMED TEACHING PRACTICES
FOR PERSONAL NARRATIVES

DRAFTING (Generating Ideas)	PUBLISHING (Making Writing Public)
Prompting highly transitional children to quickly name people and places is daunting.	A child may be more comfortable sharing with you than with any of their classmates, let alone anyone outside of your classroom. Check in before . . .
• Tell students a day in advance that they will be brainstorming personal stories. • Try to center the classroom in your writing prompts. School is a common denominator among students. REVISION and EDITING When prompting narrative writing, we are not asking a student to relive an event once. Throughout revising and editing, students will experience that event again and again.	• Posting their writing on a bulletin board or online. • Sharing their writing with their families. • Asking them to read aloud. • Sharing with other teachers, administrators, or instructional coaches.

We tend to think of community-building exercises as fun, get-to-know-you icebreakers we do for a few days at the beginning of each school year before we dive into "content." To be honest, this was my approach for many years. Instead, we need to think of community building as something we do every day: **every class period is an opportunity to strengthen the bonds between students—or weaken them.** While the strategies that follow are useful in building community at the start of the school year, they also become touchstones to facilitate continued learning for the rest of the year.

As you review these strategies, note that I do not necessarily do all of these within the first few days of school, but do try to use most of them within the first few weeks and revisit throughout the year.

"Getting to Know You" Name Tents

Nothing seems to start a relationship with students on the right foot more than just knowing their names; often students express surprise and smile a little wider when they see me make the effort. This was especially important when I taught ninth graders who were already panicked about navigating an unfamiliar space. It seems like such an obvious and simple thing to learn students' names—*and to pronounce them correctly*—but if there's anything worth prioritizing early in the year, it's this.

To get student names right, I have asked students to record themselves saying their name aloud using a simple app like FlipGrid or even using the audio recording feature in my school's learning management system. If I ever needed to check or double-check a pronunciation, especially a last name during parent-teacher conferences, I then had these recordings as reference. In addition, a link to these recordings can also be provided with a class list to make sure that substitute teachers had access to the correct pronunciation of student names. As someone whose former last name was Bagamasbad, I would have appreciated this extra care when a substitute teacher called my name out in class.

I've had students make name tents for years and they are still the easiest and fastest way for me to learn student names, which comes in handy when you're teaching 125 students a year. Using a folded 8 ½ · 11-inch paper, students write their names—first names or nicknames—in big letters so that I can read it from across the room. I also ask students to write their name on both sides of the name tent so I, and their peers, can see it from multiple angles. Students also draw three to five pictures or words on the name tent to tell me and their classmates a little something about them. Students keep their name tents up during class. Whenever I call on them, I make it a practice to say their name

twice: once when I call on them and again when they are finished, and I thank them. I collect all name tents at the end of class. When students are writing in their notebooks at the start of class the next day, I use that time to individually match each student to their name tent.

Math teacher Sara Venderwerf helped me to take name tents a step further: following her lead, I include a chart like the one in Figure 2.3 inside the name tent. During the first week of school, I take two minutes at the end of each class for students to write down a note to me: an observation, question, small reflection, anything. I take them home each night and write a brief note back to each student (see Figure 2.4).

To be honest, I spend much of my prep periods that first week writing back to every student individually: even though my responses are usually no more than a sentence or two, responding to each student takes time, so I must prepare for all my classes ahead of time that week. It's been worth the payoff: I learn *so* much more about students and remember their names much more quickly than before I tried Sara's method. Then, after the first week of school, we move to end-of-the-week reflections in the form of Critical Incidents Questionnaires. (See page 84.)

FIGURE 2.3 "GETTING TO KNOW YOU" NAME TENTS

It's back-to-school time! At the end of each class this week, feel free to write me a brief note to let me know how things are going, if you have any questions, if you just want to share something about yourself or if there is just anything I should know.

MONDAY	TUESDAY	WEDNESDAY	THURSDAY	FRIDAY
Student:	*Student:*	*Student:*	*Student:*	*Student:*
Teacher:	*Teacher:*	*Teacher:*	*Teacher:*	*Teacher:*

FIGURE 2.4 "GETTING TO KNOW YOU" NAME TENTS

picture/sketch of something that represents yo

Monday, August 28	Comr
Comments: (student)	
I'm excited that we are getting to know everyone in our class' names, because I think that is very important. I LOVE Harry Potter and I hope we read lots of fantasy, but I like reading almost everything as long as there is a good story. Also sorry I was late, I don't know where I am, and I'm usual very punctual!	
Response: (teacher)	R

POSSIBLE QUESTIONS TO RESPOND TO: How do you feel about English like about reading, writing, or this class? What are you fearful of? Wh picture/sketch of something that represents you.

Monday, August 28	Tuesday, August
Comments: (student)	Comments:
I enjoyed class today.	
Response: (teacher)	Response:
Thank you. I'm glad, and I hope you enjoy class every day. ☺	

picture/sketch of something that represents you.

Monday, August 28	Tue
Comments: (student)	Comment
I had fun in this class. Today I got lost, ~~what~~ a lot, & hope I get used to it	
Response: (teacher)	Respons

Tuesday, August 28
Comments:
You are already making me feel more confident as a writer by making us write that reflection right away

Because of the open-ended nature of the prompt, students' responses to the name tents vary—but, in a way, that is exactly the point of the name tents. They provide a small opportunity for students to know their voices are heard in the opening days of school. Some students, like the one on the left, were open and revealed many interests over the course of the week, while others, like the one on the right, weren't sure what to say, which is okay, too. My hope is to open the doors in those opening days for students to share whatever they are willing.

Interview Activity

A few years ago, I realized that many of my students still didn't know each other's names several months into the school year. So I made it a priority to make sure that students learned each other's names and a little bit about each other as quickly as possible from day one.

On the second or third day of school, I pass out a sheet with a long list of interview questions, enough for every student in the class. The questions, as you can see in Figure 2.5, vary from your typical ice breaker question—what's your favorite flavor of ice cream?—to deeper, more thought-provoking questions—why do you think people are mean to one another? And of course, these questions can and should be adapted to suit the needs of your own students.

Because it is the beginning of the school year, as we looked at earlier in this chapter, it's critical that our questions do not ask students to disclose overly personal information—or at the very least, that our questions are open-ended enough so that students can reveal as little or as much as they like in ways that feel safest for them. While we cannot know everything about our students, especially at the start of the year, consider your student population and community and use that knowledge to inform the questions you decide to use.

Many teachers also use similar "getting to know you" questions in surveys they ask students to complete at the beginning of the year. I did this as well, although I shifted to exchanging letters with students instead (see page XX). Although surveys for the teacher are generally more private than interactive activities like the identity inventory mentioned here, we still need to be sensitive about the questions we ask. Author of *Equity-Centered Trauma-Informed Education*, Alex S. Venet has a very useful set of guidelines for teachers to consider before asking students to share personal information at the start of the year (or really, at any time of the year). Venet cautions against asking students for information that teachers are unprepared to handle. Instead, she recommends that instead of asking students to disclose what they wish teachers knew, we can ask students what they wish their teachers would *do*. Read more of Venet's suggestions at the QR code provided.

Read Alex Venet's "What I Wish Teachers Knew About 'What I Wish Teachers Knew'"

Next, I assign each student a number, which then corresponds to the interview question that they will be charged with asking all the other students in the class. I've found that it takes about as many minutes as students in the class—twenty minutes for a class of twenty to twenty-four students—for students to have enough time to interview each other. When they're finished, each student will have a data sheet comprised of every classmate's answer to their question.

After students take a few minutes to look at their data, I ask them if they notice any surprising or notable patterns. Students share their findings with each other, either through whole group discussion or in small groups using a discussion protocol for turning and talking (see chapter 4, "Listening and Speaking: Critical Conversations").

For an extension of this activity, I have also asked students to create a visual representation of their data (Figure 2.6) which we can post and refer back to in later units (this is especially useful when we begin discussion of what it means to have an "American" identity when I teach American literature).

FIGURE 2.5 INTERVIEW ACTIVITY

1. If you were given a lifetime supply of one kind of food, what would it be?
2. What was your favorite TV show as a little kid?
3. What is one of your goals for the new school year?
4. If you could wake up tomorrow having gained a new ability or skill (not superhero), what would it be?
5. What is a movie you've seen (not necessarily in theaters)?
6. What is the last song you listened to?
7. What do you believe is the most important job in the world?
8. How do you spend a typical Saturday?
9. Who is a person that you know in real life that you admire and why?
10. If you were given the power, what is a new law that you would create for the country?
11. If you could add any class/subject to the school curriculum, what would it be?
12. What do you believe is the number one reason that people are mean to each other?
13. What is the most important quality that you look for in a friend?
14. What is an interesting or unique thing about your family?
15. What is a phobia of yours?
16. Do you identify with a culture or ethnic heritage, and if so, what?
17. If you could get everyone in the world to do one thing, what would it be?
18. If you could be any fictional character, who would you be?
19. What is something that you are really good at?
20. What is the first book you remember reading?
21. What is your favorite flavor of ice cream?
22. What is your dream vacation?
23. If you could live in any type of house, what would it be?
24. If you were going to donate money to a charity or cause, which one and why?
25. If you could live in any other historical time period, what would it be and why?
26. What is your favorite holiday and why?
27. What superhero would you most like to be and why?
28. If you could live anywhere in the world, where would it be?
29. What is a word that has always sounded funny to you?
30. What is your favorite word?

FIGURE 2.6 INTERVIEW ACTIVITY INFOGRAPHICS

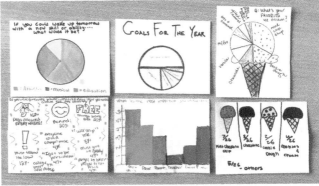

Although this activity has already accomplished quite a bit—it's given each student a unique role and an opportunity to connect with every other student in the class—the key here is the *reflection* I ask students to engage in toward the end. Specifically, I ask students to reflect a little more deeply on what the information we've found might say about us as individuals and as a class. In this way, we're opening up discussions about identity and what it is that makes us who we are. Below are some of the questions I ask students to reflect upon in writing and discussion. These questions, especially the last one, can serve as the seeds for longer narrative writing later.

- Which questions do you feel best represent who you are as an individual person? Why?

- Which questions do you think least represent who you are? Why? What's the difference between these questions and the previous?

- What does this information about each other tell us? Can we draw any conclusions about us as individuals or as a class?

- If we really wanted to get a sense of who we are as individuals or as a group, are there any questions that are missing? Which ones? What could they tell us about ourselves and each other?

- Choose a question that resonated with you. What memories or stories come to mind? Why might this story be important to you? How does this story help you to better understand yourself?

Interview Activity—Jenga Edition

I can't emphasize enough how critical it's been in my own classroom to give students time to get to know each other and opportunities to ask each other low-stakes but potentially meaningful questions. (This need for structured social interaction and play has become even more evident since the pandemic.)

Another way I use the interview questions from Figure 2.5 is by having students play Jenga in small groups of three to four students per group. Each Jenga piece corresponds to one of the interview questions (Figure 2.7); each time a student pulls a Jenga piece from the tower, they have to answer that question and then ask their teammates to do the same. While I tell students that the "competition" is to see which group can build the tallest tower within a time limit, I know that my goal is to have students get to know each other.

As with the previous interview activity, the most meaningful part of the process is in the *reflection* we do afterwards. This time, our reflection questions are focused on the team dynamic that emerged during the activity:

- How did it feel to play this game? Why?

- What made your team successful? Why?

- What challenges did your team have? How did you approach them?

- When did you feel most supported by your team? How did you support your team?

- What can we learn from this activity in terms of what we want from each other in our class this year?

In our debrief, students almost always comment on how good it felt to cheer each other on, and in turn, how good it felt to be supported by their classmates. Every time I've walked around the room, I see kids encouraging each other and celebrating when their teammate takes a turn without tipping over the Jenga tower. Because they often might not even notice that they're doing this, I make sure to notice and name this for students. One year, "be a builder" became a mantra in one of my classes, a shorthand for whenever students wanted to playfully remind each other to be supportive of each other.

FIGURE 2.7 INTERVIEW ACTIVITY–JENGA EDITION

My first Jenga blocks are pictured here. Immediately after writing on two hundred blocks, I realized I could simply number the blocks and have the numbers correspond to a handout with numbered questions. In this way, I could easily adapt the activity for different sets of questions, as I did later with discussion questions about something we were studying or review questions related to a unit.

Shared Reading

As many elementary teachers know, a shared read-aloud can be an effective way to set a positive and welcoming tone in the beginning of the school year. For many years, the first shared read-aloud in my class was the course syllabus. I would pass out the copies of the syllabus and highlight the most important points, often to a room of blank or confused expressions staring back at me. This did little to set a positive and welcoming tone.

While it's no doubt important to establish expectations for the course, building a sense of community—finding ways to communicate to students that they are seen and valued—is perhaps the most important thing and, really, the only thing we need to do in those opening days. Reading off a list of rules on the opening day also sends students the message about whose voice is valued (the teacher's) and establishes a power dynamic that prioritizes what a teacher wants versus what students need. Consider the difference between a teacher reading a syllabus and teachers and students unpacking a shared reading: **the former tells students,** *I will tell you what we will do* **while the latter communicates,** *Let's read and learn about something together.*

Two shared texts that I've found particularly useful in my classroom are Clint Smith's TED Talk, "The Danger of Silence," and Dr. Margaret Wheatley's essay, "Willing to be Disturbed." Because we will likely discuss some contentious or controversial issues over the year, I begin with both of these texts as a way to remind students to keep an open mind when engaging critically in issues with multiple perspectives.

"The Danger of Silence"

In Smith's TED Talk, he outlines four core principles for students that he believes are necessary in today's world:

1. Read critically.

2. Write consciously.

3. Speak clearly.

4. Tell your truth.

Watch Clint Smith's TED Talk, "The Danger of Silence"

We watch the TED Talk in class and then discuss these principles. I ask students to write individually about what they think each of these principles mean. We then compile our ideas using sticky notes and large poster paper for each principle (Figure 2.8). After a gallery walk to view the posters, students return to their seats to write again; this time, I ask them to reflect on what they've read and to write a personal commitment to themselves about how they might abide by these principles. I also post these four principles on the wall in my classroom so that we can return to them throughout the year.

"Willing to be Disturbed"

In this essay, Dr. Wheatley argues that in order to foster a more civil discourse in our society, we need to start from the position of being open to being disturbed—in other words, to listen to the opinions of others with whom we disagree, even profoundly.

Read Margaret Wheatley's "Willing to be Disturbed"

Before we read the essay, I first ask students to consider the denotations and connotations of the word *disturbed*. We brainstorm synonyms, and as you might expect, most students conclude that the word is negative, especially in the contexts that are most familiar to them such as "disturbing the peace" or "mentally disturbed." We discuss how each of these instances prioritizes maintaining the status quo or what is considered "normal." I then ask students to consider contexts or situations that might need to be disturbed: When might the status quo be harmful? When is disturbing the peace necessary? Why?

FIGURE 2.8 GUIDING PRINCIPLES FROM SHARED READING

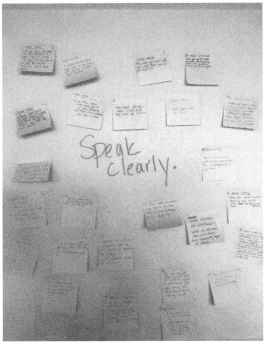

We then read aloud Dr. Wheatley's essay as a class, with every student reading one sentence at a time. This shared experience not only allows all student voices to be heard, but my hope is that by reading the words aloud, students may begin to internalize some of its key points. Students read it a second time quietly to themselves, this time marking the text for the lines that stood out to them as particularly powerful. Each student shares one line they found powerful so that we are able to hear what has resonated. Here are just a few of the lines that students often choose:

> Curiosity is what we need.
>
> We do need to acknowledge that their way of interpreting the world might be essential to our survival.
>
> When so many interpretations are available, I can't understand why we would be satisfied with superficial conversations where we pretend to agree with one another.
>
> But when I notice what surprises me, I'm able to see my own views more dearly, including my beliefs and assumptions.
>
> When I hear myself saying, "How could anyone believe something like that?" a light comes on for me to see my own beliefs.
>
> But the greatest benefit of all is that listening moves us closer.
>
> We can't be creative if we refuse to be confused.

The beauty of using a shared text like "Willing to be Disturbed" and "The Danger of Silence" is that they become touchstones that we can return to throughout the year. For example, when passions run high and discussions become heated about particular topics (which they sometimes will), I remind students of these texts and our shared understanding that we need to be "willing to be disturbed" if we are to "read critically, write consciously, speak clearly, and tell our truth."

Picture Books

I love using picture books, even with my oldest learners (who I found to love being read to!). One way I've used picture books is to retype the words from the book into a document and present the words without telling students that the words are from a picture book. Depending on the picture book, the words create a poem, but other times, the words create a short story. Students read and annotate, engaging with the meaning of the words first. Sometimes I'll ask students to draw a picture next to the words. Finally, after we've engaged with the words first, I reveal and read aloud the picture book (if you have enough

copies of the book, students can read the picture book to each other in small groups). Engaging with the picture book in this way allows students to put aside any biases they might have about picture books being for "little kids" and to encourage them to see the beauty in the art and complexity of the message found in such books.

Three picture books that work particularly well to build community and affirm students' identities, especially at the start of the school year, are listed in Figure 2.9. What's particularly beautiful about these picture books is that they each lend themselves to deeper layers of meaning for older students.

What other types of read-alouds can middle and high school teachers use? Consider the type of community you want to build in your classroom and the issues or content you'll discuss. What attitudes or dispositions will be necessary for students to be prepared to engage in those

FIGURE 2.9   PICTURE BOOKS FOR SHARED READING AND COMMUNITY

TITLE AND AUTHOR	STRUCTURE/ GENRE OF PROSE	THEME(S)
Patchwork, written by Matt de la Peña and illustrated by Corinna Luyken	Poem	Affirmation of different identities; Recognition of all the possible ways that identities can shift, change, and grow over time; Difference between social and personal identities
Where Are You From? written by Yamile Saied Méndez and illustrated by Jaime Kim	Poem	Affirmation of complex cultural/racial identities and lived experiences; Family relationships; Opportunity to discuss microaggressions around a person's name and identity *This title would work very well in a text set alongside George Ella Lyon's poem "Where I'm From," as well as Renee Watson's version, along with Gary R. Gray's picture book *I'm From*, illustrated by Oge Mora.
Your Name is a Song written by Jamilah Thompkins-Bigelow and illustrated by Luisa Uribe	Short story	Family relationships; Microaggressions; Diversity of the history and cultural backgrounds of names and relationship to identity *This text would also pair well with Sandra Cisneros' short story, "My Name," from *A House on Mango Street*, as well as the spoken word poem, "Unforgettable" by Elizabeth Acevedo, Pages Matam, and George Yamazawa.

conversations? Is there a line of inquiry or essential question that drives the course you're teaching? Then find a brief text—something that can be unpacked during a single class period or two, such as a poem, video, or even a piece of art—that invites students to think about these ideas and their application to learning. I've often used the true story of a group of kids in southern Thailand, who worked together to create a football pitch in the midst of their floating village.

Video of the 1986 Thai Football Team who created their own pitch and made a difference for the community

Class Agreements

Even though class agreements seem to be more the domain of younger grades, the truth is that all kids, no matter the age, can benefit from learning in a community where our values, beliefs, and hopes for the class are explicitly shared. I follow up our shared reading

of "Willing to be Disturbed" and "The Danger of Silence" with a discussion of classroom community: what do we all need in order to be successful as a class? Below are some prompts I've used to get kids thinking and talking about what they want from and can contribute to our class community.

- In this class and in the world, I want to be a person who . . .
- In this class, I need others to . . .
- Mrs. Ebarvia can help me be successful by . . .
- To show others respect and kindness, I will . . .
- This year, I commit to . . .

I usually project the prompts one-by-one to the board and ask students to write their response to each prompt on a separate sticky note. I also take each prompt and copy them onto large chart paper and hang them around the room to create different "stations." After writing to each prompt at their desks, they post their sticky note onto the corresponding chart paper. I then assign groups of students to each station question where they read all the sticky notes. They discuss patterns in what they see and then report out to the class what they've learned.

In her book, *Equity-Centered Trauma-Informed Education*, Venet (2021) reminds us of one agreement—a nonnegotiable—that we should hold ourselves to as teachers: unconditional positive regard. Venet writes, "The message of unconditional positive regard is, 'I care about you. You have value. You don't have to do anything to prove it to me, and nothing's going to change my mind.'" While we might have deeply meaningful conversations about class agreements, none of this matters if we don't hold this basic agreement at the forefront of every interaction we have with our students. We can actively resist the capitalist equation that measures a person's worth by what they contribute to a society by telling students, every day, that they have value regardless of what they do or don't do, what they produce or don't produce—that they have value, intrinsically as a human being, full-stop and period.

This debriefing time is critical. We talk about what conditions in the classroom would be necessary to make sure that students make class productive for both themselves and others. Students' answers will vary from year to year, but in our debriefing, I also make sure that I point out a few key conditions that I think will also be critical for our class, especially when unpacking what it means "to show others respect and kindness." I borrowed and adapted these conditions from a Learning for Justice workshop I attended in 2018 and have found that while students' responses will reflect some of these, the specificity of this language helps clarify their thinking:

1. Use and receive "I" statements with respect.
2. Respect confidentiality.
3. Embrace messiness and kindness.
4. Practice accountability (intent v. impact)
5. Be aware of equity of voice (move up, move down)

In my experience, talking through the difference between intent and impact has been the most useful in terms of being able to return to this agreement later in the year when someone in class inevitably says something that might be negatively received, even if there was no ill intention. And so not only does this class agreements activity begin to build community, it also serves as a scaffold for the type of perspective work we will be doing the entire year. As you'll see in later chapters, students will return to similar protocols to unpack and discuss more controversial issues. Building in small but intentional opportunities to ask students to 1) reflect individually, 2) consider other perspectives, and 3) come to consensus is the foundation of creating a thoughtful and informed habit of thinking.

Show and Tell

"Show and Tell" has long been a staple among elementary classrooms, and so perhaps because of this, when I tell my high school students to bring in a meaningful object for our own class "show and tell," a tangible childlike joy erupts in the room.

My directions are simple: Bring in a meaningful object. Be prepared to share a story and tell us why this object is important to you. On "Show and Tell" day, students take no more than sixty seconds each to tell the class about their object. Although students will often complain that there isn't enough time to share, I tell students that the time limit is to ensure that all voices are heard during class and all students have equal time to share. Without the time limit, what often happens in situations like this is that some students will take several minutes to share while others say very little. Limiting the time also encourages students to focus on the most important details (a skill that will come in handy in their writing later in the year).

When everyone is finished, I then have students write down the names of all the students in the class in their notebooks and the object that they each brought in. In high school, I often find that students may not know the names of their peers, even several weeks or even months into the school year, even if they've been in the same class. Because it's

critical to civil discourse that students know one another, experiences like this and simple acts like writing each other's names can be powerful steps in setting a foundation for real dialogue.

Together, learning each other's names and listening to the stories behind each other's objects helps to build community in ways that are often more powerful than I ever anticipated. Students often recall each other's objects and stories even several months later. Furthermore, this "Show and Tell" activity also leads into a longer piece of writing focused on their object as students unpack the reasons this object might carry so much personal significance for them. I have had students write about a family heirloom, their favorite pen, and a baseball. One of the most memorable essays a student shared in class described the collar their childhood dog had worn. Sometimes, these personal essays even become the foundation for students' college essays. But more than anything, these essays are an opportunity for students to share a small part of themselves in a concrete way. It's hard to be vulnerable and share what's inside to the outside world. But by focusing on just *one small thing,* we can begin.

Letter Writing

Although it seems obvious, we can't underestimate the value of getting to know our students. The first writing "assignment" I often give students is an invitation to write me a letter. I try to leave the instructions as open-ended as possible so that students can tell me anything that they feel comfortable sharing. That said, I also tell students to consider sharing with me anything that they think might be useful for me to know as their teacher: their attitudes and experiences with reading or writing, their past experiences in English class that may inform how I can best support their success this year.

I also write and read aloud my own letter to students (see Figure 2.10) so that I can model what being vulnerable might look and sound like. And yes, while these letters might serve as a writing sample, the value in them is in what they tell me about my students as individuals. I do not grade or evaluate these letters. If I am asking students to share with me who they are as a way to make them feel welcomed, safe, and seen, then taking points off for any reason can only be counterproductive. The purpose, I share with students, is for them to tell me about themselves, and with that in mind, a grade is neither necessary nor warranted.

Later in the year, we revisit letter writing as a wonderful tool to have students respond to texts and to reflect on their own identities and stances as readers and human beings (see Chapter 3).

FIGURE 2.10 LETTER TO STUDENTS

August 31, 2018

Dear 10th graders,

One question that I often get from students is why I decided to become a teacher. I'm not sure, but I think kids ask this question because maybe you're at a place in your life where you're starting to wonder what you'll do with your own, what college you'll go to and what you might want to study. Why do people choose the careers they choose? How do people end up as teachers, accountants, doctors, businesspeople, sales workers?

My answer to the question is complicated. The truth is, I never thought I'd be a teacher. Growing up, I was intensely quiet and shy. When I was in kindergarten, I remember days that I would refuse to go to school and my mom had to drag me there. Later, and throughout school, I was the type of student who could go an entire year without saying a single word in class. I would have been horrified to have a teacher call on me and I rarely, if ever, volunteered to speak. That said, I was always engaged in class, and I loved listening to what other people had to say—but I could never get my own words right. So I made up for not speaking in class by doing all my work and making sure that my writing could convey in words what I couldn't in speech.

Things changed when I got to college, mostly because I forced myself to change. Being away from home for the first time was one of the most terrifying experiences I'd had. And because I knew how hard it was for me to speak up in class, I made a rule for myself: no matter how difficult, I was going to ask or answer a question within the first week of any class I was in. I realized that the longer I went without speaking, the harder it became to speak. I also sat close to the front so I couldn't disappear. I had to be deliberate and intentional about making myself change. Sometimes my questions would be something simple, like when an assignment was due. But eventually these easy questions made asking the harder ones a little more manageable.

And now, many years later, I stand in front of a room full of teenagers and talk all day. If you told my high school self that this is where I'd end up, I would have never believed you.

But I think the real reason I became a teacher is because I wanted to do something with my life that mattered.

My first career choice was to be a doctor, and that's what I had told my family and friends my entire life. I wanted to be a doctor because I thought it was the best thing I could be—the thing that would make my parents most proud. Because my parents emigrated here from the Philippines and made many sacrifices for me and my brother, I thought that being a doctor was a way to show them that their sacrifices were worth it because their daughter had "made" it. But in college I quickly realized that I didn't actually like science very much.

Then I took a class on the history of public schooling in the U.S. and I realized that one of the most powerful ways we can perhaps change society is through schools—it's in school that we develop different ways of thinking. When it's working at its best, school doesn't just prepare kids for the world; it prepares kids to change it. That's work that I wanted to do. And because English was my favorite subject—and I have always believed in the power of reading and writing—I became an English teacher.

When I'm not teaching, I'm spending time with my family. I have three boys, and as they grow up, I've come to appreciate how important it is to spend family time together because, like all of you, they will soon be out of the house and in the world. So while I love teaching, I have been making a more focused effort in recent years to have a better work-life balance so that I can spend time with my kids, my husband, and my parents, who are getting older each day, which reminds me that our time, too, is limited. With this in mind, I invite you, too, to think about your own relationships with your family and how you might make the most of your time with those you love. School and work are important, no doubt, but I really believe that the real meaning of life comes down to the people we choose to spend our time with.

Even if English isn't your favorite subject, I hope that over the next 180 days we can talk about things that matter, that we can approach every class with an open mind and just ask ourselves, what can we learn today? And if you take nothing else from this letter, remember this: I am someone here to help. I see you, I care, and if there's anything I can do to help, my door is open.

Happy reading,

Mrs. Ebarvia

I began using Critical Incidents Questionnaires (CIQs) a few years ago after reading about them in Brookfield's (2012) *Teaching for Critical Thinking: Tools and Techniques to Help Students Question Their Assumptions*. Essentially, a CIQ is a brief five-question instrument that Brookfield, a college professor, has used to get feedback from his students about their learning and his instruction. Although Brookfield collects feedback from the CIQ anonymously, I use the five questions as reflection questions for students at the end of each week. Using my district's online learning management system (Schoology), I set up a private discussion board for each of my students that only I and the student could view and comment on, posting the questions as the standing prompt for each week (Figure 2.11).

At the end of the week, students took five minutes to open up their discussion board and answer one of the five questions. I read all the responses over the course of the following week. It would be nearly impossible for me to respond to each of them more than about once a month. In this way, each student's discussion board serves as a record of their own learning and also allows me to communicate with each student in one place throughout the year.

FIGURE 2.11 CRITICAL INCIDENTS QUESTIONNAIRE (CIQ)

REFLECTION & DIALOGUE

How's it going?

"We do not learn from experience . . . we learn from *reflecting* on experience." - John Dewey

Please take a few minutes to reflect on your learning in English class and let me know how things are going. The goal of this space is to capture your thinking about yourself as a learner and thinker - and in what ways your thinking has changed over time depending on what we're doing in class as readers and writers.

Please answer at least one of the following questions (feel free to answer more than one) for your reflection. You are also welcome to add any additional thoughts, questions, etc.

- At what moment were you most **engaged** as a learner? Could you explain?
- At what moment were you most **distanced** as a learner? Why do you think that was the case?
- Think about what we (teacher & fellow classmates) did in the class this week. **What did someone do or say that you found most helpful? Why?**
- Think about what we (teacher & fellow classmates) did in the class this week. **What conversations or actions left you wondering or confused? Could you explain why?**
- In what ways do you think you **grew** this week as a reader, writer, thinker? What caused that growth? What did you read, write, think?

adapted from Stephen D. Brookfield's Critical Incident Questionnaire (CIQ) @triciaebarvia

Adapted from Brookfield (2012)

For me, the feedback from the weekly CIQs allows me to adjust instruction as needed and gives me insight into how each student learns. That said, perhaps the most valuable part of the CIQ process is the way it asks students to reflect on their own learning. It's this metacognitive element that serves as an important building block for the deep self-reflection that will be needed when students are asked to tackle more difficult conversations throughout the year. In addition, when dealing with those more difficult topics, this reflection space gives students an opportunity to share what they might be thinking but are afraid to voice in class.

Notice and Appreciate (NAPs)

While a CIQ reflection is a way for teachers to get ongoing feedback on a one-on-one basis, NAPs (Notice and Appreciate) provide students with an opportunity to provide notes of affirmation to each other throughout the year. NAPs are simple: Students are asked to notice and appreciate something that a peer has done in class. In the examples in Figure 2.12, students submitted NAPs after reading their fellow classmates' weekly blog post entries. After collecting their NAPs in a Google form, I shared the affirmations in a digital form such as those seen here.

Making a habit of noticing and appreciating how others contribute to the classroom community and to each other's learning isn't just a "feel good" exercise, although even if it were, that alone is worth the effort. When students know that noticing and appreciating each other's contribution is a *norm* in how we treat one another, they build pro-social habits that strengthen their ability to form community connections and relationships.

FIGURE 2.12   NOTICE AND APPRECIATE (NAPS)

On Jen's "On Losing a Best Friend"

I really appreciate how raw the emotions she expressed in this piece. It was a very courageous thing to write about but the way that she wrote it in second person was very powerful. She captured the audience from the very beginning and the flow of the piece was just so well done. The word choice was astounding and I could really relate to the piece, as I'm sure many others have with going through a breakup. I am impressed by her bravery to come to terms with what happened and write about it—I could never do that.

(Continued)

(Continued)

On Amy's "On Pledging Your Soul"

I found the post (all too) relatable, since I've been guilty of ignoring the pledge most days in homeroom and never really thought about it until now. Now, I don't think that not enthusiastically reciting the pledge every morning means you hate America, but maybe we should all pay more attention to what we take for granted everyday.

I also liked the way the beginning and ending were tied together around one experience.

· ·

A STRONG FOUNDATION

When my husband and I were looking for our first home, we looked at many older homes in our area since new construction was, to be honest, out of our price range. And as any homeowner knows, the older the home, the more TLC it often needs. One piece of advice we got from many of our friends and family was to look for a house that had "good bones"—in other words, a house that had structural integrity, one that had a strong foundation from which we could build and remodel as needed.

Students don't get to choose their teachers, but they do look to see if our classrooms have "good bones." The work we do as teachers to build a strong foundation based on trust, vulnerability, and bravery in our own classrooms can create a powerful space for them—a place for their learning to not only thrive, but also where their identities and the perspectives of all can be respected and honored.

My hope is that the community building activities we do at the start and throughout the year serve as the "good bones" that we need to rely on when our discussions don't go as planned, when disagreements about what we're reading and studying might get heated, when one of us doesn't show up as their best self that day. One day, as I was cleaning up the supply caddies I had stationed at each group of desks, I noticed that several caddies included little notes students had written for each other—and not just for each other, but for the students they knew who would be sitting in their desks the following class period (see Figure 2.13). While the notes might be dismissed as doodling, I knew these notes meant more than that.

And it was a beautiful reminder that sometimes a community is built and rebuilt one post-it note at a time.

FIGURE 2.13 SMALL GIFTS MADE POSSIBLE BY COMMUNITY

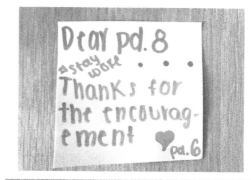

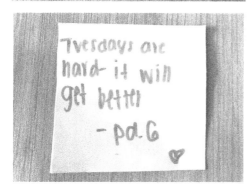

Sometimes the best feedback that I can get about how students are feeling in my classroom space are in the notes they leave behind. Students began using the post-it notes in their supply bin to leave notes for students in other class periods. It's small, unexpected but genuine gestures of kindness like these that matter. However, while these unscripted moments of community are revealing, I must also always push myself to look for the moments in my classroom where this type of community is *not* happening—and that means working persistently to check in with students and build time for the types of reading, writing, and sharing that allow students to feel welcome and seen.

How can we *get free* through **our identities?**

As we saw in Chapter 1, understanding how our own personal and social identities inform the way we navigate the world (and our classrooms) is critical in antibias education. The better we know ourselves—and where our biases reside and hide—the better equipped we are to practice a "liberatory consciousness," one that enables us "to live 'outside' the patterns of thought and behavior learned through the socialization process that helps to perpetuate oppressive system" (Love, 2018).

A first and critical step toward developing a liberatory consciousness is **awareness**, which Dr. Love describes as the "capacity to notice, to give attention to our daily lives, our language, our behaviors and even our thoughts. It means making the decision to live our lives from a waking position." As our students become more aware of their own identities and experiences, we can encourage them to move toward Dr. Love's next step, which is **analysis**, where students theorize and make sense of what they notice, why, and what can be done.

In the previous chapter, we looked at how authentic community is the foundation for relationship building and creates the brave space students need to engage with antibias work. In this chapter, we'll explore some experiences teachers can facilitate in our classrooms that raise students' capacity to become aware and analyze how the beautiful complexities (and sometimes messiness) of who they are can be liberating.

CHAPTER 3

. . . .

UNPACKING MULTITUDES

Expanding Students' Understanding of Identity

The concept of identity is a complex one, shaped by individual characteristics, family dynamics, historical figures, and social and political contexts. Who am I? The answer depends in large part on who the world around me says I am. Who do my parents say I am? Who do my peers say I am? What message is reflected back to me in the faces of teachers, my neighbors, store clerks? What do I learn from the media about myself? How am I represented in the cultural images around me? Or am I missing from the picture altogether?

—Beverly Daniel Tatum

If we teach who we are, then we also teach what we *believe*. As educators, we are charged not only with the academic and intellectual development of our students, but also the emotional, moral, and ethical development of their character—whether we are aware of this responsibility or not. Teaching is an intensely human activity; we cannot help but convey our beliefs about what is right and wrong, good and bad, valuable and worthless by the choices we make, even when they are unintentional. Schools socialize; they help young people learn about what it means to be part of a community, how to *be* among others outside of their immediate families.

And to live among others in any civil and productive way, we need to build our capacity for empathy—to be able to understand and appreciate the perspectives and experiences of others and especially for those who are different from ourselves. As we saw in chapter 1, as human beings, we possess an in-group bias for those who are similar to us: our task, then, as teachers is to help students **develop empathy beyond their biases**. Occasionally I hear adults talk about how "kids today" don't have enough empathy (notice the nostalgia bias?). In my experience, young people have tremendous capacities for empathizing with others, perhaps even more than some adults. The problem isn't a lack of empathy; it's asking ourselves, *with whom* do kids empathize (or not)?

Thankfully as English and language arts teachers, we are in an ideal position to foster empathy through the stories we share with students *and the stories we can ask students to share with each other*.

THE PROMISE AND POWER OF STORYTELLING

When the Common Core Standards were launched in 2009, many language arts educators noticed the clear shift away from narrative writing towards text-dependent analysis. While there is no doubt that helping students to use the text to support their ideas is important, the over emphasis on analytical writing at the expense of narrative writing comes with real costs. Stories, after all, are the heartbeat of who we are as human beings, and there are few, if any, areas of our lives that are not touched by stories. Even fields that seem to be obsessed with data—medicine, science, and business, for example—are, at their core, on a quest for the story behind the data, not the data itself. As part of his work in market research, my husband analyzes large amounts of data and reports back to clients his findings. And what he often finds is that no amount of data is useful without someone who can look at the data and tell its story. Stories answer the question: what does this mean? They give us a way forward.

As Chinua Achebe noted, storytelling "is considered vital by every society on earth. Humans seem to be incurable makers of stories. Whatever we do, we create a story to support it." When I share Achebe's words with my students, I challenge them to try to go a day without telling a single story. It's an impossible task. Whether it's in the hallways or in the cafeteria, online with their friends or around the dinner tables with their family, students cannot help but tell the stories of their lives: what happened in class, at practice, on the bus.

FIGURE 3.1   WHAT STORIES DO STUDENTS SEE?

In what ways does your classroom reflect the identities of the students in your room—as well as the experiences of people *not* in the room? As students engage in identity work in their reading and writing, consider the ways you might keep both "windows and mirrors" consistently and faithfully present in the learning space.

In this chapter, we'll focus on the reading and writing opportunities that center our students' stories. **By helping students to reflect on the stories that make them who they are, they can also begin to unpack the ways those stories inform their identities.** With a better understanding of their own identities—and their biases—students can then appreciate the stories of others. And by getting "proximate" to others' stories, as Ahmed (2018) reminds us, we can help students step into conversations responsibly about how we treat others and who we are as a society.

And to do that we must start by helping students get proximate to themselves and ask the following: who am I?

As you explore the strategies and lessons in this chapter, consider the self-reflection work you did in chapter 1. The better we know ourselves as educators and as people, the more we will be able to model the critical self-reflection we want our students to internalize.

NOTEBOOK WRITING THAT EXPLORES AND EXPANDS STUDENTS' UNDERSTANDING OF IDENTITY

As we continue to nurture brave spaces in our classrooms (chapter 3), we can invite students to reflect and write about their stories, about how these stories inform their identities, and, ultimately, about how their identities affect their reading, writing, and perceptions of the world. I try to flood students with **consistent and multiple *ways* of thinking about themselves and writing their reflections in their notebooks every day.** This work not only helps them to begin to see how their identities affect their outlook, it also helps them to find *moments worth writing about.* Over the next few pages, you'll find suggestions and prompts that students have often found helpful in getting them to dig deeper into their experiences.

One thing you'll notice in each of these notebook prompts is that they help to develop students' self-reflection muscles—the ones they'll need to exercise flexible, antibias thinking—and they ask students to consider multiple perspectives and ideas. Even when something in their notebook ends up focusing on one topic, students can see that it was borne from many. By the end of the year, their notebooks are filled with more ideas than might ever become fully developed, but it's a reminder to students of all the ways they contain multitudes.

Whenever they look for meaningful writing topics or find themselves facing an unfamiliar viewpoint or idea, students can look back on their reflections for ideas, points of reference, and reminders of how they have grown and changed. I've found writing notebooks to be powerful tools in my classroom, and I recommend them highly. However, if you choose to *not* use writers' notebooks, find a system that keeps self-reflection consistently accessible to students: a dedicated notebook or folder that they keep, for example.

In addition, I encourage you to write alongside students whenever possible, sharing and modeling the type of vulnerability that the writing and reflection process might require.

Although I argue for creating as many opportunities for students to think about their identities, in some cases and for some students, this reflection may bring unintended negative consequences, such as stereotype threat. **Stereotype threat** occurs when individuals—in conditions when they are reminded of negative stereotypes of groups to which they belong (particularly racial groups)—conform to the stereotypes associated with that identity, which can then affect achievement (Steele & Aronson, 1995).

Certainly writing about one's racial identity could remind students of such stereotypes. Yet we also know that giving students permission to write about their full selves is necessary. Therefore, it is critical that (1) we deepen our own understanding of stereotype threat and (2) we reduce the negative impact of stereotype threat through intentional interventions. These interventions include (but are not limited to) creating a classroom community that values diversity as well as individuality, promoting a growth mindset, and presenting role models and texts from diverse groups (Center for Teaching and Learning, n.d.)

Identity Inventory

No matter what class I teach, I frame the reading we do—whether it's primarily fiction or non-fiction—as opportunities to learn more about others and ourselves. Reading, I tell students, allows us to figure out who *we* are, what we value and believe. At the same time, who we are impacts what we choose to read and how we respond. So, with that in mind, I invite students to take an "inventory" of their identities.

Social Identities

I ask students to dedicate the first two-page spread in their notebooks to this inventory. First, we brainstorm the various elements that make up our identities and write these in our notebook in a single column. To facilitate this process, I sometimes start by asking students to consider the following eight elements of their identities, which I picked up at a Learning for Justice workshop (I added the last category, age, to the list):

1. Gender

2. Race

3. Sexual Orientation

4. National origin/Immigration status

5. Socioeconomic status

6. Home language(s)

7. Religion/Spiritual Practice

8. Ability

9. Age

Students write down these elements and then jot down notes that describe how these might apply to them. I've found that although students are familiar with these concepts, rarely have they thought deeply about them. It's common for students, for example, to confuse race with ethnicity, so as I read each element, I also take time to define them. I also use this opportunity to model by sharing how I identify within each element. If I did not feel comfortable sharing a particular element, I might offer students *possible* ways a person might identify rather than how it specifically applies to me (Figure 3.2).

FIGURE 3.2   IDENTITY INVENTORY

Identity Inventory

Gender — cis gender female

Race — Asian American

Sexual orientation — straight

National origin / immigration — U.S. citizen / 2nd gen

Socioeconomic status — comfortable Filipina middle - upper? class

Home language — monolingual English

Religion — raised Catholic

Ability — fully abled-bodied (corrective lenses)

Age — middle? GenXer

fande
sport
sport
musi
mov
tv s
fave
sup
intr
fav.
boo
hei
be
ty
bi
ey
ec
la

Before doing this activity, it is critical that teachers are familiar with each element, what distinguishes one from another, and the language you can use with students. For example, when I discuss gender identity, I explain that gender is a socially constructed identity that runs along a continuum, not a binary. I provide examples of the many ways that a person could identify their gender and explain that I identify myself as cisgender female. Take time to familiarize yourself with each of these terms using definitions from trusted organizations such as Gay, Lesbian, and Straight Education Network (GLSEN) or the glossary provided from Racial Equity Tools. Practice with a colleague how you might explain each element to students. Remember that the working definition you provide students might be the first time anyone has taken the time to explain that concept. During this activity, I also do not generally solicit ideas from students about how to define these terms because I cannot guarantee that a student will not repeat a harmful stereotype aloud in class. Instead, I try my best to provide an accurate working definition so that any misconceptions students might privately hold are corrected.

Because this can be highly personal information, I preface this writing prompt by explicitly telling students that they will not be required to share any of this information with others. The value of this exercise and creating an identity inventory is in its power to drive *self*-reflection, and therefore, students may be asked to *reflect but not to share* unless they are comfortable. I point out that these social identities are only *some* elements that make us who we are, but that none of them defines us. I also offer the following guidance:

GLSEN Glossary
of Terms

Racial Equity
Tools Glossary

- Because some of us may not be sure how this social identity applies to us, it's okay to write down whatever feels most comfortable to you.

- There is no right answer.

- How you respond today might be different from how you responded in the past or how you might respond in the future. (For example, I share that although my elderly father would have identified as fully able-bodied for most of his life, he now has accessibility needs that require him to use an elevator versus stairs.)

- It's also okay not to write down anything if you don't want to. (I guide students to answer in their head but still write down the category.)

- You are not obligated to share how you identify with anyone.

Again, it is critical to make sure that students understand that they do not have to write down how they identify if they do not feel comfortable doing so. Even though they are not obligated to share, and even though their notebooks are their private space, even the act of writing down an identity may be challenging for some students. We should never put students in a position to reveal personal information, even inadvertently, that they are not comfortable sharing.

> The value of this exercise and creating an identity inventory is in its power to drive self-reflection, and therefore, students may be asked to reflect but not to share *unless they are comfortable.*

At this point, I proceed in one of two ways:

1. Ask students to place a star next to the elements that they feel most impact the way they navigate the world and then to reflect briefly in writing.

2. Ask students to cross off the element that has the *least* impact on how they navigate the world. Then, of the remaining elements, again cross off the element that has the least impact on how they navigate the world. Students repeat this until they are left with one or two elements that they cannot cross off . . .

This second option, which is how Val Brown and Hoyt Phillips facilitated this activity at their Learning for Justice workshop, can be much more emotionally challenging for students because it asks students to literally cross off elements of their identity. When I have had students reflect on this process, they share how uncomfortable it felt to have to not only choose an element of their identity, but to *eliminate* others. "These identities are *all* part of what makes me who I am," is a common response, which is, as we discuss, part of the point here. We are complex individuals made up of any number of identities, which we carry with us everywhere we go. Our students bring in their full selves to the classroom each day, and yet how many times might we fail to acknowledge some of these identities, or worse, ask students to leave parts of their identity at the door when they enter our rooms? (Interestingly, when I have done this exercise with adults, I get the same response; in fact, some adults become angry at having to cross anything off their lists.)

At some point during our discussion of this activity, I ask students why they think I asked them about these *specific* elements of their identity. Why race? Why gender? Why socioeconomics? Students' responses vary, but one thing I point to students is that nearly every major social and political problem we face in the world right now has to do with one of these categories. They typically reexamine the list and see that it's true. I use this opportunity to point out that by understanding how each of these categories applies to our identities, personally, we can better understand how they manifest in society.

The next part of our discussion is the most important. I ask students to discuss *how* they decided which identities they crossed off first, second, and so on. I reiterate that we're not looking for *what* they crossed off but what *criteria* they used in making those decisions. For example, some students share that the ones they crossed off first (and most easily) were ones they felt like they did not really have to think about. Others share that the ones they were hardest to cross off were ones that felt very important to their identity, that they would not be the same person if this element of their identity was different.

Inevitably, this process leads us to discuss how the parts of our identity that are beneficial to us are the ones that we often think about the least. Because we think about them *least*, their impact on how we navigate the world may not be as immediately apparent. And yet, they *do* impact how we navigate the world: If we do not have to think about that part of our identity—if that part of our identity is *not an obstacle*—then that *lack of obstacle is an advantage*. And this is when students begin to recognize the privileges they hold. To see how privilege works in our lives, we can examine which parts of our identity we never have to consider when we walk through the world. Our privileges hide in what we can ignore or choose not to see.

I share, for example, that often one of the first things I cross off is home language. I am a monolingual English speaker. In my daily life, I never struggle to communicate or to understand what others are saying to me because in the United States, English is the dominant language. I ask students to name a situation in which my ability to speak one language might be more of a disadvantage, and they point out that if I were traveling abroad in a country that did not cater to English speakers, I would feel the impact of that element of my identity more deeply.

Note how this identity inventory activity encourages students to understand two critical concepts: *privilege* and *intersectionality*.

Similarly, I share that because I am fully able-bodied and have a neurotypical learning style best suited to school, I can usually cross off *ability* fairly early as well. In almost every class I've done this activity with, a handful of students will share that they could never cross off ability because they have a diagnosed learning issue that impacts every moment they are in school. They cannot *not* think about their ability to read, listen, study, and understand what is being taught. Students with more privileged identities often find themselves sitting in some discomfort around the *lack* of disadvantages their identities present them. And that discomfort is okay. It's what we do with that discomfort, how it informs our actions, that matter.

Understanding that some of our identities are disadvantaged in society while other identities are advantaged helps students to understand how intersectionality works. According to Dr. Crenshaw (2018), who coined the term, **intersectionality** is a way of "understanding that multiple forms of inequality or disadvantage sometimes compound themselves and they create obstacles that are often not understood within conventional ways of thinking about anti-racism, feminism, or whatever social justice structures we have."

To illustrate how intersectionality works using this identity inventory, I point out to students that although my partner and I both share the same racial identity (Asian American), as a woman, I *also* experience sexism while he, as a man, does not. Understanding intersectionality also helps us see why disaggregating data is so important. For example, if we only looked at Asian Americans as a single group, we would see that in 2015, Asian Americans had the highest median household income compared to all other racial demographic groups (Edlagan & Vaghul 2016). One might conclude Asian Americans are a successful group, the "model minority."

However, when the data are disaggregated by Asian ethnic groups, we see that many ethnic groups under the Asian American umbrella earn far less. In fact, the income gap between the wealthiest Asian American earners and poorest is the widest among all racial demographic groups. If we only looked at race, and failed to look at the intersection of race and socio-economic status, then this would overlook, if not erase, the financial struggles of thousands of Asian Americans. Intersectionality is a "prism" (Crenshaw, 2018) that allows us to see how multiple systems of oppression work together to create compounded disadvantage.

Expanding Social and Personal Identities

Of course, because **who we each are is so much more than these nine elements**, I always ask students to brainstorm a list of additional elements that make us who we are. We expand our inventory to include things like handedness, hair color, horoscope, hobbies and so on. Then, next to each element, students take a few more minutes writing down how this element of identity applies to them as individuals, as in Figure 3.3.

I also ask students to consider the following:

- Which identities are most important to your sense of self today?

- Which identities do you think were most important to you five years ago?

- Choose an identity that is important to you. When were you aware of this identity? What happened?

- Which identity has changed most for you over the years?

- Which identities do you think others see first when they think of you?

FIGURE 3.3   EXPANDED IDENTITY INVENTORY

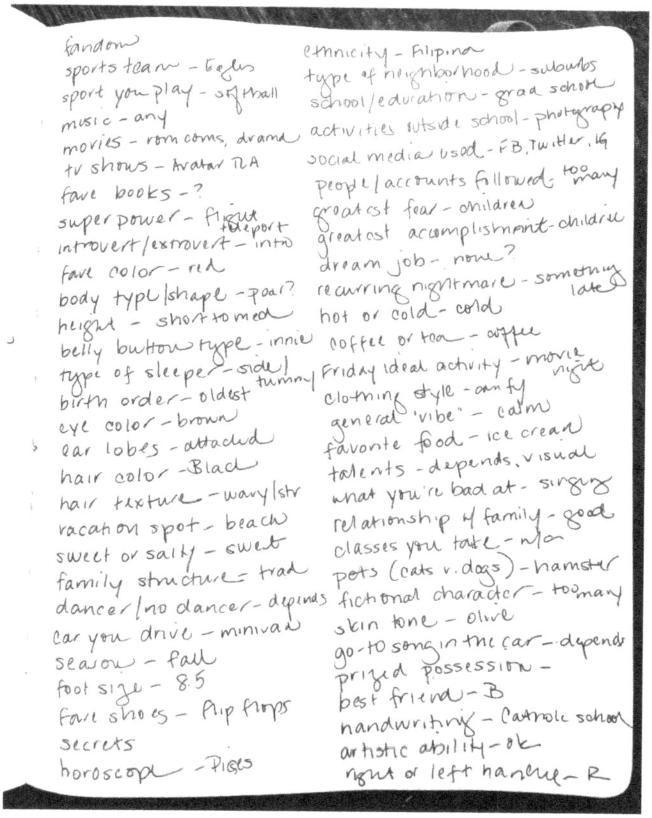

- Which identities are least visible to others?

- Which identities are ones that are advantageous to have in society? Which identities could be challenging? Why?

- Choose an identity and tell a story related to it.

Throughout the year, we return to this identity inventory, as we look for inspiration in writing personal narratives and especially when we analyze our identity lenses as they relate to our response to reading various texts and in constructing arguments.

My hope for students in doing this identity work is multilayered and complex (see Figure 3.4). Research has shown that when people are reminded of their multiple racial or social identities, they engage in more flexible, creative thinking and problem-solving (Gaither et al., 2015; Velasquez-Manoff, 2017). Given the depth and scope of the issues facing us today, no doubt we could use more creative problem-solvers.

One way to have students further analyze their identities is by looking at both inventories—the nine social identities we originally discussed as well as our expanded list—and discuss which are *most easily visible to others* and *which are not*. We might use the familiar iceberg metaphor to classify which parts of our identities are located in the visible part of the iceberg, which are not, and what the implications might be.

FIGURE 3.4 COMPLEXITIES OF IDENTITY

IDENTITY . . .	FOR EXAMPLE . . .
• is both personal and social	Some elements of our identity are ones we can fully choose for ourselves and are personal (musical taste, favorite movies, fandoms we love). Other elements of our identity, however, are also defined by other people or institutions (race, social class, age, national origin).
• can be flexible and subject to change for a variety of reasons	Although the personal elements of our identity can change as we grow and our tastes shift, even social elements of our identity can also change over time. We might become disabled. We might become fluent in another language. Our financial situation may change, along with our socioeconomic status.
• depends on our context	Some of our social identities are *socially* constructed; they may change depending on the *societal norms* we navigate. Racial categories in the United States are different from other countries. (For example, although I am considered Asian American in the United States, that category has less meaning if I were to move to the Philippines. There, people would be more interested in my ethnicity versus racial identity.)
• can be advantageous or challenging	Some parts of identity are privileged in different circumstances. An individual's socioeconomic status where the cost of living is not high would have a tremendous advantage when it comes to their ability to buy a home or car. That same individual, however, may experience some challenges if they were to move to a large city where their cost of living might double.

List and Lean In

Generating lists and writing about something from that list might be one of the most simple, versatile, and powerful notebook writing prompts we can use. The strategy is simple:

1. Provide students with a topic or category for their list.

2. Give students one to two minutes to try to make the longest list they can with one simple rule: don't overthink it. The goal is to

write down as much as they can, quantity over quality. This will give them more to choose from in the next step, and as I tell students, you never know when something unexpected but perfect ends up on your list.

3. Star three items from their list that stand out to them, for any reason.

4. Choose one of their starred items and free-write about it for five minutes.

These lists serve as additional ways for students to take an inventory of their identities throughout the year. Sometimes the lists can sow the seeds for some future essay—for example, creating lists of places they've been before writing a longer essay about a meaningful place, or creating a list of favorite foods before writing about food memory narrative. Sometimes the lists help students make a connection to a text we're studying, like creating a list of people or places we go to for the truth just before we begin reading *1984*. And sometimes the lists don't go anywhere at all beyond their notebook. **The purpose is *generative*, and to support students in the habit of considering *many* ideas as a default starting step in their thinking.** During the school year, when our discussions turn toward tasks such as generating solutions to research questions or trying to better understand a character's motives, I remind students of the value and benefit of generating many possibilities.

What lists can students create in their notebooks? Anything!

- Places they've been
- Places they want to go
- People they see every day
- Words they love
- Words they hate
- Comfort foods
- Foods they would never eat
- Childhood toys
- Childhood television shows or characters
- Superpowers
- Books
- Fictional characters
- Modes of transportation
- Emojis
- Expressions/Slang

- Apps on their phone
- Websites often visited

Drawing Our Selves

Identity maps—a tool that Sara Ahmed shares in her books—and other visual representations of our identities can be powerful tools for self-reflection, *if we allow them to be*. If we ask students to reflect on their identity, draw their selves on a page, display their webs on a bulletin board, or keep them tucked in a notebooks, but never revisit them, never connect them to what they're experiencing, reading, and writing—then what have we really done to help students unpack the intricacies of who they are? Instead, as Ahmed (2018) reminds us, deep, meaningful identity work is complex, and we need to take the time to honor those complexities:

> Many of the students you spend the better part of your day with live a hyphenated life. Indian-Americans, Mexican-Americans, Latinx-Americans, bi-racial, multi-racial, religiously hyphenated, gender hyphenated, culturally hyphenated. Maybe you do as well.
>
> [A]s one of those kids, though we all have varying degrees of visibility, I tell you that it's not easy growing up hyphenated in America. The duality of your existence is questioned by implicit or explicit messages around you. You can be seen as just one of "us"—or quickly ushered into a space of othering with one headline or news cycle, or unit taught in school. Neither of which you want. You are American when all is well, but quickly labeled by only other parts of your hyphen when convenient by the next oppressor.
>
> Kids that live a hyphenated life are constantly trying to get it right on both sides of the hyphen as Jhumpa Lahiri puts it. They spend their day, their life, code switching through different norms, different spaces because of the way we default to center one race, one gender, one ability, one religion, one relationship, in this country. (Ahmed, 2018)

The power of drawing is that visuals can often help students capture the contradictions and dualities of their identities in ways that words cannot. Students who stumble over their words or feel limited by the lines on a page may find clarity and freedom by brainstorming through a web or sketching pictures and piecing them together.

In addition to identity maps, I've also had students draw visual autobiographies, using James Gulliver Hancock's *Artists, Writers, Dreamers, and Thinkers: Portraits of Fifty Famous Folks and All Their Weird Stuff* as a mentor text. Some of my favorite student examples can be seen in Figure 3.5. After sharing our visual biographies, students tape them into their writer's notebook and refer to them to mine for those moments worth writing about.

FIGURE 3.5 VISUAL BIOGRAPHIES

Of course, a few of my all-time favorite visual writing exercises are maps—heart maps, hand maps, and home maps. Maps help us make sense of the world, and most importantly, they can help orient ourselves when we feel lost. Heart and hand maps can be especially effective ways to help students to think about what they hold close to them inside and the variations of heart maps.

While heart and hand maps help students identify what's important to them, I've found that home maps help unearth memories. For home

maps, I ask students to choose a physical place that they call "home." Some students might draw a map of their bedroom; others might draw their entire house, and still others might draw their neighborhood or their backyard or a local park. Then, once they draw the map of this place they call "home," students annotate the map. "Review your map," I guide students. "Let your eyes move from left to right, top to bottom, slowly through the space on the page. Think about what memories come to mind as you do this and mark these moments on your map." Then students reflect and write, usually for anywhere from five to ten minutes. I usually split this notebook writing into two days, with the first day focused on drawing their picture and the second day focused on the reflection.

Two other texts that I love to use to help students draw their selves are Grant Snider's *The Shape of Ideas: An Illustrated Exploration of Creativity* and Mari Andrew's *Am I There Yet?* Both Snider and Andrew are visual artists whose work is rich for writing inspiration and can serve as beautiful mentor texts for students' own reflection. Figures 3.6 and 3.7 show some of the visual essays mentor texts that I have often used with students. Because personal writing can be daunting, starting with images and small writing can be a more inviting and accessible entry point for students.

FIGURE 3.6 GRANT SNIDER MENTOR TEXTS

Source: Snider (2016, 2019).

FIGURE 3.7 MARI ANDREW MENTOR TEXTS

Andrew (2019).

A student's own visual representation of something they are grateful for.

Andrew (2018). p. 12.

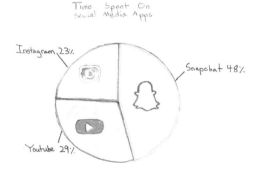

Using simple pie charts as visual notebook prompts has been particularly engaging for students because of their many possibilities. After my students create a general "what makes me me" pie chart—perhaps inspired by their identity inventories—they might zoom in on any individual aspect of it and create a new pie chart. Below are some examples of topics for more specific pie charts:

- what worries me
- my hopes and dreams
- what it means to be a friend
- things I'm working on

- my writing process

- my childhood experiences

- favorite school subjects

What I appreciate most about these pie charts is that they allow students to see the complexities in any area of their identity or otherwise. Any time we can get students to recognize the complexities behind their identities increases their capacity for reading texts with a greater self-reflection. Students' childhood experiences, for example, help to shape many of their driving beliefs about how the world works and why; if students can uncover that, make connections between their experiences and their values, attitudes, and beliefs, they can become more critical thinkers.

More Than the Average Joe

Another one of my favorite notebook prompts simply asks kids to think about things they know about—topics, issues, hobbies that they are an "expert" on, or at the very least, those things that they might know a little bit more about than the "average" person, however they define that. In order to inspire kids to think out of the box, I share how I believe I am an expert on eating cereal. I pour my milk first, and then add only enough cereal to cover the surface area of the milk. I eat that cereal and when finished with that first layer of cereal, I add a little bit more to the bowl, again only enough to just cover the surface area. Then I eat that. I repeat this process until I run out of milk. In this way, I can avoid one of the things I hate the most about my favorite breakfast food: soggy cereal.

As you can imagine, I get a lot of strong reactions to my process: some students cry blasphemy at my pouring the milk first, while other students who, like me, also hate soggy cereal, think I'm a genius. With this example in mind, I hope to show students that they can be "experts" on things serious and things not so serious, on things big and on things small. Students write their list, and then after a few minutes, we whip around the room and have each student share one thing they know better than your "average Joe."

I use this notebook prompt as a way to introduce the idea of *ethos* when teaching arguments. Ethos refers to the credibility of the writer, and when writing, it's important to consider the extent to which a writer might need to establish their authority on the subject at hand. Or perhaps by virtue of who they are (for example, a known expert), they might have automatic ethos with the reader. As writers, students need to think about their own sense of ethos: about what topics do they have authority to speak about, and how? We pick up this idea again when we analyze arguments (see chapter 6).

Questions for Memoirists

Although I prompt my students' notebook writing each day, choosing prompts that I know will connect to other reading or writing we might be doing, sometimes there is no need to reinvent the wheel when it comes to developing questions that can inspire students to reflect on their experiences.

Early in the year, long before I tell students we will be writing personal essays, I share Atwell's (2002) Questions for Memoirists from *Lessons that Change Writers*. I copy Atwell's questions on quarter sheets and have students paste these into their writer's notebooks (Figure 3.8). Sometimes, when I'm pressed for time or on Friday "free-write" days (when I offer students the option to write whatever they like at the start of class), students can choose from any of Atwell's questions.

FIGURE 3.8   QUESTIONS FOR MEMOIRISTS

- What are my earliest memories? How far back can I remember?
- What are the most important things that have happened to me in my life so far?
- What have I seen that I can't forget?
- What's an incident that shows what my friends and I are like?
- What's an incident that shows what my pet(s) and I are like?
- What's something that happened to me at school that I'll always remember?
- What's a time when I had a feeling that surprised me?
- What's an incident that changed how I think or feel about something?
- What's an incident that changed my life?
- What's a time or place that I was perfectly happy?
- What's a time or place that I laughed a lot?
- What's a time or place when it felt as if my heart were breaking?
- What's a time with a parent that I'll never forget?
- What's a time with a grandparent that I'll never forget?
- What's a time with a brother or sister that I'll never forget?
- Can I remember a time I learned to do something, or did something for the first time?
- What memories emerge when I make a time line of my life so far and note the most important things that happened to me each year?

The Stranger in the Photo

Within the first few weeks of school, I ask students to bring in three to five photographs of themselves that are meaningful to them from at least three distinct periods in their lives, spread out over time so that

there is some range in the photographs. We then read Don Murray's essay, "The Stranger in the Photo is Me." In this essay, Murray reflects on an old photograph of himself from his days as a soldier. Looking at this photo, Murray feels both connected and disconnected with the young man he once was. It is one of my favorite mentor texts to use with students early in the year, as it builds community when students share their photographs with one another and also inspires some beautiful essays.

Read Don Murray's essay, "The Stranger in the Photo is Me"

Asking students to write from photographs also gives them practice in thinking from both a bird's-eye view and an "outsider" stance. Students then invite classmates to take this "outsider" stance when they share their photographs with each other. For example, in pairs, Student A gives their picture to Student B. Student B then writes down three things they notice in the photograph and then three things they have questions about. Then they switch roles and repeat this process. Doing this can help students notice things in their photograph they might not have before and perhaps give them another entry way into writing. This "Stranger in the Photo" essay is often one of the very first essays students write.

Some prompts I might use as students write and reflect on their photographs:

- What's the story in this photograph in ten words or less?

- What do you notice now in this photo that you hadn't before?

- What other memories come to mind from this time period?

- Who's missing from this photograph (or in the background)? Write about them.

- What happened just before this photograph was taken? What happened afterwards?

- Describe this photograph through your five senses. What do you notice?

- Who or what is the subject of this photograph? If you took a photo of this same scene with a different subject, who or what would that subject be? How would it change the story?

What I also appreciate most about this writing is that it reminds students that their identities can shift and change over time. Reminding students of the flexible nature of identity can be helpful when they encounter new ideas and change their opinions as we read and discuss various texts later in the year.

Figure 3.9 highlights a photograph I use with students when writing beside them for this assignment. Before I explain anything about the photograph, I ask students to tell me what they *think* is going on: what *story* does this photograph tell and how do they know? Before reading on, try this out for yourself. Pause and look at my photograph: what do you think is going on here?

FIGURE 3.9   THE STRANGER IN THE PHOTO IS ME

If you're like most of my students, the story you see might go like this: My younger brother is trying to give me a lollipop, which I refuse, as our mother looks on. I also ask my students which "character" in the photograph they are inclined to be more sympathetic toward. They almost always agree that I look like I'm the one who's being difficult in the photograph, while they feel more sympathy toward my brother.

After they consider their initial readings of this photograph, I share what I know to be the story behind this photograph, at least from my own (perhaps imperfect) memory. I also model what close *noticing* looks like as I think aloud:

In this photograph are me, my mom, and my younger brother. Since I know that we were at the World's Fair in Tennessee, which took place in 1982, I also know that I'm six years old in this photograph. If you don't know the backstory, you might look at this photograph and think that my brother was trying to give me a heart lollipop and that I was refusing to take it. But although I don't remember much else from this

day, I do remember that the lollipop was originally mine. My brother wanted to trade his lollipop with mine (his was a rainbow swirl lollipop), so we traded. I also remember invoking the "no tradebacks" rule, which he ignored by trying to give me back my original lollipop. I think this photograph shows a little bit of our dynamic growing up. I was the older sister who was a bit stubborn, and he was the younger sibling who I found annoying. Then there's my mom, who always played the role of peacemaker when my brother and I fought. My dad, while not in the picture, is the one taking it, which I think says a lot about how he tried to capture moments like this from childhood.

The detail that catches my eye most when I look at this photograph, however, isn't the lollipop. It's the blue bag sitting on the ground by my mom's legs. Although you can't see inside it, I know that inside the bag are the snacks that my mom brought with us to the fair that day. My parents were immigrants, and one of the rules my mom always lived by (and still does) was not to waste money on unnecessary things. Instead of buying food at the fair, I imagine that the blue bag contains fruit (likely oranges), juice boxes, and probably some Filipino snacks to keep my brother and me content throughout the day. In fact, that we were allowed to buy lollipops was unusual!

I point out to students that there's more to this photograph than they initially thought, and again, I use it as yet another opportunity to point out the importance of **intellectual humility**, and how our initial observations and readings are almost always not only incomplete but sometimes wrong.

After I talk through my photograph, I ask students to share the photographs they've brought with them and do the same with a partner. After a few minutes, I ask them to take another look at my photograph and remember what I shared. I ask them to identify elements of my identity that seem relevant. I prompt students to go back through their identity inventory in their notebook and determine which parts of my identity are revealing themselves in my photograph. Among the many possibilities, here are just a few:

- birth order
- family structure
- national origin / immigration status
- gender
- ethnicity
- socioeconomic status
- sibling relationships

Next, students turn to each other and identify what parts of their own identities are revealing themselves in their own photographs. In doing this, I want students to develop a habit of taking a second and third look at a text, noticing how more is revealed the closer we look. I also want students to internalize the self-reflection needed to consider how their identities are revealed in both the moment captured in the photograph and the way they "read" that memory.

Other variations of this writing might include the following:

- If pressed for time, instead of bringing in photographs, I've also had students simply write about three different moments in their lives using simple sentence starters like "When I was 5 years old" or "When I was 10 years old . . . "

- Another simple sentence starter that I use is "When I was . . . I used to think . . . Now I realize . . . "

- Or yet another, "I thought I knew everything about . . . but now I realize . . . "

When students keep track of their thinking and how it can change over time, they become less fixed on absolutes. This will be a critical skill we revisit throughout the year.

Another way to use photographs is to ask students to browse their photos on their mobile devices and choose three photos that represent who they are in some way. After giving students a few minutes to choose their photos, I then have them share their photos with one another in a "musical chairs" format—a practice I learned at a Learning for Justice workshop. Students move around the room as the music plays, and then as soon as the music stops, they share their photos with the person closest to them. We repeat this for a few rounds and then follow-up with some writing in our notebooks.

Introducing students to photo essays *as a genre* can also be a powerful entryway into writing about identity. While you can find many examples of photo essays online, one particularly beautiful mentor text I have used with students is Phillip Toledano's photo essay *The Reluctant Father*. The combination of photographs and prose can invite students to think about the powerful interplay of visual and text, as well as rich discussion of how the identities of the author are reflected in each medium.

What's in a Name?

Of course, one of the most important parts of our identity is also the most obvious: our names. Asking students to share something about

their names and how their names represent parts of their identity is something that many teachers do. I offer it here as a reminder of how important names are. First names, middle names, family names—each of these may hold special significance for students.

Read and view Phillip Toldedano's photo essay, "The Reluctant Father"

As you may recall in chapter 2, page 67, getting to know each student's name and making time for students to know each other's names (and pronouncing their name correctly) is an important piece in creating community. To encourage thinking more deeply about the importance of names, I anchor our exploration about names with the beautiful spoken word poem, "Unforgettable" by Elizabeth Acevedo, Pages Matam, and George Yamazawa. First we watch their performance, and then I provide each student with a copy of the poem. The second time we read the poem, we listen and read along. Students mark lines in the poem that stand out to them. Because the poem can elicit strong reactions from students, I sometimes use the Courageous Conversations Compass to help students identify what they think, feel, believe, and want to do in response to this poem (see chapter 4, page 166). I then invite students to expand on their responses by writing in their notebooks. Although these are brief reflections, these notebook entries often become the inspiration for a longer piece about their names. We share our responses in pairs or small groups before sharing with the class (see chapter 4 for additional conversational strategies).

Of course, there are many other mentor texts about the importance of names, and perhaps you already have a favorite. One that many teachers (including myself) have used is "My Name" by Sandra Cisneros's *The House on Mango Street*. Students can also be invited to explore the essays curated in Cheri Lucas Rowlands's "'Names Have Power': A Reading List on Names, Identity, and the Immigrant Experience" and explore how one or more of these essays both mirrors and expands on the themes in "Unforgettable." Or, perhaps after reading Jerrine Tan's "What Chinese Calligraphy Taught Me About Myself," students can do what the author does and explore what they can learn by writing their own names, over and over again, perhaps in different ways. Finally, Ilaria Parogni's "What Matters in a Name Sign?" from the *New York Times* provides a beautiful exploration of how "Name signs, also known as sign names, are an important component of 'capital D Deaf' culture." One year, several of my students who had cultural names responded strongly to Jami Nakamura Lin's essay, "Does My Child's Name Erase My Identity?" Finally, Adryan Corcione's "How Transgender People Choose Their Names" in *Teen Vogue* highlights the many different reasons transgender individuals choose their names and why. No matter what mentor texts you choose, providing students with the opportunity to understand their own names and others can be a powerful invitation for self-reflection and developing empathy for others' experiences.

Literary Inspiration

I've found using children's books and poetry to be effective and inviting ways to inspire students to reflect and write about their personal experiences. Because both are relatively brief, we can read the texts in their entirety within a few minutes, leaving ample time for students to write and reflect.

My hope with any children's book or poem I teach is that the text inspires a "flashbulb" memory for students that can inspire rich thinking about their experiences. These small pieces of writing are also wonderful because they allow us to zoom in on craft as well: conversations about a single word choice can help students become more thoughtful and precise in the words they choose and claim as they write about their own experiences.

FIGURE 3.10   CHILDREN'S BOOKS & POETRY TO INSPIRE REFLECTION ABOUT IDENTITY

Children's Books

- *Roxaboxen* by Alice McLerran
- *Drawn Together* by Minh Lê
- *Crown: An Ode to the Fresh Cut* by Derrick Barnes
- *Amy Wu and the Perfect Bao* by Kat Zhang
- *Saturday* by Oge Mora
- *Stacey's Extraordinary Words* by Stacey Abrams
- *When Lola Visits* by Michelle Sterling
- *The Remember Balloons* by Jessie Oliveros
- *Thunder and the Noise Storms* by Jeffree Ansloos and Shezza Ansloos

Poetry

- "When I Grow Up I Want to be a List of Further Possibilities" by Chen Chen
- "We Real Cool" by Gwendolyn Brooks
- "Sonrisas" by Pat Mora
- "The Way It Is" by William Stafford
- "We Wear the Mask" by Paul Laurence Dunbar
- "Famous" by Naomi Shihab Nye
- "To Be of Use" by Marge Piercy
- "The Weight of Sweetness" by Li-Young Li
- "Allowables" by Nikki Giovanni

Figure 3.10 offers some suggestions for titles for children's books and poetry, but even brief excerpts from a longer piece of writing—a novel or essay—can be equally powerful. For example, I've had great success with brief excerpts from Tim O'Brien's *The Things They Carried* when I taught that novel in one of my classes. Consider the following sentence in which O'Brien describes war:

> *War is hell, but that's not the half of it, because war is also mystery and terror and adventure and courage and discovery and holiness and pity and despair and longing and love. War is nasty; war is fun. War is thrilling; war is drudgery. War makes you a man; war makes you dead.*

There is so much to unpack in the sentence structures and repetition, the use of contrasting ideas and the deliberate choice of abstract nouns. After students study these sentences closely, they then imitate these sentences and use their rhythms and structure to describe something about themselves or something that is meaningful to them. I direct them back to reflect on their identity inventory or pie chart. Below are a few examples of writing inspired by the passage above:

> Soccer is hell, but that's not the half of it, because soccer is also magic and rhythm and communication and courage and grit and teamwork and friendship and speed and love. Soccer is pain; soccer is joy. Winning is everything; winning is nothing. Soccer fills you up; soccer takes everything away.

> Dance is beauty, but that's not the half of it, because dancing is also spinning and laughing and hip hop and jazz and twists and turns and plies and pirouettes. Dancing is holding on; dancing is letting go. Dancing is freedom; dancing is a prison. Dancing is who I am; I am more than dancing.

Life Graphs

For this "way in," I ask students to look at the identity inventory and to choose a few elements of their identity from these lists. On the board, I draw a graph with an X and Y axis.

I label the graph, "Teaching," and then I say to students, "As you know, teaching is something that I know a little about. Here, I'm going to graph my teaching life." I label the X axis for time: "I'm going to start my graph at the year 2000, because that's the year I did my student teaching." I end the X axis with the present day.

"I'm going to use the Y axis," I continue, "to measure the quality of my teaching—how awesome or meh I think I was as a teacher over the years." I label the highest point on the Y axis "awesome," and the lowest point, "Meh." (To be funny, I once extended the line below the X axis into negative territory and labeled the end point, "What am I doing?".)

I then think aloud as I plot points on my graph and connect them to make a line. As I plot away, I say things like, "I was mostly trying to survive as a first-year teacher, so I'd rate myself close to the "meh." I then add another point and say, "I remember that I had a really great second year of teaching because I could fix everything that had gone wrong the year before." A few years later along the X axis, I add a much higher point and say, "I remember trying out blogging for the first time with my students this year and it went really well. My students produced some of the best writing I'd ever seen up to that point."

I talk through these "life graphs" and explain to students that we can find some "moments worth writing about" by looking at the way the line moves up and down. "Look," I tell them, "for the plot points that are both high and low. Ask yourself, what happened here? It's at those plot points—those moments—that can provide the richest material to write about." I also point out that when you do several of these life graphs that you can start to see patterns and correlations. For example, I joke that the minute my third son was born in 2010 that the overall quality of my parenting declined. I point out that my teaching life graph is a bumpy one, which is to be expected, but that the overall trend is upward. One student points out, "It looks like the better you got at teaching, the worse you got at parenting." I had to laugh. (See Figure 3.11)

FIGURE 3.11 LIFE GRAPH

As I walk around the room to watch students creating their own life graphs, I see that their faces are focused, intent. I see life graphs titled: relationship with my parents, self-confidence, playing tennis, artistic life, friendships, and so on.

Whenever I have done this activity, students marvel at the up and down trajectories of their lives. Again, I guide students to look at the peaks and valleys, and I ask them to reflect in particular on how a low point turned around for them. I still remember Chris, who during a writing conference told me that he would write about his middle school experiences.

"What made you decide on that?" I ask.

"Actually, I got the idea from the life graph we did in class. I did a graph on 'self-confidence,' and I noticed that I had a huge decline during middle school." He smiles. "So I think that's something worth writing about."

Indeed.

Circles of Self

Because who we are is intimately connected to the people around us—whether by choice or not—I ask students to think about their identity in relationship to the people in their lives. First, I ask students to write down a list of all the people they come into contact with in their lives. For this list, I remind students that in writing this list, they are not creating a list of people they are "closest" to, but simply a list of people they encounter. To help students, I ask them to think about the different spaces they occupy: school, home, church, family, neighborhoods, and so forth. I ask students to page through their notebook for previous writing that might be helpful.

Next, I ask students to draw three to four concentric circles, placing themselves in the middle. Then I ask them to consider the list of people in their lives. Students then place each of these people in the circles, with those with whom they feel "closer" close to the middle, and those they might not know well in the outermost circle (or even outside the circle). See Figure 3.12 for an example of how I model this for students.

Some follow-up questions for writing to dig deeper:

- Describe someone close to you, someone in your inner circle. What makes your relationship close?

- How did you feel as you listed and noticed how people in your life are in different circles?

FIGURE 3.12 CIRCLES OF SELF

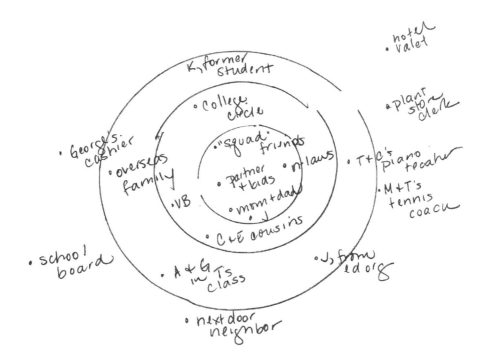

When I model the circles of self, I try to show students the many different people in my life I might encounter on any given day. Like many of the other writing activities in this chapter, the point is not the end product but the process of noticing who is in your life and thinking deeply—and honestly—about their relationship to you and you to them.

- Are there any people in your circles who have changed position in recent years? Perhaps there is someone who used to be in an outer circle but is now in your inner circle, or vice versa. Why? What accounts for this change?

- Consider those who are in the outer circle. Why are they there? Is this intentional? Is there anyone in the outer circle you'd like to bring in closer? What's stopping you?

- Looking at these concentric circles and the people inside them, how else could we label or describe this visual? For example, perhaps this visual can be better described as circles of *influence*—and if so, what does this say about who we listen to and who we don't?

A similar reflection is the "Universe of Obligation" lesson from Facing History & Ourselves, a nonprofit organization that uses history to challenge teachers to stand up to bigotry and hate. In this lesson, students are asked to also draw concentric circles and within those circles, to identify "the individuals and groups toward whom obligations are owed, to whom rules apply, and whose injuries call for [amends]."

Learn more about Facing History's "Universe of Obligation"

Later in the year, we revisit this page in our notebook when we consider multiple perspectives in arguments. For example, we might consider an issue, review these circles, and then ask ourselves, *is there anything in my relationships with others that helps me to better understand this issue—or prevents me from understanding it better?* Or, in a similar protocol, rather than placing ourselves at the center, we might name an issue and consider which people (and the points-of-view they represent) are "closest" to this issue and why, drawing similar concentric circles to visualize this. We can ask whose voices occupy the center of an argument and whose voices are marginalized (and why).

To Be or Not to Belong

While the previous notebook prompt asks students to consider the relative strengths of their relationships to others, this next writing treads similar ground but focuses more deeply on *group* identity. After all, so much of adolescence is focused on not just figuring out the answer to *who am I?* but also in asking *and where do I belong? Who are my people?* In other words, to what group identities do our students subscribe? With what community or social groups do they identify?

For this notebook prompt, I ask students to revisit their identity inventory. This time, I invite students to look for the elements of their identity that relate to groups they belong to. For example, if one element of their identity is their love of sports, then they might see themselves as also belonging to a group of "athletes" or perhaps more specifically, "soccer players" or "runners."

After students choose a group identity, I ask students to create a list of characteristics of that group. In other words, what makes that group a *group?* What shared interests, connections, personality traits do its members have? Are there common physical characteristics or personal experiences among its members? I might prompt students with sentence starters like, "When people think of ____, they usually think . . ."

Then I ask students to write on the extent to which they, as individuals, fit in with this group identity. After students share in small groups, we reflect on how group identities are useful in thinking about ourselves and what the limits of these group identities might be. We return to this idea of group versus individual identities when we study characters in literature as well (for example, in *Things Fall Apart*, to what extent does the character Okonkwo fit into Ibo society? Or in *A Raisin in the Sun*, to what group identities does the character Beneatha belong to and to what extent?)

More Than the Worst Thing

As you might notice in the prompts I've shared up to this point, my hope is to help students see their identities—and the stories behind them—as flexible and changing, to see that there are always multiple ways *into* a story about who they are and that who they are is complex and nuanced.

▶ "Proximity has taught me some basic and humbling truths, including this vital lesson: Each of us is more than the worst thing we've ever done."

—Bryan Stevenson

To emphasize this point, I ask students to write in their notebook two lists and two stories.

First, I ask students to compose two lists. In the first list, they should write down some facts about themselves—a simple, bulleted list of "neutral" facts, things like where they live, go to school, and who's in their family. They might refer to their identity inventory to find some of these items. In the second list, I ask them to write their opinions—a bulleted list of favorites, likes or dislikes.

Next, students write down a positive story about themselves, a story that makes them proud, the kind of story they'd want to be read at their funeral. It must be a true story. David Brooks's TED talk, "Should you live for your resume or for your eulogy?" is a helpful resource for introducing this concept. Conversely, students then write a negative story about themselves, a story that makes them ashamed or embarrassed, perhaps about a time when they were unkind, mean, impatient, the worst version of themselves. Again, the story must be true. I clarify for students that I will not ask them to actually share the content of these stories unless they volunteer, especially the negative one.

Watch David Brooks's TED Talk, "Should You Live for your Resume or your Eulogy?"

I ask students to review their two lists and two stories. I ask the following question, guiding students to briefly reflect in their notebooks:

- If others only knew one piece of information or one story about you—something that people would always associate with you— which piece of information or story would it be? Why?

- Which piece of information or story would you least want others to know about you and why?

As you might expect, most students want to be remembered and known for the positive story and would prefer the negative story to be forgotten. And sometimes the stories or parts of our identity are neither positive or negative. For example, Grace, a ninth grader I had a few years ago, chose the seemingly neutral fact of "student" as something she didn't want people to know. "I'm so much more than just a student," she explained. "I wouldn't want that to be the only thing that people knew about me." Again, note that I do not ask students to actually share the content of these stories unless they volunteer, especially the negative one. It's enough that students reflect on the power of these two lists and stories to define who they are.

In our reflection, I push students to think about their responses. I point out that the negative stories are just as true as the positive ones. Are they not as valid? (Later when we analyze arguments, I remind students of the importance of multiple perspectives when seeking truth and consensus. After all, sometimes contradictory perspectives are also both true.)

This is when I share one of my favorite parts from Bryan Stevenson's book, *Just Mercy,* a memoir about his work trying to abolish capital punishment. In the introduction of his book, Stevenson shares how getting to know death row inmates, many who have committed atrocious acts, opened up his "understanding of human potential, redemption, and hopefulness" (Stevenson, 2014, p. 11). In fact, getting to know these condemned individuals taught him a valuable lesson, that "each of us is more than the worst thing we've ever done" (p. 17). I pose the hypothetical: **what it would be like to be defined by the worst thing they'd ever done.** You can imagine the discomfort that sits in the room—and we sit with it.

We then go back to the lists they've created and ask ourselves: Which pieces of information here could be interpreted as positive or negative? By whom? Why? By unpacking our identities in this way, students begin to see the ways in which no story exists in a vacuum or on a page. Context—and narrators—matter.

Then I pose the following thought experiment:

Suppose someone else was going to write a biography about you. Which pieces of information would you share? Which would you keep private? And who would you trust to write your life story?

At this point, we start to make connections to the various stories we've heard our entire lives and think about the ways in which these stories, too, are incomplete. We discuss fictional stories like *The Wizard of Oz* and consider how our view of the Wicked Witch as "evil" is challenged when paired with a story like *Wicked*—not to mention how our view of the author Frank Baum is challenged when we learn that he promoted racist and hateful policies toward Native people (Pierpoint, 2018). Or we consider the story of *The Three Little Pigs* from the wolf's point-of-view as in Jon Scieszka's children's book, *The True Story of the Three Little Pigs*.

While these stories are fictional, we consider, too, the danger of the dominant historical narratives. For example, what are the stories that are most associated with (and often define) Christopher Columbus or Thomas Jefferson?

By taking students through this process of thinking, our hope is that they again see the ways in which their stories—and the stories of others—require multiple perspectives. When we have few stories about people, especially about people different from us—what Vietnamese American writer V. T. Nguyen (2018) calls "narrative scarcity"—we are susceptible to creating stereotypes. I have often used this process just before we are about to launch a unit on argument or discussion of a controversial issue as a reminder that in spite of whatever we *think* we know, there is always more to uncover and learn.

Above and Below the Line

In my training around Courageous Conversations About Race (Singleton, 2014), one of the critical things I've learned to think about more often are the dominant narratives and counternarratives that exist around any issue and, in particular, about any group of people. Borrowing from Singleton's work here, I ask students to consider what is "above" and "below" the line of awareness for themselves and others regarding their identity. See page 251 for how to apply this to analyzing texts and arguments.

I start by asking students to draw a horizontal line on their page. I explain that anything above the line is information that is considered generally "known" about them to outsiders. Information that they write below the line is that which is generally "unknown" about them, except for those who might know them very well, such as close friends or family. Another version of this prompt is the familiar "iceberg" analogy. Often, only the tip of the iceberg is seen (or "known") by outsiders while the vast majority of the iceberg lies beneath the surface (or "unknown"). What is above the line are the **dominant narratives** about who they are, while what is below the line are the **insider** or **counternarratives** about their identity (Figure 3.13).

To illustrate this concept, we read an excerpt from *Writings on the Wall*, a collection of essays by Abdul-Jabbar (2016). Here, in the

introduction, Abdul-Jabbar reflects on the dominant narratives that exist about his own identity:

> Despite the fact that I've been writing about social issues longer than I played basketball, many of my critics on social media begin their comments with "Stick to basketball, Kareem." However, aside from having played basketball a couple of decades ago, I am also an American, a father, a businessman, an education advocate, a journalist.

As you can see, Abdul-Jabbar's memoir invites students to think about how the identities they possess—how the above the line, dominant narratives that others have of them—are often constructed and determined by others. This push and pull of social versus personal, group versus individual identities, provides students with rich terrain to write about. After we read his essay, students complete an Above-and-Below-the-Line exercise using the information Abdul-Jabbar shares, similar to that in Figure 3.13.

I then use a personal example related to my parents' immigrant story to illustrate the power of dominant (above-the-line) narratives and counter (below-the-line) narratives. Recall what I previously shared in Chapter 1 about my parents' story when we discussed the *just world hypothesis bias* (pages 28–31). Figure 3.13 captures the dominant narrative about my parents' immigration story, the "American Dream." And yet, as I remind students, the below-the-line, counter narrative tells the more complete picture.

After sharing these examples, students are ready to consider how this exercise applies to themselves. When doing this exercise with your own students, I encourage you to think about what examples from your own experiences you might also share.

This writing exercise is particularly useful because it helps students think about the parts of themselves that they choose to share with the world and those parts of themselves that they choose to keep hidden. I encourage students to think about how they might use their personal essays to unpack what's below the line (to the extent they feel comfortable). Another mentor text I've used that is helpful for students is Nicole Chung's *All You Can Ever Know*. In this excerpt from her memoir, Chung reflects on the ways in which she was told a singular story about her adoption: that she was lucky to have birth parents who gave her up so that she could have a better life. This "family lore" is the dominant narrative about her life, but as she implies (and later explores in the rest of the memoir), there is so much more below the line in her story.

Family lore given to us as children has such hold over us, such staying power. It can form the bedrock of another kind of faith, one to rival any religion, informing our beliefs about ourselves, our families, and our place in the world. When tiny, traitorous doubts arose, when I felt lost or alone or confused about all the things I couldn't know, I told myself that something as noble as my birth parents' sacrifice demanded my trust. My loyalty.

When I share this excerpt, and this passage in particular, I ask students to reflect on what "family lore" they too have heard and how this lore might be only one part of their story.

FIGURE 3.13 ABOVE AND BELOW THE LINE

TOPIC	
ABOVE THE LINE What is seen What is known What "we" are "conscious" of	DOMINANT NARRATIVES
BELOW THE LINE What is invisible (or not seen) What is unknown What we are *not immediately* conscious of	INSIDER PERSPECTIVES COUNTERNARRATIVES

Kareem Abdul-Jabbar	
ABOVE	*Basketball Player · LA Lakers · "Dumb jock" · Basketball Commentator*
BELOW	*American · father · businessman · education advocate · journalist · charity organizer · history buff · filmmaker · novelist · former global Cultural Ambassador for the U.S. · political activist · Muslim*

(Continued)

My Parents' Story

ABOVE

Immigrants · "American Dream" · Successful, steady jobs · Sacrifice and Determination

BELOW

College educated · Colonial relationship with the U.S. · Family already in U.S. · Exanded Immigration Laws · U.S. Labor needs · "Model Minority" Stereotype · Bilingual, fluent English speakers

YOU

ABOVE THE LINE
What is seen · what is known · what "we" are "conscious" of

*What is the **dominant narrative** about you? And to whom? What are the first words, adjectives, or assumptions that people make?*

BELOW THE LINE
What is invisible (or not seen) · unknown · what we are *not immediately* conscious of

*What is the **counternarratives** about you? What are the things that only those closest to you know? What **insider perspectives** do they have?*

Figure 3.14 summarizes the notebook prompts shared so far. Notice the *cadence:* students explore the complexities of their own identity(ies) *and then can apply to their analysis of the identity(ies) of characters as well as their analysis of social issues in their communities and greater world.*

FIGURE 3.14 SUMMARY OF NOTEBOOK WRITING PROMPTS

NOTEBOOK PROMPT	WHAT STUDENTS LEARN	HOW THIS CAN BE APPLIED
Identity Inventory (p. 93)	• Emphasizes the multiple layers of identity • Provides working definitions and clarity around different social identities students have • Develops an understanding of the concepts of intersectionality and privilege	• Connection between social identities and social issues • Analysis of literary characters through their social identities (for example, the internal conflicts characters experience may reflect the social identity they possess) (p. 113)

NOTEBOOK PROMPT	WHAT STUDENTS LEARN	HOW THIS CAN BE APPLIED
List and Lean In (p. 100)	• Develops a habit of generating many possible ideas before narrowing down or focusing on a single area	• Encourages students to default to considering many different possibilities in literary analysis and argument writing before drawing conclusions
Drawing Our Selves (p. 102)	• Encourages visual, creative thinking to inspire writing	• Visuals biographies or other visual mentor texts can be used in character analysis and to outline arguments
More Than the Average Joe (p. 106)	• Highlights students' strengths and areas of expertise	• Introduces students to the idea of ethos, can be used to analyze in other writing
Questions for Memoirists (p. 107)	• Inspires reflection about small and meaningful moments in their lives	• Most questions can be applied to character analysis or when reading memoirs
The Stranger in the Photo (p. 107)	• Encourages "looking again" at photographs to unpack memories and experiences	• Visual analysis skills can be applied to photo essays and journalism
Literary Inspiration (p. 113)	• Engages students with mentor texts for identity in various genres	• Craft analysis can be applied to multiple forms of writing
Life Graphs (p. 114)	• Reimagines the use of timelines to reflect on experiences	• Can be applied to character arcs in fiction
Circles of Self (p. 116)	• Encourages students to consider their relationships with and positionality to others • Makes concrete and visual the concept of who/what is centered and who/what is marginalized	• Can be used to analyze the relationships and positionality that characters in stories have with one another (p. 118) • Can be applied to argument analysis when researching social issues (p. 118)
To Be or Not to Belong (p. 118)	• Draws the connection between individual identity markers and group identities • Encourages students to analyze the fluidity or rigidity of group identities	• Examination of literary characters through the lens of their group identities and their impact
More Than the Worst Thing (p. 119)	• Encourages students to think beyond the binaries of positive v. negative, good v. bad • Develops both pride and humility	• Provides a touchstone activity to remind students not to jump to conclusions (about a character or issue)
Above and Below the Line (p. 121)	• Develops understanding of dominant versus counternarratives • Encourages students to identify dominant narratives and seek counternarratives • Reminds students not to rush to conclusions or judgment	• Can be applied when students engage in character analysis, researching issues, and analyzing arguments

PROVIDING MENTOR TEXTS FOR IDENTITY

Throughout these pages, you'll find many invitations for students to write about their identities. As you consider using these in your classroom, remember the why of this work with students. Although many educators may invite students to write about their identities at some point during the school year, the purpose of this identity work in antibias education is so that students can make the connection between who they are and the potential biases they carry because of their identities and experiences (or lack thereof). The clearer students see themselves, the brighter the light they can shine on the biases that might lurk beneath the way they read and write their world.

In order to help students think and write about their identities, they need thoughtful mentor texts: personal essays that are rich in craft lessons to improve students' writing, but that *also* model the type of deep, self-reflective thinking about identity that we wish for our students. Asking students to simply write about who they are and what's important to them can be an intimidating experience. Exposure to a rich variety of personal essays, however, allows the abstract to become concrete.

Sometimes students don't know what they can write about until they've been given permission through another person's writing. Over the years, I've had several students who have had initial reservations about writing about their racial or gender identities, especially on college essays, and were discouraged from writing about these topics by their families and friends for fear of discussing something "controversial." But issues that relate to our identities are not controversial—they are *human* issues, and education, at its heart, is about what it means to be human beings living among and with one another.

Guidelines for Choosing Mentor Texts

Although there are countless personal essays out there, I use questions in Figure 3.15 to help guide me in selecting texts for my students. Notice that these are questions that can be used to choose *any* text being used in the classroom.

FIGURE 3.15   TEN QUESTIONS TO ASK WHEN CHOOSING IDENTITY MENTOR TEXTS

1. What are the identities of my students in my class?
2. Does this text speak to the diverse identities of the students in my classroom? in the school? in the community?
3. Is the text written by someone from within that identity group(s) or an outsider?

4. Can this text provide meaningful insight to students about identities with which they are unfamiliar?

5. In what ways can this text help to develop a positive social identity for my students?

6. How can this text challenge incomplete or harmful dominant narratives about different identities?

7. Does this writer treat their subject with complexity and nuance and avoid stereotypes?

8. In what ways could students be potentially and negatively spotlighted in their identities if I use this text? How can I mitigate any harm associated with stereotype threat? (pp. 93)

9. What craft moves can I teach using this text?

10. What does this text *not* do or include that I will have to supplement with another mentor text? What counternarratives will my students need *after* this text?

With these questions in mind, ultimately, I select mentor texts that will provide students with an opportunity to **build empathy for the experiences of others** and **speak to their own**. I look for mentor texts that can help students look beyond the sound bites and headlines of their social media and news feeds—essays that will bring students closer to the lived experience of others and provide crucial "mirrors and windows" for understanding (Bishop, 1990).

This is also why getting to know students as quickly as possible through their identity inventories, writing conferences, and other writing early in the year can be so valuable. The more we know about our students, the better able we are to select material in the curriculum to meet their unique needs. Better yet, we can also ask students about identities or experiences they might be interested in reading more about and bring those voices to the classroom.

One caveat I'd like to make here: in choosing mentor texts related to racial or gender identities, be mindful about the potential impact that these texts might have on the students in your room. Depending on the situation, some students of color and LGBTQIA+ students may feel like that part of their identity is being spotlighted in a way that makes them uncomfortable. This might be especially true if a student is the only student in the room who identifies a particular way. Yet at the same time, to build understanding, we also need to find a way to allow all students to learn about as many identities and experiences as possible, just not at the expense of students who may already be marginalized.

The stronger our relationship with our students, the more they are willing to trust us in leading potentially difficult conversations as we navigate these texts that explore identity, including ones that mirror

their own. Our relationships with students can inform how we navigate those conversations in more responsible, meaningful ways. For example, when I considered sharing an essay that involved a racist incident between a White man and a Muslim woman, I knew that it could potentially make the one Muslim student I had in class uncomfortable. So I gave her the essay a few days in advance, told her I was thinking about using it in class, and asked her to let me know if she would be comfortable with it. In this case, she was, but I think that because of the relationship that we'd built that she would have also been comfortable telling me if she wasn't.

Figure 3.16 lists a few mentor texts—compelling and beautiful essays that invite students to think about various identities in new ways— that I've used with my own students. As you can see, the essays listed encompass a wide range of identities.

FIGURE 3.16 MENTOR TEXTS FOR IDENTITY

Essays:

- "Raising a Black Son in the United States" by Jesmyn Ward
- "Black Men in Public Spaces" by Brent Staples
- "On Fear and the Superhero" by Gene Luen Yang
- "What 'White Food' Meant to a First Generation Kid" by Lisa Ko
- "Why I Write: Making No Become Yes" by Elie Wiesel
- "How Rugrats Made Me Feel Comfortable in America" by Edward Delman
- "I'm More than An 'Other'" by Meghan Markle
- *The Last Jedi* Killed My Childhood, and That's Exactly Why It's Great" by Rob Bricken
- "I'm Ghanian-American. Am I Black?" by Yaa Gyasi
- "'Maddy' Might Just Work After All" by Jennifer Finney Boylan
- "The Perfect Body Is a Lie" by Lindy West
- "Bridging Troubled Waters" (Introduction to *Writings on the Wall*) by Kareem Abdul-Jabbar
- "The Changeling" by Alexander Chee
- "Why Pope Francis Makes Me Cry" by Andrea Bocelli
- "Being Muslim Is" by Maheen Haq
- "Sandra Cisneros Inspired Me to Live Life As a Wild Woman" by Lizz Huerta
- "Blessed are the White Trash" by Joshua Wilkey
- "Korean as a Second Language" by Spencer Lee Lenfield
- "How Disney's Animated Movies Awakened my Queer Imagination" by Manuel Betancourt
- "When Your Family Wants You to be 'All Boy'" by Nick White
- "Coming Out" collection of video essays from *The New York Times*
- "Conversations about Race" collection of video essays from *The New York Times*

Unfortunately, our current political climate has created an atmosphere of fear when it comes to using texts that highlight the authentic and lived experiences of historically marginalized groups, particularly Black, Brown, and LGBTQ+ communities and individuals. As I write this, laws in some states, notably Florida, have made the teaching of any text that is deemed "controversial" for any reason almost impossible as book challenges remove texts from classroom libraries and school curricula. Many of the texts I suggest above, for example, may be considered unacceptable to those who cannot tolerate, much less understand, the experiences and existence of others unlike themselves. While these book bans and challenges make teaching during this time particularly challenging, these threats are nothing new. In March 2023, Dr. Sonja Cherry-Paul and I recorded a webinar for Learning for Justice in which we share strategies for navigating this pushback while still advocating for diversifying our classroom texts. Scan the QR code to watch the webinar.

WRITING OUR STORIES, OUR SELVES

When students write about their own personal experiences, they are never *just* telling a story. When students write personal narratives, they are composing themselves and claiming identities. Writing personal

Watch my webinar with Dr. Sonja Cherry-Paul on "Diversifying Texts" in your classroom.

narratives, at its core, is about answering the question, *Who am I?* As Roozen (2016) points out,

> Through writing, writers come to develop and perform identities in relation to the interests, beliefs, and values of the communities they engage with, understanding the possibilities of selfhood available in those communities. The act of writing, then, is not so much about using a particular set of skills as it is about becoming a particular kind of person, about developing a sense of who we are.
> (pp. 50–51)

Storytelling is a superpower. And like all superpowers, storytelling can be used for good and for harm. When we allow students the opportunity to write their own lives, to imagine themselves as they want to be imagined, to take control over their stories, they become authors—they claim authority over who they are and who they want to be. I can't emphasize enough how powerful this is, especially for students of color, queer students, students of targeted religious identities, and others whose experiences have been too often told by others in, at best, inauthentic ways, and at worst, dehumanizing ones. For so many students who have been rendered voiceless, or who come from

communities that have been silenced or marginalized, storytelling is a revolutionary act. As Villanueva (2016) reminds us:

> Writing provides a means whereby identities are discovered and constituted. Yet those are never clear cut. We carry many identities, choosing to foreground one (or some) depending on the context, the audience, and the rhetorical task at hand . . . Identity politics tends toward the construction of a single identity. But we know that identities are multifaceted. One can be liberal on social issues but conservative on fiscal issues. None of us is ideologically "pure." Or one can be a gay man of color, wherein sets of different conflicts and different power relations can occur. (pp. 57–58)

Like us, our students embody complex and sometimes contradictory identities. Supporting students in writing that helps them to make meaning of these identities can empower them to not only understand themselves better but also others. And of course, storytelling is also about how we tell stories about others and the power that comes with it.

Conferring as Relationship-Building

One of the most powerful ways we can get to know students is through conferring. I consider conferring to be a nonnegotiable when students are writing about parts of their own identities.

Within the first few weeks of school, I try to sit down with every student for just a few moments for prewriting conferences. By asking students to tell me what matters to them and what's worth writing about, I can get a sense for how comfortable a student might be in their identities (See Figure 3.17 for some possible questions to use during prewriting conferences that can inspire students to reflect on their identities.)

I understand, for example, that my own identity as a woman of color—and as an Asian American woman—also plays a role in the way I am able to connect with students. Yet no matter what identities I might possess, we can signal our support for all students through our choices in the classroom, by being intentional about the voices we feature on our classroom walls, the books we have available in our classroom libraries, or the pronouns we use in our language. Students are watching; every day is a test to see if we are worthy of their trust, if our classroom is a space that is safe enough for them to be brave.

To help students narrow down topics, I remind students that we have many identities and many stories inside of us. One question that has been helpful for students to narrow down is this one: which of these do you feel "calling to you" at this time to write about? Why do you think that might be?

FIGURE 3.17 IDENTITY PREWRITING CONFERENCES

To help students generate topics for writing about their identities, I ask students to bring their writer's notebooks with them to our conversation, marking words, phrases, or whole entries that stand out to them and that they are willing to share (recall my advice about the sanctity of writers' notebooks in Chapter 2).

Some questions that can encourage students to deepen their thinking:

- Could you tell me why this particular word, phrase, entry stood out to you?

- In thinking about the person you are today, what do you think drew you to this topic?

- What do you think you might have written about this topic a few months ago, a year ago, five years ago? Why? What's changed, if anything?

- What are the elements of your identity that are most integral to who you are today?

- When you think of this part of your identity, what memory or moments most stand out to you?

Finally, remember this above all else: the goal of this identity prewriting conference is not to "convince" or worse, to compel a student to write about a part of their identity that they are not willing to share on paper. In fact, students may very likely be willing to share with you verbally but be unwilling to put what they've shared onto the page. Our one-on-one conversations with students should be considered sacred; when I speak with students, I try to encourage, engender trust, and build confidence in *their* ability to choose what to write, to maintain their own agency as a writer. Again, recall the guidelines for a trauma-informed writing workshop shared in the previous chapter (p. 80).

Invitations to Write, Explore, and Expand Students' Sense of Self

Figure 3.18 provides a list of personal essay prompts that can help deepen students' thinking about themselves and especially how they came to be the person they are today. For each personal essay, I include a brief description followed by authentic mentor texts that students can use.

FIGURE 3.18 WRITING OUR SELVES—PERSONAL ESSAY POSSIBILITIES

ESSAY	DESCRIPTION	MENTOR TEXT(S)
Indelible Moment	The word indelible means "that which cannot be erased—marks that may not easily be removed." Indelible moments are those moments that imprint on us so deeply that we would not be the same person without them. These moments are so profound that we might even define our lives by before this moment and after this moment.	• "Shame" by Dick Gregory • "Raising a Black Son in the United States" by Jesmyn Ward • "The Most Important Day" by Helen Keller • "The Meanings of a Word" by Gloria Naylor

(Continued)

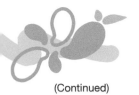

(Continued)

ESSAY	DESCRIPTION	MENTOR TEXT(S)
	Similarly, psychologists refer to moments like these as "flashbulb memories"—which are highly detailed, vivid moments that we remember because something happened around us or to us that was not only out of the ordinary, but perhaps even life-changing. Writer Willa Cather once wrote that "most of the basic material a writer works with is acquired before the age of fifteen." In those fifteen years, what have been your indelible moments? Your flashbulb memories?	
Definition Essay	Often our strongest values, attitudes, and beliefs are tied to the way we define, personally and individually, what is abstract. Often, abstract nouns like *love, courage, justice,* and *equality* are the hardest to define but the most critical to understand. In this essay, define the abstract through the concrete—write about specific experiences and moments in your life where you've come to understand an abstract idea or concept. What does *love* mean to you? What is *justice*?	• On hope: "Hope is an Embrace of the Unknown" by Rebecca Solnit • On being "woke": "What It Really Means to be 'Woke'" by Giselle Defares • On hunger: "What We Hunger For" by Roxane Gay • On gender: "I Want a Wife" by Judy Brady • On language: "Mother Tongue" by Amy Tan and "How to Tame a Wild Tongue" by Gloria Anzaldua
A Meaningful Place	Revisit in writing a place that means something to you. What meaningful events, moments, or memories took place here? What does this place symbolize for you or for others?	• "Watching the World Pass By from a Train Car" by Connor Fahey • "Buying a House" by Sean Prentiss
Someone who . . .	Write about a meaningful person—who is someone in your life you admire, care for, love? Who is someone who challenges you, inspires you, makes you better? Or who is someone who fascinates you? Who is someone you'd like to get to know better by researching and writing about them? For this essay, you might also consider the most important relationships you have in your life. What has this relationship meant to you? Why? In what ways has this relationship changed you—for better or for worse?	• "You May Want to Marry My Husband" by Amy Krouse Rosenthal • "The Essential Man" by Chris Jones • "Foreign Affairs; My Favorite Teacher" by Tom Friedman • *The New Yorker* profile essays

ESSAY	DESCRIPTION	MENTOR TEXT(S)
What You've Learned	Write about a time you learned something important . . . or even unimportant. We spend so much of our lives in schools, in classrooms, cafeterias, and hallways, and we're surrounded by friends, teachers, frenemies—and in that time, we've accumulated lots of stories. You might tell a story related to school—put us there, in the moment, to feel what you felt, to think what you thought—and then describe what it meant or could have meant to you as a person. Or you might write about a serious learning experience, as Dick Gregory wrote in "Shame." Or perhaps take a cue from David Sedaris and write about a humorous learning experience.	• "Shame" by Dick Gregory • "Me Talk Pretty One Day" by David Sedaris • "I Just Wanna Be Average" by Mike Rose • "And the Orchestra Played On" by Joanne Lipman • "On Being 17, Bright and Unable to Read" by David Raymond • "White Lies" by Erin Murphy
Our Bodies, Our Selves	Write an essay about your body—or more precisely, parts of your body. Write about the scar on your knee, the freckles on your arm, the hair that never stays in place, what your hands mean to you. Describe, tell a story.	• "The Clan of the One-Breasted Women" by Terry Tempest Williams • "On Having Curly Hair" by Grace Lanouette (see the full text at the end of this chapter)
The Ties that Bind	Write about your family. Families are complicated and messy, but writing about our family can also help us make sense of some of the most important relationships in our lives. Write about your family as a whole, or zoom in on one person—your mom, dad, brother, sister, aunt, uncle, grandparents.	• "Ties," a New York Times collection of essays about family. • "Disco Papa" by Karen Russell • "Praying for Common Ground at the Christmas-Dinner Table" by Reza Aslan • "The Subject of a Sibling" by Susan Senator
Falling in Love	Think about something you love. Or consider something you loved in the past. Children, as you might know from your own experiences, often develop interests and passions, perhaps so obsessive that these feelings can only be described as love. Make a list of the things you love/loved. You might try thinking back to a specific age or time in your life—perhaps when you were in the second or third grade—and ask yourself, what did I love back then? When my youngest son was five, he loved to collect coffee cups. Whenever he saw me drinking my Wawa or Starbucks coffee, he would keep the cup when I was finished. Eventually he had amassed a long line of a dozen or	• "What We Hunger For" by Roxane Gay • "The Strangest Discoveries that Made Me Fall in Love with Science Again" by Esther Inglis-Arkell • "Remember When You First Fell In Love with Cars?" by Simon de Burton • "How Falling in Love with Harry Potter Shaped My Life" by Chelsey Pippin • "You Can Never Go Back: On Loving Children's Books as Adults" by Anya Jaremko-Greenwold • "Writing About Charlie Brown Feels Like Writing About Myself" by Chuck Klosterman

(Continued)

(Continued)

ESSAY	DESCRIPTION	MENTOR TEXT(S)
	so coffee cups which he kept lined up on the dining room window sill. What did these coffee cups mean to him? I'm not sure. After a few weeks, his interest faded and he was onto another obsession, but he still likes to collect things—small knick knacks here and there, and keep them in his latest favorite cardboard box which serves as his makeshift treasure chest. My middle kid loves superheroes. My oldest? Basketball. Me? Photography. What do you love? Describe and tell the story of how you fell in love with it— make us fall in love with it, too, even if for just a few moments.	
Falling Out of Love	Sometimes the best experiences to write about aren't about falling in love, but falling out of it. Think back to something you used to love and write about how you fell out of love with it. Tell about what made you fall so hard, and then what made you realize one day that what you thought you loved wasn't really everything you thought it was. This prompt invites you to think about what it felt like to realize something you loved, admired, or enjoyed wasn't all it was cracked up to be. It's a prompt that invites you to think not about loss, although there is some of that, but really about growth. After all, in order to grow, sometimes we need to let go of the things we used to love, to leave behind some things in order to make room for others.	• "I've Fallen Out of Love with Music" by Sophie Heawood • "Why I've Fallen Out of Love with Football" by Simon Kuper • "The Seven Stages of Falling Out of Love with Your Fandom" by Esther Inglis-Arkell • "Leaving Fandom: Why I Gave Up Sports, Why You Should Consider It, and How to Start" by David S. Heineman • "How I Finally Moved On from my Childhood Crush, Holden Caulfield" by Tatiana Ryckman • "The Last Jedi Killed My Childhood, and That's Exactly Why It's Great" by Rob Bricken
What Keeps You Up at Night	When I was little, I was scared of the dark. I needed a night light to fall asleep—to make sure that I could see if a monster was coming. I needed to have my closet door fully closed—to lock inside any monsters who might be hiding. But I needed the bedroom door open so that I could make a quick run to my parents' room if necessary. I don't need a night light anymore, and the monsters may not have been real, but they were real to me. Write about a problem you have or had—perhaps something that you never figured out.	• "On Getting My Shit Together" by Peter Brown • "Difficult Girl" by Lena Dunham

ESSAY	DESCRIPTION	MENTOR TEXT(S)
	Focus on the problem—describe it, animate it, how this problem has irked you, haunted you. Consider the roots of this problem, its causes, its sources. Wonder about it. The problem could be physical, mental, emotional. It could be abstract or concrete, an idea or a person, real or imagined (but it *feels* real, and so it is to you).	
This American Life	This American Life is a radio program dedicated to telling stories. Each episode has a theme and brings you two to four stories on that theme. Browse through the This American Life archives to find a theme you might be interested in. Think of each episode description as a writing prompt, an invitation for you to tell your own story. Be sure to listen (or read) a few, too!	• This American Life (curated list on a website of the same name) • "13 Brilliant This American Life Episodes You Can Hear Right Now" Eric McQuade, Laura Standley, and Devon Taylor
What's Saving Your Life Right Now?	On her blog site, author Anne Bogel writes: "This is a tough time of year for a lot of us. The days are short, and relentlessly dreary. Everyone has the flu, or if they're lucky, the sniffles. Budgets are tight. And spring feels a long way away. "Winter is a challenging season for me. To preserve my sanity during the cold and gray days, I adopted a habit a few years back. I started keeping a list—an actual, physical, pen-and-paper list—of the things that were actively giving me life in my least favorite season. "The idea comes from author Barbara Brown Taylor. In her memoir Leaving Church, Taylor tells about a time she was invited to speak, and her host assigned her this topic: 'Tell us what is saving your life right now.' "Most of us know what's killing us and can articulate it, if asked. Some of us are overwhelmed with hurry and worry; some of us face crushing poverty; some feel utterly paralyzed. "But few of us stop to note what's giving us life. Taylor says it's too good a question to not revisit every once in a while: what are the things—big or small—that are saving us?" So what's saving you right now? Write about it.	• "9 Things Giving Me Life Right Now" by Anne Bogel • "I Couldn't Read While Grieving, Until I Found These Books" by Veronica Henry • "Finding Solace in the Words of Furious Women: Or, How to Smile at Men Who Tell You What You Want" by R. O. Kwon • "Spider-Man Taught Me How to Live, Comics Taught Me How to Write" by Nikesh Shukla

(Continued)

(Continued)

ESSAY	DESCRIPTION	MENTOR TEXT(S)
The Do-Over	Write about a time you failed at something, perhaps spectacularly or quietly, publicly or privately. Go beyond thinking about the typical failures of adolescent life, like a school test or your driver's license test (though that might make for a good story), and consider the other multiple and varied ways you might have experienced failure: perhaps the time you failed to remember your sibling's birthday, or the way you failed to speak when you knew you should. Write about a time that you wish you could do-over—a time that you failed in some way, small or big, that you regret. Tell that story. Then tell what you would do if you had the chance for a "do-over."	• "Her Name is Azeb" by Julia Torres • "And Now, for an Encore" by Adrienne Starr
Meaningful Object	Consider the material objects in your life—things you own, perhaps given to you, perhaps you earned. Of these things, which are most valuable to you? Don't think of it in terms of monetary value, but consider its personal value to you. Another way to think about this: if you could only save one thing among your possessions, what would it be? That said, a meaningful object might be meaningful for less-than-positive reasons. Consider something that you wish you didn't own or have. Tell about the tension there. Write about this object. Tell the story of how you came to have this object and why it's important to you.	• Excerpt from An American Childhood by Annie Dillard • "The Jacket" by Gary Soto • The Object Parade: Essays by Dinah Lenney • "Object Lessons" series from The Atlantic
Letter of Recommendation	Unlike the open letter, this essay isn't an actual letter, but refers to the letters in the literal sense. Write an essay in the spirit of The New York Times's wonderful column called, "Letters of Recommendation." These are essays that are "celebrations of objects and experiences that have been overlooked or underappreciated." Browse the site for examples and brainstorm your own.	• Letters of Recommendation essay column in the New York Times (so many great examples!) • "The Useful Dangers of Fairy Tales" by Amber Sparks • "In Memoriam: Harry Potter" by Tricia Ebarvia • "Em-dash, How I Love Thee" by Tricia Ebarvia
How-To	Share something you know how-to do. In this process analysis essay, share some advice or create a guide for how your reader might do something— and why.	• "How to Be Friends with Another Woman" by Roxane Gay • "Mindy Kaling's Guide to Killer Confidence" by Mindy Kaling

ESSAY	DESCRIPTION	MENTOR TEXT(S)
		• "How to Listen to Music: A Vintage Guide to the 7 Essential Skills" by Maria Popova
		• "How to Survive the College Admissions Madness" by Frank Bruni
		• "To Fall in Love with Anyone, Do This" Mandy Len Catron
		• "The Real Guide to Making Friends in College" Bizzy Emerson, Glenbard West, Veronica Hannsberry King
		• Essays from *The New York Times* collection, "Well Guides"
		• Essays from *The New York Times* collection, "Tip"
		• Essays from Real Simple's collection, "Life Strategies"
Food Memories	Food is such an important, driving force in our lives. We share and create some of our most important stories surrounded by food. It comforts us, nourishes us, and heals us. So far, I haven't met a student who didn't have one special dish or fond food memory to look back on. That's what the food memory narrative is about. Write a memory that centers on a favorite or memorable food experience. In addition to telling the story of this food and your experience, you might consider sharing the recipe, too.	• "Savoring Memories of Sunday Dinner" by Susan Russo • "Jerusalem: A Love Letter to Food and Memories of Home" by Bilal Qureshi • "What 'White Food' Meant to Me as a First-Generation Kid" by Lisa Ko • "I Became a Thanksgiving Orphan" by Jessica B. Harris • "Memories of Meals Past" collection from The New York Times • "The Magic of the Family Meal" by Nancy Gibbs • "Poor People Deserve to Taste Something Other Than Shame" by Ijeoma Oluo • "Over Easy" collection of essays from The Cut
Listicle	Write a listicle. What is a listicle? You might not have heard of the term, but if you've spent any time on the internet, then you've certainly read them. *Listicle* is a portmanteau of the words list and article. Listicles are pieces of writing that combine the best elements of lists and articles. Think of them as essays in whole or partial list form. Unlike traditional lists, listicles spend some time developing ideas about each item on the list and their meaning. Think about a topic that you know about that would work well in listicle form and write about it.	• "5 Reasons Listicles are Here to Stay, and Why That's Okay" by Rachel Edidin • "6 Things You Should Know About My Brother, Steph Curry" by Jessica Camerato • "Top Ten Reasons to Make (and Love) Top Ten Lists" by Dan Kois • "20 Reasons Why Harry Potter is the Best There'll Ever Be" in *Vogue magazine* • "The 10 Best Actors of the Year," annual series in the *New York Times*

(Continued)

(Continued)

ESSAY	DESCRIPTION	MENTOR TEXT(S)
This I Believe	This I Believe is an international organization engaging people in writing and sharing essays describing the core values that guide their daily lives. Over 125,000 of these essays, written by people from all walks of life, have been archived here on our website, heard on public radio, chronicled through our books, and featured in weekly podcasts. The project is based on the popular 1950s radio series of the same name hosted by Edward R. Murrow.	• This I Believe website, with curated lists by themes

Reconsidering, Reframing How to Assess Writing

Entire books, grounded in research and scholarship, have been written on how to assess student writing; this book has neither the space nor the breadth to cover everything that can and should be said about best practices in this area.

That said, there are some crucial things to consider when assessing a student's writing when that writing is about their identities and the meaningful, perhaps even painful experiences associated with them. One of the worst things that could happen would be a student conflating the grade they earn on an essay with their value as a person. *A student is not a grade.* When we assess student writing, we are not assessing students' value as human beings or even their worthiness as writers. We must start with the premise that whatever our students' *skills* might be, they are all *writers*. Period. They are writers who may have room to grow, but they are writers *regardless* of what skills they do or don't have . . . *yet*.

> One of the worst things that could happen would be a student conflating the grade they earn on an essay with their value as a person. A student is not a grade.

That *yet* is critical, and it's a mindset that we can help students to internalize. If they struggle with a particular craft move, instead of saying I'm not good at [fill-in-the-blank skill], they can say I'm not good at that *yet*. Writing is an art, of course, but it is also a *craft*, one that can be improved with practice, feedback, and experience.

So where does assessment come in?

Assessment is necessary to the extent that *feedback* is necessary for students to grow as writers. To navigate some of the challenges of assessing personal writing, I offer a few general guidelines:

1. Distinguish between assessing student *writing* (the product) versus assessing student *writers* (the person).

2. Develop shared language and expectations around the specific areas of focus or skills to be assessed.

3. Practice looking at writing craft together as a class using mentor texts.

4. Provide multiple opportunities for students to self-assess and talk through their own writing.

5. As a teacher, embody the role of *reader* versus evaluator when assessing writing.

While these guidelines are ones that I use with all student writing, I have found them to be especially important when it comes to students' personal writing.

First, we must make clear the distinction between assessing the *current skills* a student has regarding writing *and who they are as a person—and we have to make this distinction clear to students*. I have had colleagues who struggle to assess students' personal essay writing because they don't want their assessment to be seen as a judgment of a student's character. I understand and have struggled with this, too—which is why I think it's important to name that tension for students in as transparent a way as possible. For example, what I say to students goes something like this:

> I know it's hard to write about things that are deeply personal to us, especially when it has to do with an identity we hold that we are sensitive to or feel protective of. Writing is hard enough without feeling you're being graded as a person. My goal as your teacher is not to judge you as a person but to provide feedback that helps you improve as a writer. Each of you has amazing ideas, feelings, and experiences to share. The purpose of assessment is to give you the feedback you need so that each piece of writing you compose lives up to its own unique potential.

In my experience, the best way to prevent students from confusing the assessment of their writing with their identities as writers or as people is to **make sure that criteria we're using to assess writing is clear.** By criteria, I do not necessarily mean formal rubrics or checklists-pretending-to-be-rubrics. By criteria, I mean coming to a shared understanding of (1) what elements make up writing and (2) how each of those elements might be executed effectively given the student's chosen purpose and audience.

For example, several years ago, I was introduced to the 6+1 Traits of Writing through my local National Writing Project site, and I began this framework with my students. In case you're not familiar, the

framework identifies six elements of writing and offers criteria for how each of these elements might be executed successfully:

1. Ideas
2. Organization
3. Voice
4. Word Choice
5. Sentence Fluency
6. Conventions

Learn more about the 6+1 Traits Model of Writing

What my students and I appreciated most about this framework was that these elements of writing are, more or less, *universal*. In other words, we can read *any* piece of writing and examine it for its *ideas*. We can look at an editorial and a piece of fan fiction and examine the ways they each *organize* those ideas. Every piece of writing, regardless of genre, has a *voice*. And so on. As my students and I read mentor texts for identity, such as those shared earlier in this chapter, we talk about the ideas, how they're organized, how the writer develops their voice, and the diversity of rich craft moves they use. In other words, we *practice* how to talk about writing that explores complex and nuanced explorations of identity.

Furthermore, by using shared language and a consistent framework, students' ability to assess their own writing (even *while* they're writing) more naturally transfers across genre and task. In personal writing, assessment becomes less about the identities and experiences they're writing about and more about the extent to which they're able to effectively communicate their thoughts, feelings, and insights about these identities and experiences.

I also position myself as a reader versus judge and jury. I tell students, I am a reader of their writing who can share how their words impacted me. Now, I happen to be a reader with a lot of reading experience, so that can not only be helpful but will also inform what I see as possibly working or not working in any piece of writing.

With all that said, the truth is the most effective way I have found to assess students' personal writing (and really, most writing) is through **collaborative writing conferences**. I meet with each student after a piece of writing is turned in. I read it ahead of time and make some notes for myself on a separate sheet of paper, *not marking up the original work*. (Why? I've found that if I've already marked up their paper, students will focus all their energy trying to read the notes on the page rather than what I'm saying, and this conference is a conversation, not a monologue.) Together, we sit and look at their writing together. We walk and talk through it, paragraph by paragraph or section by section. I celebrate the choices the writer made that were effective for me. I ask questions where my understanding as a reader was challenged. I share wonderings in places where there might be an opportunity to explore and develop an idea further.

At the same time, students will share their thoughts as they were writing and what they hoped for in the choices they made. We talk about places where writing may not have had the effect they hoped for. Where there is a gap, I make sure *not* to locate the fault of that gap in something the student did or didn't do but acknowledge the ways in which my own identities and experiences as a reader may be playing a role. For example, instead of telling the student they didn't include enough description of the setting in their personal narrative, I share how I imagined the setting based on what they *did* include and the experiences I was bringing to the text as a reader. When the student sees the discrepancy, they can make the choice as a writer to add the necessary details. Protecting and nurturing student agency when it comes to writing is *always* important, *but especially when students are writing essentially themselves onto and into the page.* We *both* take notes on the paper throughout our conversation.

> *Where there is a gap, I make sure not to locate the fault of that gap in something the student did or didn't do but acknowledge the ways in which my own identities and experiences as a reader may be playing a role.*

After we finish reading through the writing together, we then look at the framework we're using to guide our assessment. Rather than me *telling* a student how they developed or explained their ideas, I ask them to determine how well they think they did, what areas they feel they shined in, and what areas they still feel like this piece of writing needed more work on. In my experience, 90 percent of the time after we confer, students are harder on themselves than I would be if I were to assess their writing alone. We end our conference with goals for what they would like to work on in their next piece of writing.

Some recommended reading on teaching and assessing writing:

- *Craft in the Real World* by Matthew Salesses

- *The Antiracist Writing Workshop: How to Decolonize the Creative Classroom* by Felicia Rose Chavez

- *Antiracist Writing Ecologies: Teaching and Writing for a Socially Just Future* by Asao B. Inoue

- *Rethinking Rubrics in Writing Assessment* by Maja Wilson

- *The Writer's Practice* and *Why They Can't Write: Killing the 5-Paragraph Essay and Other Necessities* by John Warner

WRITING THROUGH IDENTITY LENSES

Just as students can reflect on the ways in which their various identities might inform their reading responses, students can also reflect on the ways in which their identities inform their writing choices and topics. As students keep track of which identities they are writing *from*—their *voice* or *stance*—they can reflect on the ways they are growing not just as writers, but as human beings. I have often shared with students my belief that "we are what we read," but the same, of course, is true for writing: **we are what we write, and what we choose to write can illuminate much about how we see the world, even if unconsciously.** I can't tell you how many times I've sat down with students during writing conferences and in our conversations about their writing, they come to realize that the words on the page revealed truths they hadn't yet recognized about themselves, others, and the way they see the world. Writing, like reading, can be powerful ways in which we make whole the pieces of our memory or the fragments of our identities.

Who is the I who writes? How do my identities inform what I choose to write about and how? If writing is thinking, then what can I learn about the different dimensions of my identity during the writing process?

After students have written several pieces (the length of each piece doesn't matter), I ask them to reflect on how their writing was informed by different elements of their identities. I do not tell students in advance that we'll be reviewing their writing through their multiple identities; instead, we do some writing and then see where our identities might have naturally revealed themselves as we wrote.

As you can see in Figure 3.19, each column is dedicated to a different element of identity, which are listed across the top. Each row corresponds to a different piece of writing. I recently took the last eight published pieces on my website and decided to track where my identities are showing up in my own writing, just as I have done in the past for both myself and with students.

Each piece is grouped according to how generally satisfied I was with it. The top set of pieces are those marked "loved, most proud," the second group are pieces that I "liked," and the last set of pieces are those that are "promising but needs work." Across the top, in each column, I chose the following elements of my identity (L to R): gender, race, sexual orientation, nationality, language, socioeconomic status, daughter, wife, mother, teacher, ability, friend. As you can see, I pulled these elements from earlier identity inventories. Then I reflect on each piece and consider the extent to which that identity was present when I was writing:

✓ = this identity was "top of mind" as I was writing

— = this identity was present, but in the background

0 = this identity did not inform this piece of writing

The goal of this exercise is not to use more or fewer identities in any given piece. Instead, the goal is to have students take a moment to reflect and "listen" to what parts of their identities have found their way into their writing. Sometimes our decision to write about a particular part of our identity is intentional, but sometimes it is not, and it can be illuminating to consider what that might mean, especially if students see a pattern. Below are some questions I ask students to consider, first by themselves and then share with a small group. Sharing their results in a small group allows students to see the different ways that their peers responded to and approached this exercise.

- What was surprising or not surprising about how your identities informed your writing?

- Was there an element of your identity missing from your chart that you know played a role in your writing? Which one?

- What patterns do you notice? What might these patterns suggest?

- Does this data inspire you to write about anything in particular for your next piece of writing? If yes, what? If no, why not?

- What have you learned about yourself as a writer or as a person after doing this exercise?

As you look at my own writer identity chart, what do you notice? (If you are curious, you can read each of these pieces on my website.) Here are some of my own noticings and wonderings:

- It was not surprising that my "teacher" identity was most present in most of my writing. After all, these pieces were published on my professional educator website.

- I was surprised how few of my identities were ever "top of mind" when I was writing.

FIGURE 3.19   WRITER IDENTITY CHART

Writer-Identity Stance

Decide which writing pieces you loved, liked, or thought were just okay. Consider the identities that you accessed while you wrote. Mark those identities that were most "top of mind" during the writing process with a checkmark (✔), a dash (—) if you thought about that identity a little bit, or a zero (0) if you know that identity wasn't part of your writing experience at all.

		gender	race	ability	ethnicity	language	socioeconomics	daughter	wife	mother	teacher	friend
L O V E D	"Driving Lessons"	✓	✓	✓	✓	0	0	—	—	✓	—	0
	"one year later"	—	—	—	—	—	—	—	—	✓	✓	✓
	"We Teach Who We Are"	✓	✓	✓	✓	✓	✓	✓	—	—	✓	—
	"how do we show up"	✓	✓	✓	✓	✓	✓	—	—	—	✓	—
	"connect the dots"	✓	✓	✓	✓	✓	✓	—	—	—	✓	✓
L I K E D	"Why Diverse texts Are not Enough"	✓	✓	—	✓	—	—	—	—	—	✓	—
	"Beyond either/or"	—	—	—	—	—	—	0	—	—	✓	—
	"Lessons from Mario Kart"	0	0	✓	0	0	0	0	0	✓	✓	0
O K A Y	"Building Blocks for online learning"	0	—	—	0	0	—	0	0	0	✓	✓
	"Notice and Note: Invitations..."	0	0	0	0	0	0	0	0	0	✓	0

FINDING (SELF-)WORTH IN WRITING WHAT MATTERS

In a 2018 blog post, library educator Torres (2018) notes, "Adolescence is a time rife with uncertainty and feeling misunderstood—like one's life is not one's own. Why not make room for both old texts that preserve voices from our history and those that bring the lived reality of various cultures and traditions to the forefront?"

Although here Julia is speaking specifically about bringing diverse voices of color to our curriculum, her point about honoring the "lived reality of various cultures and traditions" cannot be overstated. Too often, we relegate students' lived experience to the margins of their school experience. But as we've seen in this chapter, we can help students see their identities as having value and their stories as being worth writing about. When we ask students to do the deep identity work described in chapter 2, they develop a deeper appreciation for the ways in which we bring our full selves to any reading, writing, or conversation we engage in: What are the identities and the experiences that have shaped them? Because it's these identities that we bring to every single reading experience. Because it's these identities that are the vehicles for bias and prejudice.

Consider, for example, the identity inventories from earlier in this chapter. As my students brainstormed elements of identity to add to their inventories, one student suggested "hair texture." At first, many other students in the class were puzzled, wondering in what ways hair texture could affect one's identity and how they might navigate the world. One student then shared how she had recently seen news coverage on social media about a young boy who was turned away from school on the first day in September because his hair "violated" the school's grooming policy. The boy had medium-length dreads that the school claimed were in violation of its policy that all students have short, neatly groomed hair. For many of my (mostly White) students, this was the first time they had ever even considered something like hair texture through the lens of racial identity.

So with that in mind, I want to close this chapter with an essay from a former student, Grace Lanouette, who wrote beautifully about the love-hate relationship with her own curly hair (Figure 3.20). I hope that her words on the following pages can inspire all of us to think about the power that students can wield to tell their truth when they reflect and write about their identities.

FIGURE 3.20 ON HAVING CURLY HAIR

By Grace Lanouette

I was bald until I was two.

Well, not bald, technically. I had some hair—some very fine, hardly noticeable, almost blonde hair that barely showed up in pictures. I was (nearly) bald for so long that my grandmother once asked my mom "Is that child ever going to grow any hair?" This question has become famous in my family. By the time I turned three I had grown a full head of thick, tightly curled hair, and every time from then on that my mom had to detangle said hair before I went to bed she cursed my grandmother under her breath.

As a young child I never paid much attention to my hair. In fact, was generally unconcerned with my appearance for the better part of twelve years, much more interested in playing out in the mud, or climbing trees, or participating in other activities that required comfortable, boyish clothing and hair that I didn't have to worry about messing up. My mom, if not annoyed then at least dissatisfied with my fashion choices, bickered with me constantly about clothing and hairstyles. She usually caved in, blow drying my hair so I could quickly pull it back and looking the other way when I preferred shorts and a t-shirt to skirts and blouses (unless it was a special occasion or church, then she was a stone wall). Until the start of seventh grade I was perfectly content with perpetually messy hair and comfortable clothing, paying minimal attention to the fact that other girls were already starting to wear makeup and dresses to school, to the fact that my classmates were starting to connect social status with appearance. Until seventh grade my hair wasn't an issue—I wore it straight or curly, up or down, it made no difference to me. But there comes a point for most girls when appearance starts to matter. There comes a point when looking just like everyone else becomes an essential form of camouflage, necessary for survival in the jungle that is middle school. Now, this is not to make a generalization about all girls everywhere. I assume, or would like to assume, at least, that there are some girls out there who spend their entire lives perfectly happy with being themselves.

Believing they exist comforts me.

I wouldn't consider myself particularly bad looking. And looking back at old pictures of myself, I wouldn't consider middle school me especially unattractive either. But the fact of the matter is that I look different. I was born in Oakland, California, but I went to school and spent most of my time in Berkeley until my family moved across the country right after my tenth birthday. I grew up in an area that is around 50 to 55 percent Caucasian. The area I live in now, a wealthy Philadelphia suburb, is around 85 to 90 percent Caucasian. As a point of reference, the United States as a whole is 63 percent Caucasian.

It is likely apparent by now that I am not Caucasian. Not entirely, at least. My mom is African American and my dad is Caucasian, meaning that I am "kind of white."

In other words, to white people I look mostly black and to black people I look pretty white. My half-blackness is enough to make me look much darker than many of the kids I attend school with. It is also enough to give me hair that might as well have come from another planet.

When I was finally admitted into the world of teenage insecurities in the seventh grade the first thing I noticed was that my hair was wrong. It was too short. It was too frizzy. It was too curly. By that point my mom had already started blow drying my hair, but as anyone who has thick curly hair knows, blow drying and flat ironing are too very different things. Blow drying involves (obviously) a blow dryer and takes about twenty-five to thirty minutes. Blow dried hair is frizzy. Flat ironing involves (of course) a flat iron and takes upwards of two and a half hours. Flat ironed hair is smooth and straight. It is almost long enough and almost straight enough and almost looks like everybody else's. I was willing to settle for almost.

I wore my hair straight to school almost every day of the seventh grade. I secretly wished my mom would let me get it relaxed, a chemical process rendering hair semi-permanently straight which would allow me to shower and swim without the unwelcome curls returning. But she always dashed my silent hopes, talking about how beautiful my curls were, and how someday I'd be glad for them. I would smile and agree with her while mentally counting down the days until I could get a relaxer on my own.

In eighth grade I got busier. With every day seemingly shorter than the last flat ironing my hair fell to the wayside, becoming more of an afterthought than a first priority. I allowed my hair to stay curly more and more as my self-confidence grew, almost managing to forget my anxieties from the year before.

Almost.

Almost as in up until the day the boy I liked at the time said to me [I] like your hair better straight. "You should wear it like that more often."

It felt like I slammed full speed into a brick wall. Just like that, my fragile self-confidence: crushed.

Once again, I exaggerate for effect.

Of course, my self-confidence was not entirely dismantled in that moment. However, a large part of it crumbled and I wouldn't be able to entirely rebuild it again for almost a year.

As I write this essay, my hair is curly. Today, I wore it to school curly. Tomorrow, I will wear it to school curly. I will wear it curly until I decide to straighten it, for whatever reasons I will have at the time.

I have come to realize that there is importance in my hair far greater than anything I could have imagined as a young child. There are women standing behind me who have struggled, fought, and lost their lives to give me an opportunity to love my curly hair. There are women who continue to fight to this day to ensure that I never have to give up that opportunity. My hair is bigger than my self-image—it is a representation of my heritage. It is a representation of centuries of suffering and pain and hard work and growth. It is a constant reminder of everything I can become.

There will always be a part of me that believes I am better when my hair is straight. I can't banish the little girl in me who wants to look like everybody else—she is here to stay. There are days I love my hair and days I don't, just like there are days I'm cheery and days I'm cranky. But I happily admit that my mom's prediction has come true: I am glad I never got rid of my curls for good.

When I look at myself now I hardly ever see all the girls I'm not. Instead I see the girl I am. I see a girl who has learned to love the things that make her different. I see a girl who doesn't need to change herself anymore.

Most of all, I see a girl who feels free.

And I know she is sitting up somewhere right next to the little girl who is begging me to do everything I can to fit in. I know she is here to stay.

How can we *get free* through **conversation?**

Everywhere we look, it seems like there are fewer and fewer examples of civil discourse; whether it's in the news, on social media, or at school board meetings, talk is less about a meaningful exchange of ideas and more about who has the consistently loudest voice.

Of course, we know it doesn't have to be this way.

By turning our attention to the ways we can listen, learn, and exchange ideas that deepen our understanding of ourselves and others, we teach students the skills that they'll need to resist the toxic patterns of "discommunication" that dominates so much public discourse. If we have any hope of finding solutions to some of our greatest challenges—racism, sexism, religious bigotry, homophobia, transphobia, and others—we need to be able to talk about these challenges with honesty and an earnest pursuit of truth. White supremacy, hate, and discrimination thrive when we avoid these hard, necessary conversations. But when students step in our classrooms, we have the opportunity to build a community where authentic, meaningful critical conversations are not only possible but practiced every day.

CHAPTER 4

····························

LISTENING AND SPEAKING

Critical Conversations

The fact that we are here and that I speak these words is an attempt to break that silence and bridge some of those differences between us, for it is not difference which immobilizes us, but silence. And there are so many silences to be broken.

—Audre Lorde

Democratic discourse means providing time and space . . . for [everyone's] perspective and experience to be listened to and affirmed. When this occurs, everyone at the table feels validated and respected. With personal validation comes a greater willingness to honor the opinions and view of others, no matter how different they may be. Affirmation also enables us to enter into conversation less rigid and more willing to challenge a tightly held personal belief, entertain a different perspective, and transform unproductive behavior.

—Glenn Singleton

I am an introvert. If you had told five-year-old, ten-year-old, or even seventeen-year-old Tricia that I would spend my life standing in front of one of the toughest audiences out there—teenagers—there is no way I would have believed you. I was the type of student who could go an entire day without speaking in class once.

When I look back, I see many reasons why I never spoke up. Sometimes it was a lack of confidence, afraid to be wrong. Sometimes it was self-consciousness, afraid that as the only student of color in the room that all eyes would be on me when all I wanted was to blend in. And other times, it was out of habit. The less I spoke up, the more I couldn't bring myself to.

To be honest, I'm not sure how many of my teachers encouraged me to speak up—at the time, I was also grateful they never forced me to. Instead, I focused on my writing, where my voice could be heard, on my own terms and at my own pace, and not at the pace of a teacher's question-and-answer rhythm in the classroom.

How would things have been different if I had teachers who created inviting ways to make space for my voice in the classroom? Because here's the thing about not using my voice: The less I spoke, the less confident I was that I had something important to say.

I wish I could say that I was the exception, but every year, I meet students who are just as hesitant to speak up as I was. I have students who have the most insightful things to say in their writing but don't have the confidence to share in class. Maybe these students are in your classrooms, too. How can we make space for their voices to be heard? (And how might we coach the loudest voices to stop and listen?)

In English classrooms, speaking and listening skills have traditionally taken a backseat to reading and writing, the skills that are most often assessed. Yet, when we consider the powerful and enduring messages that students internalize as a result of not being heard, or of not learning to listen, we can see why we must teach listening and speaking skills if we want a truly equitable classroom.

Making critical conversations central to our work means creating a space in which every student has the opportunity to listen, learn, and speak their truth in ways that move our collective understanding forward with respect, humility, and empathy. This is not easy work. How many times have we seen students interrupt or talk over one another? How many times do students' hands go up while another is speaking? How many times do students engage in side conversations?

On the surface, these behaviors might look like classroom management issues, which might lead us to enacting more rules and structures to ensure that there would be fewer interruptions and more "on task" behaviors. But **a quiet room doesn't guarantee listening, just like a loud room doesn't mean chaos.** Countless things will compete for our students' focus. And we cannot always control—nor should we want to control—their attention. The question then is how we can create conditions that invite students to *stay in* the conversation, to be present for one another.

So let's get talking.

LEANING INTO DIFFICULT CONVERSATIONS

One substantial barrier to making critical conversation central to our classrooms is worry—our own and our students'—that the conversations may become uncomfortable: What happens when students disagree? When does one student's opinion impinge on another's identity?

It's up to us to make space for students to navigate conversations even if they are potentially difficult, to unpack their thinking about the issues that matter to them and in the world. Thus, each year, I survey my students to ask what issues they're most interested in learning about.

What comes up? Among their responses: the environment, sports, media studies, gender, education, politics, racism, and more. (Note that many of these issues are related to the identities included in the identity inventories from the previous chapter.)

It's easy to see how any one of these issues might be difficult to navigate given students' various beliefs, opinions, and ideas (even more so when these issues intersect, as they often do). And yet, issues like these are the ones that matter to students, and so these are the issues they need the ability to speak about in a way that is curious and humble. In the words of James Baldwin, "Not everything that is faced can be changed, but nothing can be changed that is not faced."

While most of us agree that critical conversations are necessary for a healthy democratic society, it can be tempting to opt to disengage from potentially difficult conversations, citing "civility" as a reason. Or teachers might hesitate to engage in these conversations out of an abundance of caution, especially if they feel ill-prepared to discuss complex issues related to identity. This can be particularly difficult in situations when there are only a handful of marginalized students in the classroom—which is why it's so critical for teachers to continue to educate themselves (and for schools to support this learning in meaningful ways). Given the contentious and increasingly polarized ways our public discourse has evolved, we might see students become quiet and disengaged when certain topics come up, or they might become defensive and agitated.

When engaging in conversations about issues related to identity, we must never put the burden on a marginalized student with the responsibility of being a spokesperson. We cannot ask them to speak on behalf of their communities, nor do we have the right to use their experiences in class to make a point. We can invite students in without inflicting additional harm.

But again, avoiding potentially difficult conversations does nothing to help the students in our care develop the skills necessary to navigate these issues. If anything, **avoidance perpetuates our inability *to engage*, diminishing our capacity to hold the discomfort necessary for growth,** further guaranteeing that the biggest issues we face will continue to go unresolved. Furthermore, **calls for civility have been historically used against people of color and other marginalized communities as a way to dismiss their valid grievances.**

Also consider the possibilities if we took the same practices that we know work in helping students to read and write and applied them to engaging in conversations about difficult topics. We know, for example, that in reading and writing, volume matters. The more students read, the better they get at reading. The more they write, the better they get at writing. There is, of course, much more than reading and writing alone—but without volume, students lack the necessary practice. When students struggle to read or write, we help them work through their discomfort, assess what skills might need attention, and provide more opportunities to practice, with guidance and with support. Do we do the same for students who struggle with speaking and listening? Are we just as purposeful, intentional, and explicit?

Given the problems we face in the world today, it is crucial that we make space and time in class for students to discuss issues that they will not only face in the world but that they face *right now*. Regarding race and racism, Cherry-Paul (2018) also reminds us in a piece for *Hechinger Report*, "Research shows that, by preschool age, children recognize and understand that whiteness is more valued in U.S. society." Our youngest students experience racism, sexism, homophobia, and other forms of discrimination. If our students are capable of experiencing these things, then I'd argue that it is part of our responsibility to help them navigate these issues and to discuss them with others in ways that deepen their own and others' understanding. One reason some issues are harder to discuss than others is because we are simply *unpracticed* in discussing them. We can give our students time, space, and guidance so that they know what to do when they are pushed to revisit and reevaluate their previously (and tightly) held beliefs.

A CALL FOR RADICAL OPENNESS

Over the years, I've noticed many students immediately think of any conversation about a potentially controversial issue as a *debate*. After all, many common library databases that students use for research often organize their articles as *pro* and *con*. Students' mentor texts for conversation in public discourse are pundits and assorted talking heads talking past one another, whether that's on a cable news program or sports analysis. Televised political debates are less about listening and more about making newsworthy soundbites. And unfortunately, debate, particularly in social studies classes, still seems to be a dominant, if not predominant, mode of discourse.

While I recognize the value of debate, my own discomfort and hesitation using it as an instructional method is because of the way **debate promotes *binary* thinking: affirmative and negative, yes and no, pro and con, winners and losers. Many, if not all, of our most pressing issues facing us today cannot be reduced, much less solved, using such binary thinking.** Binary thinking leads to the oversimplification of complex issues. Nuance and exceptions to the rule, which always exist, are pushed to the margins in favor of neat, simple, clear solutions, which may or may not always be correct.

Furthermore, framing discussion as *debate* compels students to choose sides, regardless of whether that "side" is defensible (or only defensible in ways that could be potentially harmful). In the best-case scenario, debate *might* offer students an opportunity to understand another perspective that they might not necessarily agree with. This is an essential skill to have and intentional perspective-taking is critical to taking an antibias stance.

But **when debate is framed to force students to choose one of two opposing sides, as it almost always is, then debate becomes less about *understanding* the complexities of issues and more about *winning* the argument.** And I don't know about you, but I've yet to meet an adolescent who doesn't want to win an argument (or at least not lose, especially in front of their peers).

We raise the stakes of conversations when we force into the binary construction of debate. The goal of debate is to *win*. **Yet to apply an antibias lens requires us to lose—to seek and to acknowledge the ways in which our thinking is limited or even wrong.** To truly deepen our understanding of the ways in which our identities, experiences, and biases inform the way we read texts and argue, we need to be intentional in defining *argument* as an exercise to *deepen our understanding and seek truth* rather than to *debate and win*. I have frequently heard teachers talk about how "engaged" students are during debates and use this engagement as a reason to continue this practice. I pose this

question in response: *What does it say that we have to use debate as the way to get our students engaged? Aren't there other ways to get students engaged?*

> To apply an antibias lens requires us to lose—to seek and to acknowledge the ways in which our thinking is limited or even wrong.

Furthermore, there's no doubt that the issues we face today will need us to call on all available means to deepen our understanding of the complex and complicated problems we face if we can even hope to address, much less solve, them. As activist Wheatley (2009) reminds us:

> we will succeed in changing this world only if we can think and work together in new ways. Curiosity is what we need. We don't have to let go of what we believe, but we do need to be curious about what someone else believes. We do need to acknowledge that their way of interpreting the world might be essential to our survival.

As you'll recall from chapter 2 (p. 75), I use Wheatley's call for us to be "willing to be disturbed" at the beginning of the year (along with Clint Smith's TED Talk) as a touchstone text, one that we return to repeatedly throughout the year. When we discuss issues that I anticipate will challenge students' thinking or beliefs, I remind them of Wheatley's call. Actually, often a student will offer the reminder, which is always more authentic and meaningful.

It's this "willingness to be disturbed" that can lead us to what hooks (2010) calls "radical openness." Rather than "become attached to and protective of" our existing viewpoints and to "rule out other perspectives," we need to be willing to "acknowledge what we don't know." This type of openness—borne from intellectual humility—is critical. Our problems are too big and too deep to not consider all that is fully possible, but to do so, **we must embody a radical openness to lean into conversations in all their complexities and, often, their messiness.**

SETTING THE TABLE FOR RADICAL OPENNESS IN OUR CONVERSATIONS

Educators know how important critical thinking is, yet the term *critical thinking* has become so ubiquitous in schools, lesson plans, and strategic plans that it's in danger of becoming meaningless. What does it really mean to think *critically*? And by extension then, what would it mean to engage in *critical conversations*?

Over the years, defining terms has become an integral part of my teaching practice. One issue that often prevents productive dialogue is that those in conversation with one another are working from a different set of definitions and assumptions. So, early in the year, I ask students to define what it means to have a conversation. Inevitably, we land on something like this: conversation is any exchange of ideas and thoughts that involves speaking and listening.

Because it's an *exchange*, conversation is inherently dialogical, open to and actively seeking contributions from all participants. Conversations can be structured or flexible, but at no time are they *mono-logic*, in which the flow of ideas would be one-way. (In the context of the classroom, I explain to students that whenever I start talking too much, this is a monologue: if I'm doing all the talking, we're not having a conversation. While there will be times that I'll need to give directions and provide information, I enlist students' help in making sure that we prioritize conversation and dialogue over lecture and monologue.)

> *Conversation is any exchange of ideas and thoughts that involves speaking and listening.*

But having a *critical* conversation requires more than an exchange of ideas—it requires us to take a critical look at ourselves, each other, and the world. The key to keeping critical conversations productive lies in the values we bring to those conversations.

What Values Lead to Meaningful, Critical Conversations?

We are always teaching from our values, whether we realize it or not. What we believe is good and right in education will show up in every instructional decision we make and whose voices we center and decenter in class conversations. If we value order, then our class discussions are going to reflect that value: We might have little patience when it comes to talking out of turn, even if students are still engaged in the discussion. Or if we value control, even if we don't admit it, we may be unlikely to show vulnerability in front of students and restrict conversation to only those ideas and issues which we are comfortable discussing.

It follows that if we want authentic, meaningful, and rigorous critical conversations, we need to consider what values we rely on. The values that have been the most helpful guides to me are the following:

- **open-mindedness,** to consider other points-of-view

- **flexibility,** to allow our minds to wander, to stretch, to change and adapt to new ideas

- **curiosity,** to seek out opinions that are different from our own, to lean into responses that both confirm and challenge our own perspectives

- **care**, not about what others think, but to care *for* each other. This means that when our words have a negative impact, even when unintentional, we care enough about one another to remedy this harm

- **humility**, because we know that there is always more to learn that we do not yet know.

The last value, **humility**, can be hard to find these days, especially if you're looking at the news. If anything, students today are bombarded with the exact opposite: talking heads on cable news who often have little background on an issue and yet claim expertise—and claim so with confidence, if not arrogance. And that's *if* students are engaged in watching cable news. Most students rely on their social media feeds for their news, usually some combination of YouTube, TikTok, and Instagram, where their news exposure is brief and fleeting as they scroll. Research shows us that the less a person knows about a subject, the more confident they become in speaking about it—a phenomenon called the Dunning-Kruger Effect. Because they don't know what they don't know, they are more confident in the little they *do* know.

Furthermore, even when the content on their social media feed is accurate and educational (I know several teenagers who use TikTok to keep up with social justice issues), the content is typically delivered *monologically*: someone talking to an audience of literal followers, a one-way conversation. As students and most social media users know, the comment section on videos and news articles aren't the best mentor texts for how to hold a meaningful conversation either.

Because these are the mentor texts students often see, it's easy to see how students might conclude that the way to have a conversation is to have an opinion and state that opinion with confidence, repeatedly, no matter what others might say. We see this version of "conversation" everywhere, from talk show panels to sports analyses, popular content creators on YouTube to presidential debates.

This style of non-conversation is, of course, nothing new, but because of social media and the increasing power of 288 characters to drive news and discourse, many of our students may be less practiced in the types of long, complex, and exploratory conversations that can lead to more informed learning. But when we, students and teachers together, approach conversations with a sense of *humility*, we open ourselves up to growth. When we adopt a stance of humility in our discourse, we acknowledge that we don't know everything, and that this lack of knowledge, rather than being a liability, is an opportunity to learn from others.

The longer I teach, the more convinced I am that it's *humility*—and not necessarily mastery of content—that is the mark of a lifelong learner. Coupled with *open-mindedness, flexibility, curiosity,* and *care,* humility is what allows us to enter critical conversations from a learning stance. And I think we can all agree that the problems that we and our students face today need more individuals committed to a learning stance.

How Can We Turn Challenges to Opportunities?

Once we have established our values, we can turn to the question of how to make productive critical conversations happen in our classrooms. All of us can likely recall being a student or a teacher in a classroom when a discussion or conversation goes wrong. While there are many unique reasons why classroom conversations might fall short, professors Stephen D. Brookfield and Stephen Preskill give us a succinct list of categories for what can go wrong:

- Unprepared students (and teachers)

- No ground rules

- Lack of teacher modeling

- Counterproductive reward systems

As I think back over the unproductive conversations and discussions I've seen in classrooms, all of them have their roots in some—if not all—of these four categories. For example, in an effort to get more students to "talk," early in my career, I kept

▶ Think about a discussion in class that was especially challenging. Do the challenges mentioned here feel familiar? How might things have gone differently and better?

track of the number of times students spoke during class discussions. Unfortunately, knowing this, students jumped in to speak even if they didn't necessarily have something meaningful to add.

Instead, we can reframe these challenges as guidelines. In order to engage in critical conversations successfully, then, we can:

- Be prepared

- Establish ground rules for discourse

- Model and promote a learning stance
- Support students with structures for conversations that legitimately encourage engagement

In the pages that follow, we'll look at some ways to put these guidelines to use.

BEING PREPARED FOR CONVERSATIONS THAT MATTER

The work outlined in the earlier chapters of this book—considering our own biases, building a safe community, and considering our own identities—is all strong preparation for engaging in critical conversations. In addition, we can prepare ourselves by viewing student voices with respect, by steeping ourselves in the topics of discussion, and by being ready to support students when a conversation turns to race.

Respect Students' Voices

It's not uncommon to hear well-intentioned teachers say that we need to "give students a voice." In fact, I'm sure that I've used these exact words. But language matters, and when we claim, as teachers, to "give students a voice," we reinforce problematic patterns when it comes to power. As Dr. Lyiscott (2017) points out:

> When we operate with the mindset that we are "giving" students voice, we align ourselves with a deeply problematic and historical orientation. So much of the rationale for oppression through slavery, colonialism, and imperialism had to do with "giving" civilization to people who were "less fortunate."

We do not "give" students a voice; they have a voice—many voices, in fact—the moment they walk into our classroom. For students of color and students from marginalized communities, the issue has never been about not *having* a voice. As writer Arundhati Roy pointed out in her 2004 Sydney Peace Prize lecture, "We know of course there's really no such thing as the 'voiceless'. There are only the deliberately silenced, or the preferably unheard." It is our job, as teachers, to hold a space in which all voices can be heard.

Bring a Strong Understanding of the Content

Because the world is our curriculum, we might feel compelled, and rightly so, to bring the outside world into our classroom. For example, we might see or hear about an incident in the news and, in an effort to make learning relevant for students, we enter into a discussion for which we are actually unprepared. When I sense that students want to talk about something that's recently happened, and it's something I haven't had time to prepare for, I'm honest with them. I might say something like, "I sense this is something you want to talk about and it's important to you. I don't know much about this yet, and I want to learn more so we can have a good conversation. Give me a day or two to learn more and we'll circle back."

Furthermore, if we expect students to consider multiple perspectives, we need to do the same. While it's unrealistic to be completely prepared for every issue that might come up in class, we can at least talk with colleagues to gather their perspectives and how they anticipate students may respond. We can learn from colleagues what they know, what they're hearing, and what we need to think about. Being ready for the possible directions a conversation might take can help us to better navigate it.

Be Ready to Support Students When a Conversation Addresses Race (Among Other Identities)

Even if a conversation does not begin on the topic of race, the fact that race permeates all aspects of modern-day American society means that an honest and critical conversation on nearly any topic could turn to a discussion that involves race. No matter our own or our students' racial identities, conversations about race can be some of the most challenging we encounter. **If we are going to enter into conversation about race or racism, how much have we ourselves read and learned and reflected? How much have we examined our own racial identity or racialized experiences?** That said, although we may never feel fully prepared, we cannot shy away from such issues. If you are committed to the power and role that schools have to disrupt and dismantle injustice, being prepared to engage in these conversations is critical.

While no single book can fully explore the tensions around race conversations, the following books (in addition to the titles mentioned in chapter 2) may be of help in navigating conversations about race.

- *Courageous Conversations About Race* by Glenn Singleton
- *Race Talk and the Conspiracy of Silence* by Derald Wing Sue
- *So You Want to Talk About Race* by Ijeoma Oluo
- *Teaching Race* by Stephen Brookfield and associates

As discussed in chapter 1, understanding your own varied and multiple identities and how those intersect with power and privilege can also help you to be prepared to engage in discussions of race.

Finally, as you prepare for critical conversations in your classroom, it is also helpful to understand why these conversations can be wrought

with so much difficulty. As Sue (2016) points out in *Race Talk: The Conspiracy of Silence*, conversations about race can be uncomfortable for a variety of reasons, including but not limited to the following:

- There's a general "disinclination to participate" which can lead to "rhetorical incoherence" (fumbling our words in discussions about race)

- Conversation can be highly emotional, including feelings of defensiveness, anger, shame, and fear

- Participants may attempt to "dilute, diminish, change, mystify, or terminate the topic"

- Participants see talking about race as impolite.

- Participants believe that talking about race isn't "academic."

- Participants believe that simply talking about race is racism.

- Conversations about race are filtered through White, Eurocentric norms and power dynamics, which can be particularly difficult for people of color.

► As you look at the list above, what's familiar?

While these points do not map out a clear path forward, they give us an idea of the terrain ahead. Knowing—and even anticipating—these responses and understanding that they are part of a larger pattern of deflecting away from conversations about race has actually been helpful for me in my own practice. I have seen all of these problems unfold in real time in conversations with kids, parents, and colleagues. When I notice one of these behaviors taking place, I remind myself that this avoidance is expected and I do not take these reactions as a personal affront. Instead, I take a deep breath and try the following:

- I name what I'm noticing in their reaction. ("I notice you think that talking about race is impolite" or "I'm sensing you don't want to talk about what race has to do with this.")

- I ask them to confirm my observation.

- If they confirm yes, then I ask them to tell me more. If I'm wrong, they'll tell me more regardless.

Depending on the situation, I try to repeat this pattern of asking for clarification. Oftentimes, we end the conversation without closure, and that's okay. My goal isn't to change their mind but to extend the conversation just long enough that the other person has to practice putting their thoughts into words. When we put our thoughts into words, it's a way of testing to see if we believe them. In the classroom, students who are listening to the conversation are also learning, figuring out what they agree with and what they do not. Otherwise, the thoughts that stay in our heads risk becoming hardened truths.

While my approach is to start with curiosity when students share their perspectives, I also know how important it is to firmly correct inaccuracies and address any misinformation or potentially harmful comments a student might make. If I sense a conversation may shift in a heated or personal direction, I might say something like, "Let's pause here for a minute. Before we go on, there are a few things I want to make sure we're clear about." At that point, I try to validate what I can in what students have said but I also make sure that facts are shared clearly and matter-of-factly.

ESTABLISHING GROUND RULES FOR DISCOURSE

The community-building work discussed in chapter 3 is foundational to establishing ground rules for discourse, and no attempts to give students rules will be fruitful without that community in place. At a training I attended, Sarah SoonLing-Blackburn, a facilitator for Learning for Justice, explained, "Time spent building community is not time wasted." Community building requires constant vigilance and maintenance, checking in and asking students: how's our community doing?

Teach Students the Difference
Between Opinion and Informed Knowledge

Take a moment to consider what "having a voice" means to you and in the context of your classroom. Then, consider **whose voices in your classroom are most often heard and whose are least often heard, whose voices are "preferably unheard," and whose voices are even silenced.** When we take a moment to recall these voices, we're often reminded that while having a voice is critical, *having a voice does not mean all opinions are necessarily equally informed or valid.*

Early in the year, I share the following distinction between opinion and informed knowledge with students so that we're working from a definition we can return to during the year. It comes from *Is Everybody Really Equal: An Introduction to Social Justice Concepts* by Sensoy and DiAngelo (2017).

> Mainstream culture has normalized the idea that because everyone has an opinion, all opinions are equally valid . . . Reality shows invite us to vote on the best singer or dancer, implying that our opinions are equal to the opinions of

professional dancers, singers, choreographers, and producers. While we *might* have an informed opinion, our response certainly does not depend on one. Thus we can easily be fooled into confusing *opinion* (which everyone has) with *informed knowldge* (which few have without ongoing practice and study). (p. 8)

Furthermore, Sensoy and DiAngelo go on to describe the challenges that confusing opinion for informed knowledge can create in classroom settings (emphasis added):

> Because of this socialization, many of us unwittingly bring the expectation for opinion-sharing into the academic classroom. However, in academia, opinion is the weakest form of intellectual engagement. **When our comprehension is low and critical thinking skills underdeveloped, expressing our opinion is the easiest response.** (p. 9)

▶ Ask students: Is that your opinion? Or do you have informed knowledge?

With a shared understanding of the difference between opinion and informed knowledge, students approach discussions in the classroom with a sense of humility. This is also why, I remind students, it's important for them to come to class prepared having done any required reading: it's not about "completing the homework" but about having the power to participate fully—to speak from a position of informed knowledge versus opinion—in class conversation.

Ask Students to Name What Makes a Good Conversation

In creating ground rules for discourse, I know that many teachers ask for student input in this process. In theory, I agree with any practice that centers student voice in a way that increases ownership and responsibility. *That said, I do not initially ask for student input when it comes to creating class agreements or ground rules.* Whenever I tried doing this in the past, students would often either regurgitate classroom "rules," which are different from agreements, or they would offer what they thought teachers wanted to hear.

Instead, I use a text such as Headlee's (2016) TED Talk, "10 Ways to Have a Better Conversation," as a starting point and then invite student voice by asking students how the ideas in Headlee's text may benefit our class conversations. Depending on how things work out, we watch together in class or students watch at home and respond in an online discussion board. While there are many texts that provide conversational tips, students have found Headlee's talk accessible as the tips are easily recalled throughout the year.

FIGURE 4.1   10 WAYS TO HAVE A BETTER CONVERSATION (SELF-REFLECTION)

ON A SCALE OF 1 TO 5, RATE HOW EASY (1) OR HARD (5) EACH OF THESE IS FOR YOU PERSONALLY.					
1. Don't multitask.	1	2	3	4	5
2. Don't pontificate.	1	2	3	4	5
3. Use open-ended questions.	1	2	3	4	5
4. Go with the flow.	1	2	3	4	5
5. If you don't know, say you don't know.	1	2	3	4	5
6. Don't equate your experience with theirs.	1	2	3	4	5
7. Try not to repeat yourself.	1	2	3	4	5
8. Stay out of the weeds (details).	1	2	3	4	5
9. Listen.	1	2	3	4	5
10. Be brief.	1	2	3	4	5

Adapted from Headlee (2016)

I ask students to rate each guideline on a scale of 1–5 (see Figure 4.1) to determine which they believe will be easiest or hardest for them. Interestingly, most students overlook number 9, overestimating their ability to listen. I point out the Stephen Covey line that Headlee quotes in her talk—"Most of us don't listen with the intent to understand. We listen with the intent to reply"—and then ask students how many times they raise their hand during class discussions while another student is still speaking. **Are they students listening, *really listening*, or are they simply waiting for their turn to talk?**

We often return to our established class agreements, but we also introduce additional guidelines or corollaries to keep in mind as our conversations deepen. Just as community building is a yearlong effort, so too must we develop, deepen, and adapt our class agreements and ground rules for discourse as the year progresses. In my own teaching, I've found that there are often opportunities to highlight each of these guidelines in ways that are organic and purposeful. I know, for example, that when we are about to discuss a potentially sensitive topic—or one that might elicit particularly emotional responses—I point out that listening well means not just listening to what a person means (intent) but also listening for how our words might affect others (impact). I also periodically have students reflect on their own discussion skills in their Weekly Critical Reflection & Inquiry (see Chapter 2).

Scrolling through our news and social media feeds, it doesn't take long to see that society often rewards those who speak first and speak loudest. The problem, of course, is that this bias for being *first* prevents us from taking the time to reflect, learn, and seek to understand before speaking. We might be first to express an opinion yet fail to have the informed knowledge we need for meaningful conversation.

> Listening well *means not just listening to what a person* means *(intent) but also listening for how our words might affect others (impact).*

Think about a topic or issue that is typically very difficult for you to talk about, something that is so challenging that you might even avoid the topic altogether. For example, when I hear people complain about "political correctness" or dismiss or demean "being woke," I feel my body tense up immediately. Depending on what exactly was said, who said it, and who else is there, I may or may not choose to engage. I make a quick mental calculation to determine whether speaking up will be worth my time and labor— or, as a woman of color, possibly risk my safety. And sometimes, the hardest times to engage are not when I'm in the company of strangers but in the company of colleagues, social acquaintances, or even family.

Learn more about Courageous Conversations About Race *protocols.*

But because I'm someone who believes that speaking up for justice is necessary, I try to engage more often than I don't. And one tool that has been invaluable to me is the Compass, developed by Singleton (2014, p. 29). Although Singleton developed the Compass to specifically

FIGURE 4.2 NAVIGATING OUR RESPONSE USING THE COMPASS

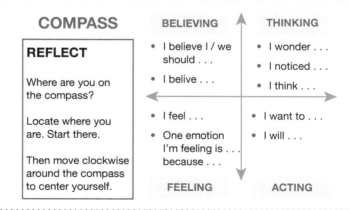

Adapted From Singleton (2014).

address conversations about race, I have found that it works for almost any topic that's difficult to discuss. In fact, if I had to choose only one tool in this entire chapter to use and practice daily with students, it would be this one.

When I introduce the Compass to students, I start by asking them what a compass is and why they'd use one. Students identify a compass as a tool that can help us understand our location in relation to where north is. In other words, a compass is a tool that can help us find our way. Then I ask students if they have ever experienced being lost in a conversation. Almost all hands go up. I share that I've often found myself lost in conversations, sometimes because I'm late to the conversation and have to catch up, or sometimes because I just don't have enough knowledge about what others are talking about. I then ask students how it feels when they're lost in those conversations and what they do. While some students might have prior knowledge to contribute, other students admit that they just don't say anything.

The choice to *not say anything* is especially prevalent when the topics of conversation are subjects such as racism and other forms of discrimination. After all, when I ask students what topics they are *least comfortable* discussing, these are the ones that come up for them (and likely for most adults).

Cue the Compass.

The Compass, I explain to students, is a tool to help us find our way when we're in conversation with others. Sometimes we might feel lost and not know what to say or not say, but the Compass helps us find something to contribute to the conversation.

Step 1 of using the Compass is locating where we personally are showing up. I project the Compass in the front of the room and say something along the lines of this:

> As you can see, there are four areas of the Compass: Believing, Thinking, Feeling, and Acting. Each of these areas represents one way we might respond to a topic.
>
> If the topic activates my sense of right and wrong, if I find myself thinking *that shouldn't happen* or *we shouldn't do that,* then I know I'm in the *believing* part of the Compass. I associate the *believing* part of the Compass with what I know in my *gut* is right or wrong.
>
> If I find myself asking questions or trying to analyze the topic, then I know I'm in the *thinking* part of the Compass. This is the part of the Compass where we spend the most

time in school. I associate the *thinking* part of the compass with my brain.

On the other hand, if I find myself experiencing any type of emotion, then I know I'm in the *feeling* part of the Compass. When I'm in this part of the Compass, I try to name exactly what feelings I'm experiencing: fear or sadness, joy or curiosity, love or anger, and so on. I associate the *feeling* part of the Compass with my heart.

Finally, if I find myself wanting to *do* something, then I know I'm in the *acting* part of the Compass. I might be moved to act by talking more with others, learning more about an issue, or speaking out in protest. I associate the *acting* part of the Compass with our hands and feet.

To familiarize students with the Compass, we start with a prompt that is often low-stakes and accessible. For example, recall the Stranger in the Photo exercise from chapter 3 (page 108). I might use the photograph that students bring in from home for that exercise and ask them what areas of the Compass they find themselves responding to. Or I might select other favorite photographs or artwork.

Poetry, particularly spoken word poetry, is especially effective, and one of my favorite spoken word poems to use when introducing the Compass is "Unforgettable" by Acevedo et al. (2014). If you aren't already familiar with this poem, take a moment to scan the QR code and watch this powerful poem. Then review the Compass: What area of the Compass do you find yourself first? Why? What other areas of the Compass do you find yourself in?

Watch "Unforgettable" by Elizabeth Acevedo, Pages Matam, and George Yamazawa

I also make sure to point out to students that they can be in multiple areas of the Compass at the same time. However, after regular practice with the Compass, they may start to notice that there might be a pattern to how they're responding. For example, when a topic is very personal to me, such as one that has to do with an area of my own identity, I tend to find myself in the *feeling* area of the Compass first.

But identifying where I am is only the first step, and I share with students that after they locate where they are on the Compass, Step 2 is to access the other parts of the Compass and reflect on how those areas are also present. This next step is *critical:* by pausing to access the other areas of the Compass, we prevent ourselves from getting *stuck* in one place.

For example, although I might start out in the *feeling* area, as I navigate around the Compass, I also access other ways of responding. I can:

- reflect on how my feelings are informed by *beliefs* that I have, then

- *think* about where those beliefs came from: what experiences, observations, or interactions with others led me to this belief?

- and finally, consider how those *feelings, beliefs,* and *thoughts* might inspire me to *act*

***This process of accessing each area of the compass is what Singleton and practitioners of* Courageous Conversations About Race *protocol call* centering ourselves.** When we center ourselves using the Compass, not only are we in tune to more parts of who we are, we are also better able to recognize where others are responding on the Compass and dialogue with them accordingly (Step 3). In other words, the Compass also allows us to be better listeners of others and ourselves.

Another way to think about this exercise is to consider what happens when we *don't* center ourselves on the Compass. We might, for example, *act* without thinking first. Or we might stay stuck in our feelings about a situation without ever taking the time to analyze where those feelings are coming from.

The beauty of the Compass is that it can be used as a response protocol for almost any text, topic of discussion, or situation that students find themselves in. Using the Compass as a scaffold for students to use when discussing difficult topics is valuable, and from a facilitator point-of-view, the Compass is especially useful when a topic might be one we feel strongly about. These can be the hardest conversations to navigate, and even more challenging is that they can happen at any moment.

As you can see from the anecdote I share on the following pages, using the Compass to center myself allowed my students and me to move through a conversation about race rather than shut it down. Notice, too, that I name the race of some of the students involved to make transparent the dynamic that can sometimes occur in classrooms in a multiracial classroom space.

Navigating a Conversation About Race With the Compass

There's a buzz in the air as I walk around the room eavesdropping on student conversations. On this day, we're discussing the introduction to Kareem Abdul-Jabbar's book *Writings on the Wall*. The prompt on the board is a simple one, "Share 1-2 key takeaways you had after reading the text."

One conversation catches my ear, and I slowly make my way over to a group of four students. This group is made up of two White students and two students of color, one Black student and one Asian. As I make my way to their table, I stop and hear one of the White students say to his group, "He's complaining about racism but then all he talks about is race." The other White student in the group nods in agreement, while the two students of color do not respond, perhaps because my appearance at their table has them looking to me for guidance. I engage.

I ask the student to tell me more, "What do you mean by that?"

"Well, all he talks about is how racism is a problem but then that's all he focuses on in the essay. He talks about his identity as a Black man and how people only see him as that."

"Go on."

The other White student adds, "He keeps saying that he's always being judged by the color of his skin, but then he keeps mentioning it."

"And that's bad because . . . ?" I ask.

"Well, because he's the one who's making it a problem because he keeps talking about it," one of the White students replies.

"Ah, so you're saying that by him talking about race, he's making the issue worse?"

They nod in agreement. The two students of color in the group look skeptical but when I make eye contact with them to see if they'd like to add anything, I can tell they don't want to say anything right now.

As the students explained their position, I found myself responding in the *believing* area of the Compass. How? When the students expressed their belief that talking about race makes racism worse, my own belief was challenged: I believe that racism can only be confronted if we talk openly about it. As that belief was challenged, I found *feelings* of frustration also surface in my body. However, I also know that their responses are not surprising given the way they may have been socialized to avoid talking about race.

Here is where using the Compass helped to move this potentially disastrous conversation to a productive one. Because I could recognize that the belief that they expressed was in direct contrast to one of my own deeply held beliefs, I knew that trying to engage with them from the *believing* area of the Compass was not going to be productive. We would just end up in a back-and-forth about beliefs and in a stalemate, at best. Instead I had to access other parts of the Compass that *might* actually have an impact in this situation. So I took a step back and moved to *thinking*.

"May I ask a question?" I asked the group. They nod.

I continue, "Do you agree that racism is a problem in society?" They nod in agreement. "And when there's a problem, whether it's racism or anything else, how do you solve it?"

After some more back and forth, they concede that one way to solve any problem is to talk about it. At this point, I offer a clarification, "I think to solve any problem, we don't just have to talk about it, we have to *study* it. And to study it, we have to talk about it."

This is where the conversation might have ended, except that I can tell that many other students in the class have stopped their conversations and have been listening in on this exchange. Another student's hand goes up.

"Mrs. Ebarvia, don't you think there are times that we can focus on race almost *too* much?"

Again, in that moment, I could *feel* my own emotions surfacing: frustration, disappointment, exhaustion as a person of color from a lifetime of having to justify why talking about race is important. Likewise, my *belief* in the importance of social justice was also coming to the surface. I could have, at that moment, acted from an emotionally charged sense of morals. But looking around the room at my students—the ones who seemed most resistant to talking about race and racism as well as the ones, mostly students of color, who seemed both anxious and eager to see what I would say—I quickly realized that trying to engage with them from an emotional (*feeling*) or moral (*believing*) place was not going to work. Having taught these students all year, I knew they tended to engage from the *thinking* area of the Compass (this was an A.P. level course, after all).

So that's what I did: I gave them something to *think* about.

"Here's why focusing on race is exactly what we need to do sometimes," I begin. "Let's think about the SAT. Our average SAT score at school is pretty high, right?"

Students nod in agreement.

"If you looked at high school rankings and saw that we had one of the highest average SAT scores in the county, what would that make you think?"

"That we're a good school," someone offers.

"Yes!" I continue, "And if our SAT scores are good, and we're a 'good' school, then that's probably not a problem we have to worry about, right?"

"What do you mean?" one student asks. By now, the entire class is listening and this has become a whole-class teachable moment.

(Continued)

(Continued)

"Well, I mean that whatever we're doing to prepare students for the SAT seems to be working. Why fix something that's not broken?" A quick look around the room and students seem to agree.

I pause, making eye contact with the student who posed the comment, "But the problem is, averages hide things." I pause before continuing, "And if we don't focus on race, then we might miss one of the things that our SAT average scores hide."

"What we need to do," I argue, "is to disaggregate the data by race to see what the average SAT score is by racial group."

"What would that do?" a student asks.

"Well," I respond, "it could tell us if one racial group is performing significantly better or worse than the average, or better or worse than another other group. And if that's the case, that means something we're doing or not doing isn't working if different racial groups are having different outcomes. But we won't find out if we have that problem if we don't focus on race . . . or really, any other demographic group. We could also disaggregate data by gender, for example."

Another student, who is White, raises his hand and offers, "I get that, but what would you even *do* with that information? Let's say you do find out some racial groups have lower or higher SAT scores compared to others. What could the school even do about that? Why would it matter?"

This is where the *believing* part of me wants to say *because that's racism!* But of course, I know engaging from an area of *belief* wasn't going to be helpful here. So continue to engage from the *thinking* space.

"Well, one thing the school could do is take a look at what activities, experiences, or classes distinguish the group with higher SAT scores from the others." I can see from their expressions that they want to know more.

"For example, we might find out that students with the highest SAT scores all took Algebra 1 in 7th grade. And when we disaggregate the data by race, we discover that most of the students in Algebra 1 in 7th grade are White students."

I pause and see students lean in a little closer. I continue.

"So, what does this tell us? What could the school do with this information? Well, one thing the school could do is ensure that more students in other racial groups take Algebra 1 in 7th grade."

Another student, an Asian student, raises her hand and adds, "The school could also ask themselves if there's some sort of teacher bias that's keeping students of other racial groups from getting recommended for Algebra 1 in 7th grade."

"Exactly."

The conversation continues from there, and I can tell that students are seeing how much more complicated the issue is than just "talking about race makes racism worse."
When I look up and see we only have a minute before the bell rings, I make two more critical points.

I ask, "Now, does having good SAT scores the only measure of a 'good' school?"

Many students shake their heads no.

"But," I continue, "we know that the way our current education system works, SAT scores *do* matter. If we focused on identifying and doing more to support students of all racial groups to do better, what would that do to the overall average SAT score for the entire school?"

"It would go up," several students reply.

"Yes, it would." And in my head, I'm reminded of the idea that a rising tide lifts all boats. I made a mental note to share that metaphor at the next class.

MODELING AND PROMOTING A LEARNING STANCE

As teachers, we can sometimes fall into the trap of thinking that we need to have all the answers. After all, we're the "experts" in the room. It's true that we might have more experience—and perhaps more knowledge—than our students. The great irony of learning, however, is that the more we learn, the more we realize how much more there is to know.

I define a "learning stance" as one that puts humility and curiosity at the center of our interactions with others. A learning stance is one where not knowing versus Knowing is the default position. Consider what it would mean for teachers to take a learning stance in a classroom where they are used to being (or expected to be) the Knower of all things. The problem with teaching from a Knowing versus *not knowing* stance, however, is that when you Know all things, you may fall into the trap of not feeling like you have anything left to learn.

And the truth is, our students have much to teach us.

How often do we position ourselves as co-learners along with our students? How often, in our dialogue with students, are we willing to model *not* knowing versus Knowing? How often do we ask questions in response to student inquiries rather than provide answers?

Additionally, how often do we communicate to students that learning is messy, that the skills they are building in making meaning are more important than having a "correct" answer, and that others' perspectives can be valuable learning tools?

Rather than hoping that students will develop a learning stance, one that encourages them to be curious listeners, we can make intentional efforts to promote this disposition.

Facilitation Frames

As facilitators of critical conversation, we can make small but important shifts in the way we talk with students that push their thinking and model what being curious—what being "willing to be disturbed" (see Chapter 2)—would look like in practice. This can be particularly tricky during whole class discussions when I'm "on stage" as the teacher and someone says something provocative. But what an opportunity we have in these moments to model curiosity! Some simple phrases I've found that have helped me exhibit a learning-versus-knowing stance with students:

• Tell me more . . .

• I'm not sure, but I wonder . . . what do you think?

• I don't know. What do you think?

• I used to think . . . but now I'm wondering . . . what do you think?

• That's an interesting point. It makes me wonder . . . does this make sense?

• When I learned that . . . I realized that . . . thoughts?

I've found that these responses can help students unpack their thinking by modeling how I unpack my own before turning the conversation back to them. That said, there may be times that students will say things that are not only disturbing but offensive, even hateful. In those cases, it's important as teachers that we're clear that hateful speech— speech that diminishes and dehumanizes another person or group and marginalizes others—has no place in our classroom. In those cases, I've offered feedback using frames such as the following:

- I'm not sure about that. After all . . . [then provide factual information to counter]

- In my experience and from what I have read . . . [then provide factual information to counter]

- What you've named is something that perpetuates stereotypes/bias. After all . . . [then provide factual information to counter]

Reflect, Revisit, and Revise

One of the most simple but intentional ways we can inspire students to listen is to reflect regularly and consistently on how what others have said has changed or shifted their thinking. This strategy includes three steps that can be integrated into any lesson, including any of the strategies that follow.

1. Before we discuss any text or issue, students **reflect** and write about the topic.

2. We move into a discussion in which students hear other points of view. Then, students go back to their notebooks and **revisit** their initial opinion. Has their perspective changed, and, if so, how?

3. More discussion follows, either in small groups or whole class. Instead of whole class discussion, I might also bring in texts that bring in additional perspectives. Then at the end of class, students return to their notebook, revisit their previous two reflections, and then **revise** accordingly. A framework I suggest for students is "I used to think . . . then I read or heard . . . which makes me think . . . "

What I Heard, Think, and Wonder

After some class discussion has occurred, I ask students to write a reflection using the following framework:

- *What I heard.* Students summarize something they heard another student say during the discussion.

- *What I think.* Students then reflect on what the other student's comment made them think about.

- *What I wonder.* Students extend their thinking to consider additional possibilities, implications, consequences, and so on.

This concept of "talking back to oneself" helps students to make a practice of revisiting their previous thinking and unpacking their assumptions.

Next, students use turn-and-talks to share what they've written. Finally, each student shares *their partner's* comments with the class. Consider, for example, one student's response (she shared this in a Critical Incidents Questionnaire Inquiry, page 84):

> As someone who is White and relatively privileged, Josh's [name changed] comment about how people assume he got into college because he's Black made me think about how these assumptions must be so upsetting. It made me wonder how I would feel if I were constantly being asked to "prove" I was good enough.

Listening Dyads

I first came across this strategy—called a constructivist listening dyad—in a Learning for Justice workshop I attended, but, like many of the strategies here, it has a long tradition in educational settings, particularly in comprehension work. In this protocol, students are partnered in pairs. An open-ended discussion prompt or question is given. Each student takes turns listening and speaking as follows:

- Student A responds to the prompt for 90 seconds (can be longer or shorter, depending on how much time is available). Student A speaks, uninterrupted, while Student B listens. If Student A finishes before time is up, both students sit and wait until the time is completed. Student B gives no feedback while Student A speaks. Student B should remain as neutral as possible both in facial expression and body language (no gestures, no nodding, no verbal affirmations).

- When it's Student B's turn, they begin by summarizing what they heard Student A say. "When we are asked to repeat what someone else says," I tell students, "it means not only do we really have to pay attention, but we have an obligation to represent what someone else said responsibly. It's important that what someone is saying is what we're hearing and by repeating it back to them, we can confirm this." After Student B finishes their summary, they ask questions to explore or deepen their understanding of something they heard Student A say. This step takes another 90 seconds.

- Student A then answers Student B's question for 90 seconds, uninterrupted.

- A few minutes of unstructured conversation then proceeds before students switch roles. The same or a new question can be posed for the next round.

What I love about constructivist listening dyads is that not only does this protocol allow students to speak *without being interrupted*, it asks students to listen in order *to understand rather than to respond*. Listening is often one of students' weakest conversational skills, so the more we can isolate it in practice, the better students can build their listening muscle.

Questions Only, Please

Too often students enter discussions under the assumption that they need to have an answer or already formed opinion. You can encourage them to instead explore ideas by requiring them to only *ask* questions. This is difficult for students as they often want to jump right

> *Listening is often one of students' weakest conversational skills, so the more we can isolate it in practice, the better students can build their listening muscle.*

into answering each other's questions. But rather than answer, I guide students to instead ask a related question that would push them to consider additional possibilities. Because this is difficult to do in live discussion, I have students use an online discussion board.

For example, consider the following exchange about a discussion of King's "Letter from Birmingham Jail":

Student 1: Why do you think King uses the word "dear" to address the clergymen if he's angry at them?

Student 2: Is it possible that he's trying to soften them up before he goes on?

Student 1: Could he be reminding them that he's also a peer?

Student 2: Why do you think he wants to remind them he's one of them?

Student 1: What do you think the clergymen will think of him?

Student 2: Could the clergymen be threatened by him?

Student 1: Where else does King address the clergymen this way?

While it might have been easier for me to give students a list of questions to answer together, when students ask questions they must stretch and deepen their understanding of a text or issue. As you can see, some of the students' questions might seem more like answers than questions, particularly the second and third questions. This is still okay as the framing of their ideas as questions still allows for other possibilities. After generating a list of questions, I often ask students to evaluate them: Which of these questions help us get to the "heart" of understanding this text, how, and why?

Shifting Four Corners

Four Corners, another strategy that is often used in comprehension work, can give students an opportunity to respond to a statement by deciding to what extent they agree or disagree. For example, when we begin our study of the American Dream, I project this following statement on the board: "The American Dream is defined by monetary success." In each corner of the room, I post the following signs—Strongly Agree, Somewhat Agree, Somewhat Disagree, and Strongly Disagree—and students stand in the corner that best represents their position on this statement. Once students move to those corners, they then discuss their position with someone in that same corner.

After a few moments, I ask some students from each corner to share. As students share—and here's the key—I encourage students to move to another corner should something they hear change their thinking. It's not unusual for students to move throughout the discussion, which we then also unpack. I often combine this strategy with the Reflect, Revisit, and Revise (page 173) and ask students to reflect in their writer's notebooks as our closing. By pausing to reflect on how their thinking has shifted, we can again encourage students to internalize a learning stance.

Two Talk, One Listens, Repeat

In this strategy, students are seated in groups of three. Two students discuss an issue or the text (or the prompt, if one is given, such as in Progressive Discussions, outlined later in this chapter), while the third student listens and takes notes that summarize (not analyze) what's being said. These notes can be more informal, written in their notebooks, or more formal, as in a typed transcript. I usually allow students to choose which method works best for them. After a given amount of time (usually only one to three minutes), I then ask the third person to repeat back to their group members what they heard. By having the third student's role dedicated to listening, they are actively engaging in a learning stance as they try to understand their group members' perspectives well enough to summarize.

HOLDING THE SPACE: CONVERSATIONAL STRUCTURES, STRATEGIES, AND PROTOCOLS

Critical conversation can be difficult—the skills necessary to engage productively are typically *unpracticed*. However, when these skills are taught, we're more likely to see conversations that deepen students' individual understanding and our collective understanding as a community. Just as we know that reading and writing are skills that can be improved with practice, so too can we create opportunities for students to practice critical conversation daily. The structured practice ideas in this section are not a replacement for independent classroom discussions—they're training for those conversations.

When we give students clear, manageable structures for their critical conversation practice, students understand their role in the conversation. When students understand when and how to participate, it's unnecessary for us to track their participation with elaborate point systems or rubrics, or to resort to cold calling—practices that emphasize public performance over thoughtfulness, that put students (especially introverts) into a heightened state of anticipation and stress, and that reinforce the idea that the teacher is the authority in class discussions.

Structures to Practice Quick Conversations

Every moment in class is an opportunity to strengthen students' conversational muscles. Starting small, with quick, low-stakes conversation protocols are an effective way to build those muscles and make talk less scary for kids. The following structures also provide an effective foundation when students are discussing more difficult topics later in the year.

Inner and Outer Circle Talk

I can always tell when small group conversations are going well when I have to interrupt students so that the whole class can reconvene. When done well, small group discussions can be powerful spaces for students to use their voice. But the truth is, for every group I have to interrupt and pull back to the whole class is another group: students who will do the assigned task independently, alongside each other, without actually having a conversation. This is typical when students don't know how to sustain a conversation with peers whom they might not necessarily know well. I'm always surprised how many students can go weeks or months in the same room yet never talk with one another. I've used this strategy throughout the year to help students talk to as many of their classmates in the room as possible.

> ► Inner and Outer Circle Talk gives students practice in having back-to-back conversations, transitioning between partners.

Instead of simply asking students to share their reflections or ideas as a whole class or in their small groups, I arrange students in two circles, one inner and one outer, and have them partner up. Students have thirty to sixty seconds to share their responses (students can have notes if they like) before all students in the inner circle shift clockwise so that they are sitting with a new partner. If there is an odd number of students, I add an "empty" seat which I call a "thinking chair." During this time, students can write in their notebooks and reflect on what they have shared and discussed so far. They then share again.

Because this may become repetitive after a few rounds, I introduce and project prompts on the board that ask students to extend or deepen their initial response. These prompts might include:

- Which word or phrase stood out to you? Why?

- What part of this text did you find most challenging? Why?

- What part of this text resonated with you most? Why?

- What connections do you see between this text and historical or current events?

- What perspectives are missing from this text? How might these perspectives deepen our understanding?

Circular Build

This protocol (see Figure 4.3) helps students practice in listening and *building* upon each other's ideas. To share their response in small groups, I ask students to share their thinking, one at a time, in a circle. The key, however, is that when a student shares, they must reference and build upon what the previous student said. This strategy can also be used when recapping a text when studying literature. The first student starts by recapping one event or development from the reading. The next student adds something new, and so on.

> ▶ Circular Build encourages students to listen carefully to each other's ideas and build upon them to create new thinking.

FIGURE 4.3 CIRCULAR BUILD

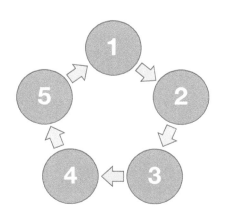

CIRCULAR DISCUSSION

- Person 1 begins with a reaction to the reading.
- Person 2 continues but **must** build upon what Person 1 said.
- Person 3 continues but must build upon what Person 2 said.
- And so on.
- Continue for 4 rounds. The challenge is to keep the conversation cohesive and "tight."

Conver-stations

Conver-stations is a structure that I use to help students move around and hear as many different perspectives as possible. In this structure, students move in pairs around the room in rounds, meeting up with new pairs to discuss a prompt (Figure 4.4). I often use this strategy in conjunction with Progressive Discussions (described later in this chapter).

▶ In Conver-stations, students collaboratively navigate back-to-back conversations.

FIGURE 4.4   CONVER-STATIONS

1. Begin in your groups of 3-4. When a queston is posted on the board, discuss as a group. Take turns, beginning with the person who is youngest in the group, then clockwise.

2. Each person shares their answer for 30-60 seconds. <u>Two</u> minutes of open discussion begins after everyone has spoken.

3. When a new queston is posted, the front (blue) pair of students moves to the next group.

4. Discuss in groups again, starting with the youngest then clockwise. Every member the group should share their response before open discussion begins.

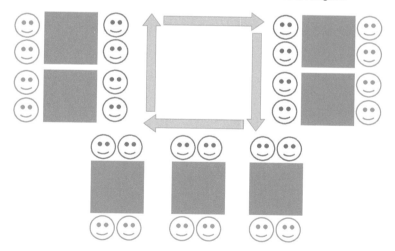

Musical Talk

▶ Musical Talk gives students practice in talking to anyone as soon as the music stops.

This is another simple protocol that I use to get students moving and talking to as many different classmates as possible. Similar to musical chairs, students walk around as music plays. When the music stops, they pair up with a

student standing near them and discuss the prompt. I have used this as a way to have students share their responses to a text, sometimes in multiple rounds with the same prompt, and other times, with different questions, integrating this strategy with Progressive Discussions (p. 191). I've even used this strategy in writing workshop in which student conversations are "prewriting" conferences in which each student might share, "Here's what I'm thinking about writing . . . " No matter what the context in which this is used, musical conversations facilitate greater interaction among students.

Jigsaw Discussions

A typical jigsaw protocol—often used in reading comprehension work—divides smaller tasks among students who then have to come back together to complete a larger goal. One of the benefits of the jigsaw is that it is collaborative.

▶ Jigsaw Discussions give students practice in piecing together multiple perspectives.

In my take on a jigsaw discussion, I start by asking students to consider what points-of-view are necessary when studying an issue. For example, when we studied the issue of gun control after the Parkland shooting, students brainstormed a list of stakeholders who would have a vested interested in this issue. These stakeholders might include students, parents, gun manufacturers, politicians, and the media. Students then researched a particular stakeholder perspective, trying the best they could to understand that point-of-view. When it was time for class discussion, students synthesized their understanding by hearing from each of these perspectives. In this way, students could appreciate how each individual, and sometimes conflicting, perspective was an integral "piece of the puzzle" in understanding the complexities of the issue.

Structures for Being Heard and for Hearing Others

While each of the strategies I've shared requires that students practice listening during discussions, the following strategies isolate the skill of active listening specifically. Consider using these strategies when you notice students may need a little more support in this area.

Listening Circle

Sometimes we need space to speak—and we don't necessarily need others to respond. In fact, there are times when the point of speaking is simply to be heard. We don't need others to validate, question, or connect to what we're saying. What we say can, instead, stand on its own. Furthermore, when we hear someone else speak their truth, we sometimes rush to affirm or connect to fill in the conversational space. Doing this, however, can sometimes not allow the other person's words to really settle in and be heard. To bring attention to this, I remind students, "Often someone else's words are a gift, and as a gift, we should simply accept. And we can be thankful for this gift by receiving it by listening and letting their words live in this space."

▶ In a Listening Circle, students make space to be heard.

I like to use a listening circle when it's enough that our words are heard and received and there is not an immediate need for discussion or commentary. I've found that the best time for this is at the end of a class in which we've had some particularly important or serious discussion. It's a way to end with everyone's voices heard and to remind each other of our most salient takeaways.

In this protocol, students stand in a circle and each person takes a turn speaking for ten to thirty seconds with "one thing they'd like to add that's important in this discussion." I let students know that there will be no commentary on what each person shares and then we begin. I've done this where we simply go around in a circle, but also when students simply speak when they feel moved to do so. Depending on the topic of discussion, I ask that everyone speak, even sharing just one small thing, or I allow students to pass.

Another powerful way I've used the listening circle is when I ask students to compliment someone else in the class for sharing something that challenged or changed their thinking.

One-of-a-Kind Micro-Share

This strategy is another tried-and-true among teachers, and it is probably one of the most common strategies I used (at least once per week). Here, each student shares something briefly. This works best when we are doing a text rendering, pulling out words or lines that stand out to us, or when whatever prompt I've given in class only requires a brief word or phrase response.

▶ A One-of-a-kind micro-share is a way to invite students to share what resonated with them without repeating what someone has already shared.

The benefit to this strategy is that every student's voice is heard *and* because I ask that students not repeat what someone has already said, it means that students really need to listen carefully to each other's responses. A "no repeats" guideline works best when I want to push students to have the broadest range of

responses as a class. As an extension, as students share, I catalogue their responses on the board or in a shared document. I then ask students to see if there are any patterns to the responses and what this might reveal about the text we're analyzing or the issue we're discussing.

Micro-Share

This strategy is exactly the same as the previous, except that I start this protocol by sharing, "It's okay to share what someone else has said. When we repeat someone else, this actually gives us an opportunity to see what resonated with multiple people." After everyone has shared, I ask students to turn and talk with a partner about what patterns they heard before launching into a larger and deeper class discussion on the text or issue we're discussing. In this way, what students have shared is a starting point, but it's a starting point that has included every student's voice.

▶ In a standard micro-share, students to can hear who has a similar take on a text

Silent Discussion

Sometimes the best way to have a discussion is not by talking aloud but by talking on paper. This strategy works best when students are closely analyzing a text. I pull several pieces of texts I'd like students to interact with more closely—a poem or parts of a poem, an excerpt from an essay or piece of fiction. I choose enough pieces of texts so that it's enough for every small group in the class to have a different selection (in a class of 28, for example, I would need 7 pieces of texts for groups of 4 students/group). I cut and paste each one in the center of a larger piece of paper or poster paper, making sure to leave space around it, then give one to each group.

▶ Silent discussions give students the option for being heard without speaking.

Students quietly annotate the text, circling and commenting on what stands out and why. After a few minutes, students move to the next selection and poster, continuing the process of silently annotating. Now that the texts already have annotations, I remind students that they may also choose to respond to someone else's comment. This strategy is particularly helpful for students who are less inclined to speak aloud but might prefer to write their ideas down. Open class discussion often privileges extroverted students who process through talk. Using a silent discussion helps to ensure that conversation is equitable.

After all the groups have finished rotating through, they then arrive back at their original text. I then ask students to review the annotations and create a summary of what they noticed. I generally ask students to share their observations about two things: what the patterns were in terms of similarities, but also what were one to two outliers they saw among the responses. Another extension of this idea is to have students go around one more time to each poster and place a star (or sticker) next to the annotation that most stands out or that they want to discuss as a class.

Curated Responses

A potential pitfall in whole class discussions is that those with the strongest opinions are those who are most often—or only—heard. I sometimes wonder if pundits on cable TV and our presidential candidates learned how to speak with such confidence and certainty in our classrooms. When there are particularly strong personalities in a room, it can be difficult for other students—especially those who may be more reserved—to offer a contrary opinion. Sometimes the first voice is the loudest, but we need to make sure it doesn't dominate. While we don't want to shut down any participants, we do want to ensure students who may not be among the first to speak are still heard.

▶ Curated Responses can help to spotlight lesser heard voices without spotlighting individual kids.

This strategy is particularly useful when you anticipate that there could potentially be strong opinions about the text or when you anticipate that some students might find it difficult to talk about a text. For example, when I first taught Jesmyn's Ward's beautiful essay, "Raising a Black Son in the United States," I knew it could be an emotional read for some students. Also, because the essay had to do with Ward's experience with race and racism, I had concerns that some students would be too afraid to say the "wrong" thing in front of the class and our whole class discussion might feel flat.

This strategy is also helpful when:

- Students have little background knowledge about a topic. Choosing which responses to highlight can amplify more informed student opinions and use these to support whole class discussion.

- The topic is potentially polarizing. By focusing on the content of students' opinions versus on the students with those opinions, the class can discuss the merits of various perspectives rather than debate each other.

- A dominant perspective has the danger of silencing the voices of students who have identities that are often marginalized or misrepresented in society or in the curriculum. Highlighting their perspectives restores the power that they may otherwise be denied.

Furthermore, in my experience, when students have little background or informed knowledge about a topic, they often revert to what they *do* know, which can sometimes mean they rely on "what they've heard" or even stereotypes. Allowing students to share uninformed opinions, especially those rooted in stereotypes, can have a potentially harmful impact on other students in the class. Reminding students about the difference between uninformed opinions and informed understanding can be of help at this point, but **it's also our job as teachers to provide a structure that minimizes harm while still allowing all students to have a voice.**

Before we discuss as a class, I ask students to respond to the text in writing, usually through an online form. I let them know that portions of their responses may be shared with the class anonymously. When I review the responses, I look for patterns, but I also look for the responses that might represent a marginalized or non-dominant perspective. For example, when we discuss *The Atlantic* writer Joe Pinsker's essay, "The Problem with 'Hey Guys,'" the majority of students—most of whom identify as cisgender—tend to underestimate the negative impact of using a word like "guys" to address a group of people that includes many genders.

In the past, when I've opened up discussion about this issue in class, it's primarily the perspective of cisgender students that dominates because these students literally outnumber others. This is how dominant perspectives dominate: because those with alternate points-of-view may be fewer in number, the "majority rules" and marginalized voices continue to be marginalized. Yet historically, if we were to rely on and act solely on the points-of-view held by the numerical majority—consider the fight for Civil Rights, for example—we would not see what progress we have made in ensuring the voices and needs of all are heard and met.

Therefore, when I review responses, I'm also looking for which perspectives can and need to be amplified. Because sometimes these perspectives can be further marginalized by the limits of school schedules—for example, there might be only one or two students of color or nonbinary students in a class—I draw upon responses from students across classes. This not only brings additional perspectives to our discussion to make it richer, it also can help to affirm and validate the responses of students in the numerical minority. Likewise, Ursula Wolfe-Rocca, a Social Studies teacher in Portland, Oregon, also uses a strategy like this to highlight minoritized perspectives. As Wolfe-Rocca notes:

> In classrooms all across this country, you will hear teachers vowing that "all voices have a place in this school." But the lesson of history is that professions of equality and opportunity, no matter how well intentioned, do not make it so. If we truly want our quiet, marginalized, and

underrepresented students to have a voice in our classrooms, we are going to have to deliberately design models of discourse that make their voices impossible to ignore.

When we consider what *equity* really looks like in our classrooms, we must have the structures and support that allow all voices, especially those traditionally marginalized, to be heard. This means, as Wolfe-Rocca reminds us, that we need to "deliberately design models of discourse" that achieve this.

The next day, I print out student responses, without names, on individual slips of paper. (When I want to invite students back into the text, I not only pass out student responses but also brief excerpts from the text itself to analyze as part of the discussion.) I share these responses and we discuss in a variety of different ways, depending on the class dynamic and what other discussion strategies we've used recently or would be particularly beneficial for students at that time. Below are a few possibilities.

Read more of teacher Ursula Rocca-Wolfe's reflection on equitable classroom discussions in her essay, "Dangerous Discussions: Voi and Power in my Classroom"

- Divide students into groups of three or four and pass out a different student response to each group. Students read and discuss the response to the text for a few minutes before they rotate the responses. This way, students are able to see all the responses, which is then followed up with some individual writing and class discussion.

- Give each student a response and ask them to take turns reading responses to the class. This allows many responses to be heard and shared without the pressure of any single student "owning" a particular opinion.

- Give each student a response and then divide students into smaller groups of three or four. Students share their responses in their groups and discuss. Students can be then prompted to discuss which response most resonates with their own experiences, readings, or observations, and why.

- Post student responses on poster paper around the room and have students do a silent discussion and annotation (page 182).

Responding Through Our Identities

This protocol builds up on the identity work outlined in chapter 3 and can be integrated into any other strategy that asks students to respond to a text or issue. Here, I ask students to be explicit about the identity

lens they might be using at any given time. Put simply, students ground their response to the text or topic of discussion in one or more of their identities:

> From where I stand as [identity] . . . I see [issue or text] as [response] . . .

Depending on the comfort level of my students, I ask them to share their response using this framework in small group discussions. For example, this can be a prompt for discussion during Progressive Discussions (p. 191), during a Constructive Listening Dyad, or in Listening Circles. That said, asking students to share aloud the ways in which their identities intersect with their response to a text or issue can be a challenge for students; it's one thing to reflect in their notebooks but quite another to share with their peers. Because of this, I usually allow students to practice sharing in small groups before opening up this type of response for whole-class discussion.

▶ Responding through Identity Lenses helps kids connect their identities to their points of-view.

Structures for Stating a Position

So far in this chapter, you'll notice that each of the protocols provide students with smaller structured opportunities to practice talking with others and active listening. The structures that follow put more emphasis on how students articulate a well-reasoned and informed position, using the listening skills they've already practiced in the previous pages.

They Say, I Say

In *They Say, I Say*, Gerald Graff and Cathy Birkenstein provide scaffolds for how to "enter a conversation" about an issue by writing in response to other voices. For example, here's some templates adapted from Graff and Birkenstein's (2021) work that students have used to respond to a text:

> The argument made by [author] is that . . . More specifically, [author] argues that [quote from text]. In this passage, [author] suggests that . . . which is important because . . .

> I agree or disagree with [author] because in my view . . . More specifically, I believe . . . After all, [provide supporting evidence]. Although some may argue [provide counterargument], I maintain . . . because . . .

▶ Using a They Say, I Say Structure gives kids opportunities to speak back to other points-of-view.

As you can see here, this template requires students to do quite a few things: they have to discern an author's purpose, provide evidence, respond with their own point-of-view, support their point-of-view with evidence, and consider a counterexample. In other words, they need to put together all the skills they have practiced in this chapter so far.

These are critical skills, and ones that need not be limited to writing. So I adapted Graff and Birkenstein's work as a conversational structure, as outlined in Figure 4.5.

FIGURE 4.5

They Say, I Say

DISCUSSION PROTOCOL

Person 1 shares opinion
uninterrupted for 1 minute

AGREE	**DISAGREE**
Similarly	However
Likewise	In contrast
In addition/	Conversely
Additionally	On the contrary
Furthermore	Instead
Moreover	On the other hand
In fact	Yet
Along the same lines	Another way to
By extension	Instead
In same way	

Person 4 continues in the same pattern:
1) Summarize Person 1, 2, and 3.
2) Signal agreement or disagreement with a transition word.
3) Share opinion.

Person 2 summarizes what Person 1 said by starting with: "According to [insert Person 1's name] . . ."

Then Person 2 determines if he or she agrees or disagrees. Person 2 **uses a transition** word to signal agreement/disagreement (see center).

Person 2 then shares his or her opinion.

Person 3: Continues in the same pattern:
1) Summarize Person 1 and 2.
2) Signal agreement or disagreement with a transition word.
3) Share opinion.

What I appreciate about this protocol is that the conversational moves students make here can then be more easily transferred to their writing. Because this protocol is more structured and encourages students to use purposeful transitions to respond to and connect their ideas to their peers' ideas, I provide students with a copy of these directions (or keep them posted on the board and in our online learning management system for easy reference).

Wait, What?

A few years ago, my former principal shared a book that she and the other administrators had read over the summer: *Wait, What? And Life's Other Essential Questions* by James Ryan. In 2017, Ryan, a law professor, delivered a commencement address at Harvard University's Graduate School of Education. In it, he argued that there were five essential questions in life that we should ask ourselves and others. These questions would later become the basis for his book. Each question is listed below, with my own description of how they can be applied to classroom conversations.

▶ Using Wait, What? questions supports kids with tools for focusing on what really matters

1. *Wait, what?* This question can be used to clarify our understanding, a way of asking for further information.

2. *I wonder . . .?* This question celebrates looking at possibilities. A simple way to practice curiosity and humility at the same time, placing the words "I wonder" at the beginning of an observation allows all participants in the discussion an opportunity to consider if the wondering is true or not or to what extent without rising to the level of debate or argument.

3. *Could we at least . . . ?* This question seeks common ground and pushes forward a discussion that might have stalled. It provides an opportunity for participants to seek agreement, even if it is about something small.

4. *How can I help?* This question reminds participants to consider what actions they might take to assist in moving the conversation forward. For example, if one student is confused, the prompt to help reminds participants to answer a question, explain a concept, repeat an earlier point, or whatever else might be needed.

5. *What truly matters?* This question works well toward the end of a discussion and asks students to synthesize their learning so far to a key takeaway: a deeper understanding or perhaps even a future action.

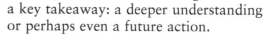
Watch Dean James Ryan's Commencement Speech.

When I use this strategy in class, my students and I begin by watching Ryan's commencement address. I then ask students to apply these questions to the text or issue we're studying at the time. Sometimes I have done this through an online discussion board or live in class by collecting questions using a tool like Socrative. We then use these questions during our class discussion, or sometimes I will integrate the questions into their Harkness discussions (see page 192).

To be honest, it's less important to me that students use these particular stems. I've found that their value—"what truly matters"—is in nudging students towards a disposition of openness and cooperation in their discourse.

Structures for Critical Introspection

When we ask students to reflect on what they've learned, how they have been challenged or changed as a result of participating in a critical conversation, we build their authentic appreciation for the benefits of critical conversations. As a result, the students develop their own intrinsic motivation for the work they do in critical conversations. The strategies that follow can help.

Critical Observer

Sometimes I create a secondary role for one or two students during discussion (especially if we are using a Harkness or Fishbowl protocol, see p. 192 later in this chapter) and ask them to act as critical observers, taking notes not on the content of the discussion but on *how* the discussion unfolded. I provide students with a list of verbs that represent *actions*—the *moves* that students make during discussions and ask them to simply tally the number of times they see their peers making these moves (Figure 4.6). While this list is by no means exhaustive, I find that keeping the list relatively slim and focused on the "big" moves makes the moves much easier for students to track.

▶ Having students play the role of the Critical Observer helps them to see how their words and actions affect the discussion.

Another way I ask students to observe our discussions is by mapping the discussion, either by hand or using the iPad app, Equity Maps (Figure 4.7). Mapping how a discussion unfolds can be very useful in noticing patterns of dominance and silence: Do some students only respond to certain students? Do students respond only to teacher inquiries or to fellow students as well? Understanding what patterns unfold can help teachers identify if there are patterns that might need to be disrupted (for example, if there are patterns related to race or gender that seem to favor some students over others).

Look at the discussion maps in Figure 4.7. What do you notice? What patterns might be present and in what ways could these be problematic? How might you then interrupt them?

FIGURE 4.6   CRITICAL OBSERVER NOTE SHEET

DISCUSSION TOPIC _____

NAME _____
TODAY'S DATE _____

MARK EACH TIME YOU OBSERVE THE FOLLOWING CONVERSATION MOVES:

_____ **INITIATE** a new line of discussion

_____ **ASK FOR CLARIFICATION** to someone's question or comment

_____ **RESTATE** what someone else has said

_____ **ADD TO / EXTEND** another person's point

_____ **SUPPORT** an opinion with evidence

_____ **OFFER A CONTRARY** point of view

_____ **CONNECT** (explicitly) to someone else's point

_____ **INVITE** someone else to speak

_____ **INTERRUPT** someone while they are speaking

_____ **CHANGE TOPICS** unexpectedly

ON THE REVERSE SIDE: COMMENT ON THE MOVES YOU BELIEVE WERE MOST IMPACTFUL DURING DISCUSSION.

FIGURE 4.7   EQUITY MAPS

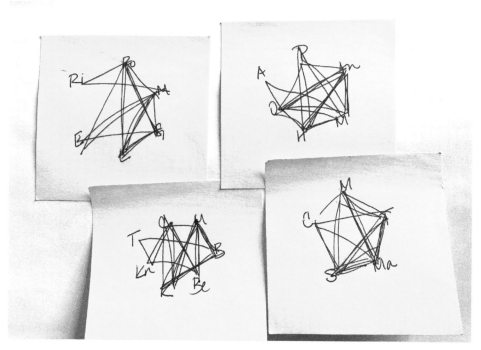

Although I have used the iPad app, Equity Maps, which provides good data on how many times individual students speak and for how long, I have also found that using simple post-it notes to track the flow of discussion are also informative and helpful for students to see.

Structures for Extended Critical Discussions

In general, I've found that the more potentially difficult the conversation—whether that difficulty is caused by the topic, student interest, time of year, or other reason—the more structure we might need to have in place. Once students' conversational skills improve, this scaffolding can be removed: in conversation, just as in construction, all scaffolds are meant to be temporary.

Facilitating whole class discussions can be tricky. I know I've facilitated my share of discussions where the conversation falls flat: I ask for a response and . . . crickets. No one says a word. There could be many reasons for this, of course, but usually when there's silence, it's not because students don't have anything to say, it's that they don't feel comfortable sharing aloud with the class.

Progressive Discussions

Progressive discussions are helpful when students are unpacking a complex topic that requires them to construct a shared foundation of understanding in order to deepen their understanding—for example, when students come to class having read something that needs to be unpacked.

▶ Progressive discussions give students a scaffold for a longer, more complex discussions.

Students sit in small groups with the text in front of them, and I project prompts on the board.

For their first prompt, I ask students to simply summarize what happened in the text (I say "simply," but as we know, summary is a skill that can be difficult, especially as text complexity increases.), or I ask students to share one detail from the reading in statement form.

Each subsequent prompt requires students to dig deeper into the text. Although there are many possibilities, I typically use prompts that focus students on a different part of the text ("In this paragraph . . ." or "On page 2, the author…"), often moving in chronological order, before ending with a prompt that asks students to consider the author's overall purpose. By structuring the discussion in this way—focusing first on the individual components before analyzing the purpose of the text—students practice inductive reasoning.

Of course, the scaffolding provided in this strategy is critical—but it is equally critical to remove the scaffolding and turn agency over to students. After doing two or three progressive discussions in class, I ask students to analyze the process itself: What did they notice about the types of prompts they were given? Did they notice any patterns to the prompts? Through our deconstruction of the protocol, students can

then see that there was an intentional design behind the organization of the prompts, and we discuss what means to think *inductively*: to examine specific examples to reach a conclusion or determine the author's purpose.

With this understanding, students then construct the prompts for the next progressive discussion. For example, students within each group might take turns coming up with prompts for their progressive discussion: one student individually creates the prompts and then facilitates the group through the discussion. Or, students might work in small groups to determine prompts for the progressive discussion. They then give their prompts to another group to use.

Harkness Discussion

The Harkness table method, founded in 1930 at Phillips Exeter Academy, is a discussion method that I use whenever we are diving deeply into a text and I want to create a smaller, more intimate discussion space. According to the school's website, [The Harkness method] is a simple concept:

▶ Use this classic method to turn the discussion over to students.

> Twelve students and one teacher sit around an oval table and discuss the subject at hand.
>
> What happens at the table, however, is, as Harkness intended, a "real revolution." It's where you explore ideas as a group, developing the courage to speak, the compassion to listen, and the empathy to understand.
>
> It's not about being right or wrong.
>
> It's a collaborative approach to problem solving and learning.

These last two qualifiers—"not about being right or wrong" and "a collaborative approach to problem solving and learning"—are what have always drawn me to the Harkness method, especially as I started to notice the way that students responded to debates in their other classes. Fresh off of a debate in their social studies or science classes, students would come to class heated about how it was unfair that they had "lost" the debate, or worse, they would blame another student as the reason for their loss. Although I was not privy to how teachers might have structured their debates, what I was seeing in the aftermath were students who saw argument as a zero-sum game of winners and losers.

Of course, as we know, the most important issues we face as a society cannot be reduced to a zero-sum game of winners and losers. In fact, doing so almost guarantees that we all lose. I'm reminded here again of Wheatley's call to be "willing to be disturbed," as she writes, "We don't have to let go of what we believe, but we do need to be curious about what someone else believes. We do need to acknowledge that their way of interpreting the world might be essential to our survival." Unfortunately, in debate, students aren't necessarily encouraged to be "curious" about the other side, only how to find its weaknesses and exploit them.

Although I don't teach at Phillips Exeter with twelve students per class, I adapt the Harkness method by dividing my class of twenty-four to thirty students in half or thirds. Students come to class with notes ready to discuss the text they were previously assigned. While I often keep note-taking requirements flexible—come with what you need to have informed knowledge, as we defined in our discussion of Sensoy and DiAngelos's work (p. 161 earlier in this chapter)—I often recommend that students have notes on the following:

- What surprised them
- What disturbed them
- Passages that challenged or confused them

As you can see, this note-taking framing goes hand in hand with Wheatley's call to be "willing to be disturbed" also echoes the three big questions that Beers and Probst (2015) outline in their book *Notice and Note: Nonfiction Signposts* (p. 81):

- What surprised you?
- What confirmed, challenged, or changed your thinking?
- What did the author think you knew that you did not?

Before we begin, I provide students with guidelines for how the Harkness table works, reminders that I post on the board and can point to as needed. As you can see in Figure 4.8, I integrate our earlier agreements inspired by Clint Smiths' TED Talk (chapter 2) into our guidelines for our Harkness table discussions.

I ask half of the students to sit in the center of the room, facing one another (I push tables together to create one larger shared space). I remind students of all the listening and speaking skills they've practiced and then they begin, referencing their notes throughout the discussion.

If the Harkness method sounds a little too unstructured—*wait, they just come together around a table and talk?*—that's because it is, and *purposefully so*. Releasing control and providing students with space and time to see where their thinking takes them is key in a Harkness

method. Although I know many teachers participate in the Harkness table, I often do not. Instead, I sit on the outside, which allows me to observe the group's dynamics and write down my own takeaways from their conversation. I interject only when I see students violating the spirit of the discussion, which is to say, I have hardly ever had to interject. Why not? Because this is the most independent and open-ended structure of the protocols I use, it is the one I try to save until students have practiced at least some of the previous strategies. In other words, by the time students find themselves at a Harkness table, they are mostly ready for it. They just need the invitation.

Meanwhile, you might be asking what the other students might be doing. Their task is to listen and take notes; after all, they will need these notes since the groups will switch after about ten to fifteen minutes. The outside circle becomes the inner circle and vice versa and the discussion continues. However, this time, the discussion must make reference to and build upon the previous inner circle's conversation. The new outside circle now listens and takes notes. At the end of class, these notes help students make sense of patterns they heard during both conversations before we launch into a full class debriefing. A written reflection that evening serves to further synthesize students' thinking.

Another option is to have students in the outside circle write their observations and comments on individual sticky notes as they listen. Afterwards, students then post their sticky notes on the board and try to group them according to patterns they noticed in the comments. This allows students to hear from almost everyone else in the class in two ways: as (1) speakers in the inside circle and (2) listeners who took good notes in the outside circle. The regrouping and pattern-seeking activity at the end allows students the opportunity to synthesize their ideas. As with many class periods, we "close" with a writer's notebook reflection on our new thinking and the questions that have emerged after the Harkness table discussions.

Fishbowl With Live Chat

The fishbowl discussion (Figure 4.9) is familiar to many teachers and builds upon the Harkness tables. In this strategy, I set it up so that a small group of students discusses the text in the center of the room; this group becomes the "inner circle." Meanwhile, the remaining students on the "outside" are tasked with having their own (adjacent) conversation inspired by what they hear from the inner circle. They do not have this conversation orally, however, as that would cause confusion. Instead, students participate in a digital back-channel

▶ In this updated version of a traditional fishbowl discussion, students receive live feedback and interaction with the outer circle through discussion board.

FIGURE 4.8   HARKNESS METHOD

The **HARKNESS TABLE** is a discussion protocol that promotes inquiry and equitable conversation in which questions are prioritized and all voices are heard.

While the "answers" that you might discover during discussion can be important, the real value of a true Harkness Table is in finding and asking better and better questions.

The goal of the Harkness Table is community-centered: rather than participate to make sure your voice is heard, participate in order to ensure that all voices are heard.

READ CRITICALLY.

- Read the text carefully, taking note of what stands out to you.
- Read like a writer, asking why the author would have written this and in this way.
- Pay attention to where in the text you find yourself confused or surprised.

SPEAK CLEARLY.

- In order for great conversations to happen, be sure that you are heard, literally. Enunciate your voice and, especially if you are naturally soft-spoken, turn up the volume on your speech.
- Speaking clearly means monitoring if what you're saying is really what you mean. Sometimes our words can get jumbled. Sometimes what we **intend** to say is different than the **impact** of what is **heard**. If that happens, revise what you said as needed to be more clear.

LISTEN CAREFULLY.

- When you are not speaking, you must be listening carefully. Active listening is evident when you build upon what the person is saying (versus waiting for your turn to talk).
- If you hear something you disagree with, it's okay to disagree. Ask clarifying questions when you're confused (If I'm hearing you correctly, you're saying that...).
- Be open and be "willing to be disturbed" as you consider ideas you hadn't before.

WRITE CONSCIOUSLY.

- Use the **Question Formulation Technique (QFT)** to write good questions for discussion (Rothstein and Santana).

Q F T
- List as many questions as you can w/out editing yourself (think freely).
- Mark each questions as closed (C) or open (O).
- Revise closed questions to make them **open.**
- Prioritize your questions by ranking them from 1 (most important) to 10 (least important).
- Take a moment to reflect on why higher ranked questions matter more than others.

TELL YOUR TRUTH.

- Share your interpretation of the text or your perspective on an issue honestly.
- That said, speaking your truth and participating in respectful discourse are not mutually exclusive.

Sample Harkness Table Discussion Map

Tricia Ebarvia (C)

discussion using various apps like Padlet or any other discussion board tool you might have. As they listen to what the inner circle of students says, they comment and talk with one another as a live stream of their conversation is projected on the board.

Because students in the inner circle (the fishbowl) can see the comments, they can also use what they see to inform their own discussion. They

might bring in the voices of others in the outer circle or address a question someone has posed. I make sure to remind students in the inner circle that their priority should be to talk with one another, not simply answer any questions that are posted in the backchannel—and that it's even okay to ignore the backchannel altogether! But having the backchannel has allowed deeper engagement for all students and facilitated some interesting overlaps in the conversations between the two groups and more times than not. While some teachers might worry about the possibility of inappropriate commenting during the live stream, I have personally had very few problems—*not* because my students are particularly well-behaved, but because of the time and space dedicated to intentional community building early and throughout the year.

FIGURE 4.9 FISHBOWL WITH LIVE CHAT

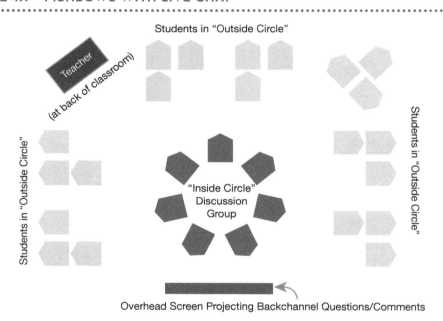

FIGURE 4.10 QUICK REFERENCE FOR CONVERSATION STRATEGIES

PURPOSE	STRATEGY	PAGE
Model and Promote a Learning Stance	Facilitation Frames	172
	Reflect, Revisit, and Revise	173
	What I Heard, Think, and Wonder	173
	Listening Dyads	174
	Questions Only, Please	175

PURPOSE	STRATEGY	PAGE
Model and Promote a Learning Stance	Shifting Four Corners	176
	Two Talk, One Listens, Repeat	176
Structures to Practice Quick Conversations	Inner and Outer Circle Talk	177
	Circular Build	178
	Conver-stations	179
	Musical Talk	179
	Jigsaw Discussions	180
Structures for Being Heard and Hearing Others	Listening Circle	180
	One-of-a-Kind Micro-Share	181
	Micro-Share	182
	Silent Discussion	182
	Curated Responses	183
	Responding Through Our Identities	185
Structures for Stating a Position	They Say, I Say	186
	Wait, What?	188
Structures for Critical Introspection	Critical Observer	189
	Equity Maps	190
Structures for Extended Critical Discussion	Progressive Discussions	191
	Harkness Discussion	192
	Fishbowl With Live Chat	194

SEEKING FEEDBACK: AUDIT YOUR OWN CRITICAL FACILITATION SKILLS

No matter what strategies and protocols we use to help foster students' critical conversation skills, our strategies or protocols are only as effective as they are responsive. In other words, we must constantly reflect and evaluate on the ways in which we are—or aren't—reaching each student and helping them to grow in their critical discourse skills. I get some of my best feedback about how these protocols and strategies are working—or not—from the weekly Critical Incidents Questionnaire (CIQ) that students respond to (see page 84). Additionally, the job of the critical observer (page 189) can also include interactions between you and your students, not only between students.

Likewise, we can reach out to our colleagues for feedback on our own facilitation skills. Although it is not always feasible, having a colleague complete an equity map and look for patterns in our interactions with students can be invaluable. In addition, just as we want to help students unpack their own biases, we need to be aware of the ways in which our own biases, identities, and experiences might be informing our response to students and what they bring to our class discourse.

In the following chapters, we'll take a closer look at how to apply some of the strategies mentioned in this chapter to better understand and deepen our reader response.

How can we *get free* as **readers of ourselves and the world?**

We bring our whole selves whenever we read. Whether we're reading a graphic novel or a poem, an episode of a favorite TV series or the headlines in our news feeds, we bring who we are to each reading experience, that moment when words, images, and sounds become more than words, images, and sounds—they become meaningful. *Filled* with meaning—and *readers* bring that meaning.

This might seem an obvious point, yet most middle and high school classrooms focus not on the encounter between reader and text—when meaning is made—but on the text itself, and *only* the text itself. When teachers use the term "close reading," this is the type of reading they're typically referring to. And thanks to standardized testing and the emphasis on "text dependent analysis," the experiences that *readers* bring to a text are pushed to the margins.

The problem with this heavy text-dependent approach is that readers bring an incredible wealth of knowledge and experiences to each text they encounter. They bring their hearts, their heads, their opinions, their anxieties, their fears, and yes, their biases, too.

To teach with an antibias lens, then, means pushing back against a text-dependent reading approach as the only type of reading that matters. Instead of limiting students' experiences with reading to *what does the text say* or *what does the author mean*, we can take a more expansive view of reading—one that honors the experiences and knowledge that students bring to a text but also helps students interrogate those experiences and knowledge. Every time we can disrupt and expand traditional and limited notions of reading, we teach against the societal bias that favors one type of reading at the expense of all the other interpretive possibilities out there. In this chapter, we'll imagine the power of reading that centers intentional perspective-taking and perspective-bending, opening ourselves to the possibility of getting free.

CHAPTER 5

RETHINKING READING

Taking an Expansive Approach

> *We are in an imagination battle . . . Imagination has people thinking they can go from being poor to a millionaire as part of a shared American dream. Imagination turns Brown bombers into terrorists and white bombers into mentally ill victims. Imagination gives us borders, gives us superiority, gives us race as an indicator of capability. I often feel like I am trapped inside someone else's imagination, and I must engage my own imagination in order to break free.*
>
> —adrienne maree brown
>
> *To say a work of fiction is unrelatable is to say, "I am not the implied audience, so I refuse to engage with the choices the author has made." . . . We must always ask: Relatable to whom?*
>
> —Matthew Salesses

When we were growing up, like most kids of the 80s and 90s, my brother and I spent Saturday mornings watching cartoons. One of our favorite cartoons was the *X-Men: The Animated Series*. My brother *loved* the X-Men, a group of mutant superheroes who had extraordinary abilities that were both admired and feared by others. And I suppose his love for them rubbed off on me, too.

If you're unfamiliar with the X-Men, they were human beings who had a genetic mutation that became the source of their powers. The character Storm could control the elements, while Iceman had freezing powers. Because they often came into these powers during their childhood or adolescence, the "mutants" (as they called themselves) needed help in figuring out what these powers meant and how to manage them. But to non-mutants, the X-Men's powers were a source of fear, even terror. Enter Professor X, a telepathic mutant himself, who opens a school for the "gifted" where these mutant human beings find a place to call home and eventually go on to become the superhero force, the X-Men.

I think some of our shared love for the X-Men was due, in perhaps no small part, to the fact that my brother and I were among the handful of students of color in our school and community, and in fact, the only Asian Americans. Even as our community of Asian Americans grew when we switched to public school, we were still among the even smaller handful of Filipino Americans. Neither one of us talked about being "minority" students very much; I think it was something we both understood without ever having to put words to it.

We were outsiders, like the X-Men.

My brother went on to become an avid reader and collector of comic books. By middle school, I turned to books like *The Babysitter's Club*. Because all my best friends growing up would babysit on the weekends, and because I wanted to fit in, it only made sense that I, too, should babysit. But to my cautious, immigrant parents, babysitting wasn't an option for their daughter. They would provide me with anything I needed, they said. But it was never about the money for me. I just wanted to be "normal"—like all the other twelve- and thirteen-year-old girls I knew—and as far as I could tell, that meant babysitting. So if I couldn't babysit, I'd do the next best thing and read about it.

Soon, I moved from babysitting hijinks to teen drama in the *Sweet Valley High* series by Francine Pascal. If you aren't familiar with the series, the books follow sixteen-year-old twins, Elizabeth and Jessica Wakefield, as they deal with what you'd expect of most tween and teen novels: friendship, romance, gossip, and sibling rivalry. I remember that Elizabeth was the "good" twin who was responsible, got good grades, and had a steady boyfriend named Todd. Jessica, on the other hand, was the "bad girl," often getting in trouble with boys and hanging out with the wrong crowd.

Most of the other details have faded from my memory, perhaps thankfully so. But I remember that I always looked forward to the description of the twins in the beginning of each book. I would read and reread the descriptions of the twins, which always fascinated me. Like this one:

> Dressed in a bright blue, skin-hugging minidress and matching tights, Jessica was an eye-catching sight. The outfit accented her long, shapely legs and brought out the blue in her sparkling aquamarine eyes. Across the room, Elizabeth, in her stylish but more casual wheat-colored pants and tan, striped shirt, also eyed her twin with admiration. Blessed with the same all-American blond good looks, the sisters appeared as alike as identical twins possibly could, but Elizabeth sometimes envied her sister's more dramatic flair.

Though I cringe rereading these words now, I cannot overstate how influential these books were to my middle school self. As many of us who have survived those years know, middle school is hard. Fitting in was an excruciating process—especially when you were one of the only students of color in the school (and one of the others was your brother). We bend and twist ourselves in impossible ways to fit in, any way we can.

At the time, I read about Jessica and Elizabeth Wakefield because I enjoyed their sibling rivalry, their romantic dramas. But looking back, I realize I was also reading their lives as a mentor text for my own. I was studying them—learning from them what it meant to be a middle-class, suburban, White teenage girl. As the daughter of first-generation immigrants from a country on the other side of the world, I didn't have the same experiences as my peers. I always felt like I was straddling two worlds. I studied *the Sweet Valley High* books to learn how to fit in.

I needed those Sweet Valley High books as a way to navigate the world around me, just as many of our students use other books to do the same. The series may not have been literary—and I'm fairly sure the teachers at my parochial school would not have approved—but I *needed* them.

As any English teacher reading this knows, books can be powerful—sometimes even life-changing. As Dr. Bishop (1990) writes:

> Books are sometimes windows, offering views of worlds that may be real or imagined, familiar or strange . . . When the lighting conditions are just right, however, a window can also be a mirror. Literature transforms human experience and reflects it back to us, and in that reflection we can see our

own lives and experiences as part of the larger human experience. Reading, then, becomes a means of self-affirmation, and readers often seek their mirrors in books.

The X-Men provided a mirror; *The Babysitters Club* and *Sweet Valley High* gave me a window. And at the center of each of these reading experiences were my own individual and social identities. Each of these texts was critical in becoming the person I am today.

Yet, I wonder . . .

While the X-Men were indeed superheroes, I wonder how my experiences would have been different if I had more mirrors—and a variety of them. What if I had books with characters who weren't blue-eyed and blond, but characters who looked and felt a little more like me? What if I spent even just a little less time trying to "be White"? What if I had characters like June from Amy Tan's *The Joy Luck Club*, Dimple Shah from Sandhya Menon's *When Dimple Met Rishi*, or Desi Lee from Maurene Goo's *I Believe in a Thing Called Love*, or even Starr Carter from Angie Thomas's *The Hate U Give* when I was growing up? What if I met a character like Jay Reguero—a Filipino American teen who unpacks what that identity means in the context of family and country—in Randy Ribay's *Patron Saints of Nothing*? Jessica and Elizabeth Wakefield taught me how to assimilate, how to fit in. But June, Dimple, Desi, Starr, Jay, and countless others?

They could have taught me *how to be me*.

These were mirrors that were missing. And as such, my approach to teaching literature—or really, any text—is informed by the need to ask *who is missing?*

No matter what race you are, it's true that readers often try to find themselves in literature. For many White readers, the *Sweet Valley High* series was just as much a window into a certain type of Whiteness as, perhaps, it was for me. But to "fit in," as individuals from a marginalized group know, to be accepted—or at the minimum, to not stand out—requires a level of contortion that is almost impossible to achieve. No matter how many times I tried, I could never, would never, be seen as White.

Now, decades later, I look at the X-Men with new eyes. As much as I loved the X-Men as a child, now I have a much deeper appreciation for it—for the messages it embodied about how we should not only accept what makes us different but also that **what makes us different can also make us powerful.** I think about that message as I raise my own kids and as I watch the news and see the ways in which we continue to treat those who are different with suspicion, cruelty, and violence.

CHALLENGING CURRICULAR BIASES

As we saw in chapter 1, it's crucial that we as educators examine the biases we bring into the classroom with us—and perhaps there is no more visible way that our biases can appear than in the texts that we choose to include in our curriculum. In fact, I'd argue that the texts we study are perhaps the most visible way we profess whose voices and experiences we value in literature, in the curriculum, and by extension, in society.

► "Nothing happens in the 'real' world unless it first happens in the images in our heads."

—Gloria Anzaldúa

Please note that unless otherwise noted, the literature used as an example in this chapter is not an endorsement of that literature. Rather, any texts mentioned here reflect my own experiences teaching literature within my context, which I hope might inspire you to think about what you may adapt for your own.

How We Got Here: Unpacking the "Canon"

In his books, *Stamped From the Beginning* and *How To Be an Antiracist*, Dr. Ibram X. Kendi argues that racist ideas spring from racist policies. In other words, when policies result in racialized differences—for example, the income gap between White people and non-White people—racist *ideas* are invented to justify why these differences exist. Often, when these differences are based on race, the justification is that non-White people are somehow *less than*—less hardworking, less intelligent, less talented, less worthy. Very little reflection on the *policies* which *created* these racialized differences is interrogated.

► "We must imagine new worlds that transition ideologies and norms, so that one sees Black people as murderers, or Brown people as terrorists and aliens, but all of us as potential cultural and economic innovators. This is a time-travel experience for the heart. This is collaborative ideation—what are the ideas that will liberate all of us?"

—adrienne maree brown

Once such racist ideas circulate, they then inform further racist actions. Thus, the cycle of racism is complete and self-reinforcing, with racist ideas informing racist policies and racist policies perpetuating racist ideas. Repeat for centuries.

Now to teaching and the curriculum.

Conversations about texts—particularly about the literary canon—are really proxies for conversations about race. When the books we assign demonstrate clear racial biases, often rooted in upholding White culture, we pass on racialized biases to our students, even if unintentionally. Furthermore, when we don't name race, making race "invisible," we normalize these racial biases. Based on Ijeomo Oluo's work in her book *So You Want to Talk About Race*, here are a few questions to ask yourself to determine whether or not something has to do with race:

- Does a person of color say it's about race?

- Does it disproportionately or differently affect people of color?

- Does it fit into a larger pattern that disproportionately or differently affects people of color?

Now reconsider these questions in the context of representation of people of color in the curricula:

- Do students, parents, and families of color say the curriculum is racially biased?

- Does the representation, or lack thereof, in the curriculum disproportionately or differently affect people of color?

- Does the representation, or lack thereof, fit into a larger pattern that disproportionately or differently affects people of color?

Reframe these same questions for other systems of oppression. For example, what would LGBTQ+ students say about their own experience with the curriculum? Is this experience part of a larger pattern? Or consider students with disabilities? How often are their experiences either misrepresented, tokenized, or erased from the curriculum?

How books became "canonized" is directly related to racialized power. Those in power—predominantly White men who had access to and control of the academy—enacted policies to maintain their power, just as almost any dominant power does. Thus, people of color and women writers were excluded, denied access to education and to the academy and other spaces of intellectual and artistic power. Because of these racist and sexist policies, racist and sexist ideas were used to justify the lack of people of color and women writers in the canon. People of color and women must be "less than"—not "literary" or "rigorous" enough. This racist, sexist thinking is used to justify the absence of people of color and women writers. This viewpoint, however, ignores the powers and policies that excluded people of color and women writers in the first place.

Over time as students and as teachers who are socialized in the "canon," we may internalize these racist, sexist ideas about what constitutes "literary value"—and then we reproduce it in our curricular choices, year after year. Studying these works is then seen as necessary in order to be "educated," and how often do we really problematize or challenge how narrow that definition of "educated" really is? Or how part of that narrow definition is rooted in racism and sexism? Additionally, because literature created by non-White artists may "break the rules" of what is considered mainstream literary—and because teachers and critics were mostly taught to read in mainstream literary ways—works by people of color are misunderstood or ignored. Add in economic factors, such as the lack of money to replace books, and the same books remain in the book closet, pulled out every year.

Here, consider the nostalgia bias we discussed in chapter 1. Recall that because of nostalgia bias, we tend to see the past through "rose-colored glasses." As a teacher, how might your own relationship with the books you read and studied in school—particularly those you enjoyed, or even loved—inform the way you make instructional decisions regarding texts?

Limited Imaginations or Imaginative Possibilities?

In *The Dark Fantastic,* Dr. Ebony Elizabeth Thomas warns of an "imagination gap"—

> I have long suspected, and I am assuredly not alone, that racialized disparities in literacy attainment among kids and teens may be ultimately rooted in a massive failure of the collective imagination.
>
> I wish to be perfectly clear here. I am not referring to any failure in the imaginations of young people. . .
>
> I am referring to the failure of adults. (Thomas, 2019, p. 6)

Dr. Thomas goes on to identify the ways in which adults—authors and other media creators—fail to imagine Black and Brown children beyond stereotypes and in ways that are instead authentic and affirmative. And as Black and Brown children continue to be marginalized, Dr. Thomas then asks, "Is it any wonder that some kids and teens of color don't like to read much?" The question for us as teachers: will we be adults who perpetuate this cycle or disrupt it?

In his book *Craft in the Real World: Rethinking Fiction Writing and Workshopping*, Salesses (2021) asks us to consider who a writer is writing *for* (and who they are *not* writing for):

> Expectations belong to an audience. To use craft is to engage with an audience's bias. Like freedom, craft is always *for someone*. Whose expectations does the writer prioritize? Craft says something about who deserves their story told. Who has agency and who does not. What is worthy of action and what description. Whose bodies are on display. Who changes and who stays the same. Who controls time. Whose world it is. Who holds meaning and who gives it. (p. 23)

We can consider Salesses's points here and apply them to the most commonly taught writers and texts in our curricula. Who was F. Scott Fitzgerald writing for? Who has agency in *To Kill a Mockingbird* and who does not? What does Nathaniel Hawthorne decide is worthy of action and what description? Whose bodies are on display in *The Things They Carried?* Whose world does *Pride and Prejudice* belong to? The choices a writer makes are not neutral but *cultural*, which means that when we teach certain texts, we are not just teaching the text, but the cultural values they carry.

Furthermore, because the publishing industry continues to be dominated by White, cisgender, heteronormative writers and narratives, our work as teachers to disrupt this norm and our responsibility to do so becomes increasingly urgent (Dahlen & Hyuck, 2019). However, because the lack of diverse representation in our curricula is a result of a series of choices, the good news is that we can choose differently.

We know from cognitive science that as we learn, we create schema, or mental models, to help us understand the world. We then use those mental models to organize and interpret new information. Why does this matter? The texts we read in class help to create the schema that students use to interpret the world around them. If the texts students read represent or reinforce a limited set of experiences (i.e., dominant White culture), then this worldview will become the mental model that students will use to interpret and evaluate new information and knowledge.

Thus, the value of more intentional and inclusive text selection cannot be overstated. *All* students benefit when they have the opportunity to have authentic "mirrors, windows, and sliding glass doors" (Bishop, 1990) in the curriculum. Students know what we value based on how we choose to spend our time in class. Which texts—and whose voices within those texts—do we spend time studying? What message does it send if these texts are not *centered* in our literary study but reserved for choice reading or optional? Is this yet another way to push underrepresented voices to the margins—to further marginalize?

All that said, simply including a more diverse and inclusive set of texts in the curriculum is only a first step, and under no circumstances should antiracist, antibias efforts be reduced to a checklist. As teachers, we must do the hard, internal work of examining the biases we bring into our classrooms, biases that are deeply rooted in our socialization. Again, **even if we have the best of intentions, we risk doing more harm than good when we do not understand the ways in which our worldviews have been informed by systems of oppression such as racism and sexism.** I encourage you to not only revisit the exercises detailed in chapter 1 but to continuously unlearn and relearn narratives about those different from yourself by reading literature and history told from the perspective of cultural insiders.

> *Students know what we value based on how we choose to spend our time in class.*

Being Good Stewards of Stories

As literacy teachers, we have a tremendous responsibility in making sure that our approach to teaching texts from communities not our own honors and respects those communities and our students. This means listening to those communities when they express concerns with how a particular text may or may not represent their community, or if our instruction, however well-intentioned, is potentially harmful. For this reason, we should listen to scholars like Dr. Rudine Sims Bishop and provide students with those necessary "mirrors, windows, and sliding glass doors." That said, we should also heed the words of Indigenous scholars like Dr. Reese (2018a) of Nambé Pueblo, who asks teachers to also consider the concept of "curtains" —

> [Curtains are] a way to acknowledge and honor the stories . . . that are purposefully kept within Native communities. Native communities resisted historical oppression and continue to preserve our culture by cultivating our ways in private spaces—behind the curtain. While Native people share some of our ways publicly in the present day, there is a great deal that we continue to protect from outsiders. Furthermore, it conveys the importance of how #OwnVoices knows what belongs within the community and what knowledge can be shared outside of our communities.

In 2015, the #OwnVoices hashtag was created by writer Corinne Duyvis who used it to indicate how she shared the same identity as that of her main character. The hashtag then became a way to let readers know that the author of a text could provide an authentic insider perspective through a shared identity as the characters.

Although we may be eager to introduce as many different texts as possible to our students, Dr. Reese's words remind us that we have a responsibility to listen to communities when they would rather draw the curtains on their stories. Sometimes I worry that when we fixate on the metaphor of "windows" that we forget that just because we can see into another culture or community doesn't mean we have the *right* to do so. Not everything is for outsiders' consumption. Instead, we might think of ourselves as practicing good stewardship of stories, taking the necessary care to share those stories responsibly.

Conduct an audit of your curriculum: how many works from authors of color, women, Native people, and the queer community are taught? How many are offered in classroom libraries? Once you have this data, what patterns do you notice?

As you consider your approach to integrating and centering more diverse and inclusive literature into your curriculum, the guidelines in Figure 5.1 may be a helpful start.

FIGURE 5.1 GUIDELINES FOR INCLUSIVE TEXT SELECTION

- **Begin with the premise that public schools never intended to educate all children equally and look for the ways in which this holds true today**. Likewise, the curriculum has never been neutral, but always ideological. In making decisions about what texts to include, look for the voices that are marginalized or missing and bring those voices into your text sets.

- **Center the counternarratives**. Although pairings of traditional canonical texts with voices of color offer rich possibilities for comparison, texts written by and represent historically marginalized groups can also stand on their own.

- **Include a diversity and scope of voices within marginalized groups**. To what extent are you perpetuating or challenging stereotypes based on your patterns of text selection? Are all stories about Black communities only about slavery and oppression? Or do you also share stories that show Black joy, love, creativity, and resilience? Are Asian American characters primarily immigrants who struggle yet succeed, or are they also complex and multidimensional? Are Indigenous peoples only portrayed as existing in the past, or are rich and varied contemporary stories also shared?

- **Be mindful of the positionality of texts and the message this positionality sends**. Are diverse voices centered in the curriculum as core and mentor texts, or are they optional? Does the entire class read *The Great Gatsby* while the books by authors of color are offered as summer reading, book clubs, or literature circles?

- **Know your purpose for adding or removing a text**. Creating a more inclusive curriculum is not simply about replacing texts written by "dead, white males." It is about addressing the racism, sexism, homophobia, and other problematic issues reflected in these texts—and choosing better.

- **Keep the issues facing people of color and Indigenous peoples current**. Racism is not a problem of the past, solved by the Civil Rights era, but a continuing problem today. Create text sets that show the complexities of these issues in both historical and contemporary contexts. Colonization was not an event centered on 1492; settler-colonialism continues today.

- **Resist color-evasive readings of texts**. If a text includes any form of bigotry, be sure to address and unpack this with students. Otherwise, students might see silence as tacit acceptance of these attitudes. Although some teachers may excuse the problems in text as being a product of its time ("That's just how it was back then . . . "), it's important to name for students that racism, sexism, homophobia, transphobia, religious bigotry, and any form of discrimination have always been wrong. What texts reflect is not what was right or wrong "back then," but what those in power believed was right or wrong. Be sure to make this distinction with students so they do not incorrectly conclude that people in the past believed that racism and other forms of discrimination were okay. This belief erases the work of generations of activists who always fought for justice.

- **Understand that not all oppression is the same**. Antiblack racism manifests itself differently than sexism. Drawing a false equivalence among them can cause more harm.

How might the **availability bias** inform our instructional choices? We tend to make choices based on what is readily available—not just what's readily available in our book rooms, but also what's readily available *in our imaginations*. Consider, too, the other biases you learned about in chapter 1. How will your knowledge of these biases help you to better advocate for a more inclusive curriculum?

Addressing Resistance

For many of us, text selection is not within our direct control. We inherit curricula that are decades old. The process for changing curriculum can be cumbersome. The cost to replace books, a determining factor. Yet we also know that the body of literature available to us—and to our students—should be dynamic and rich and varied. To maintain curricula that doesn't change with the times is a disservice to our students. Imagine the message that students receive when the books we choose to study are decades old: does this mean that nothing worthy of study has been published in recent years? Or if the books we choose to study with them are authored primarily by writers who are White: does this mean that there aren't any texts worthy of study by Indigenous and people of color? (of course not!)

As we try to change curricula to be more inclusive, we will inevitably face resistance. Some colleagues or administrators may argue that they don't care "what color the author is" as long as the work is "high quality" (but who defines quality?). Yet this argument fails to consider several critical points:

1. The racial identity of an author *does* matter and has *always* mattered; if it didn't, then Indigenous authors and authors of color would not continue to be disproportionately denied publishing opportunities.

2. The racial identity of the author *can* inform a text by providing an authentic cultural insider perspective.

3. The definition of "quality" has been historically used against people of color to exclude them from spaces of power. Who has historically defined what "quality" is?

4. Many readers—including teachers—are not practiced in analyzing or engaging in discourses that are outside of the literary mainstream.

By removing race from the discussion about text selection, this color-avoidant approach fails to address the racial bias that can and does impact the way teachers and students read and understand texts. Also note that even though it is true that many women, including White women, were often excluded from the canon, *sexism is not a proxy for racism*. Or put another way, while the growing inclusion of voices of White women into the canon may help with gender diversity, this does not address a lack of racial diversity.

As we work to move from being color-avoidant to racially and socially conscious in our text selections, we can start by being intentional about the language we use. The language we use with students speaks volumes, even in small ways, and Figure 5.2 includes some helpful guidelines.

Consider the resistance you may have faced (or anticipate) when you advocate for more inclusive text selections. In what ways can you engage in these conversations productively? In her book *The Art of Coaching*, Dr. Elena Aguilar has some useful question stems that can be helpful in these conversations, including active listening stems (What I'm hearing you say is . . . is that correct?), nonjudgmental responses (I'm interested in learning more about . . .), clarifying questions (It would help me if you could give an example . . .), and probing questions (What do you think would happen if . . .).

FIGURE 5.2 A NOTE ABOUT LANGUAGE WHEN WE TALK ABOUT IDENTITIES AND TEXTS

Be aware of biases built into everyday phrases. Consider my deliberate use of the term *color-avoidant* rather than the more familiar term of *color-blindness*. Associating the physical disability of blindness with ignorance is an example of ableist language. I have also used the word *color-evasive* as a replacement.

Be aware of when you name dominant v. nondominant groups. Reflect on the language you use when referring to texts by dominant versus nondominant groups. Regarding race, for example, do you point out that Toni Morrison was an "African American" writer but call F. Scott Fitzgerald an "American" writer? *Not* naming White as a race, even in these small instances, perpetuates Whiteness as a norm.

Model thoughtfulness, care, and compassion in choosing our words. Although it can be frustrating to know which words are the "right" words to use, especially when referring to marginalized groups, this frustration pales in comparison to the way that thoughtless language can harm others, even if unintentionally. I try to (1) remember that language matters and (2) choose the best word for the specific situation.

Consider the audience and context. For example, I personally identify in any number of ways: Asian American, Asian American Pacific Islander, Filipinx American, person of color, and woman of color. When I want to focus on the shared experiences of individuals and groups within the Asian diaspora, I use Asian American or Asian American Pacific Islander. If I want to be clear about the specific experiences of being Filipinx American, I use that term. If I want to show solidarity with Black, Latinx, and Native Indigenous communities, I use person or woman of color.

Aim for specificity versus general language. When speaking of others, I try to err on the side of being more specific than general so I don't oversimplify or reduce complex and diverse identities. When I booktalk a title like *Frankly in Love,* for example, I make clear that the author David Yoon is Korean American rather than Asian American. When I booktalk *The Poet X,* I make clear that the author Elizabeth Acevedo is Dominican American rather than Latinx. And when I booktalk Cynthia Leitich Smith's *Hearts Unbroken*, I make clear that Smith is not only Native or Indigenous, but a tribally enrolled member of the Muscogee (Creek) nation. For Native or Indigenous individuals and communities, this distinction between the general term and more tribally specific term is especially important as many students may not even realize that Native or Indigenous identity is not only cultural but also political.

Name relevant identities that are often avoided or erased. Consider the ways in which we might marginalize the identities of queer writers. While many high schools teach the work of Oscar Wilde, Tennessee Williams, or Lorraine Hansberry, how many students know that these writers were queer or brought a queer lens to their analysis of their work? Silence can be a form of marginalization and erasure. Because LGBTQ identities may not be as visibly assumed as racial or gender identities, their visibility or lack of visibility in the curriculum—especially for queer students—can be significant.

As educator Lifshitz (2020a) reminds us, "the language we use becomes a habit. And we owe it to our students to use the most inclusive language possible so that it becomes a habit before it has the potential to harm a child."

DESIGNING A PERSPECTIVE-TAKING APPROACH

The paradox of great teaching remains: the longer you teach, the more there is to learn. One of the challenges of teaching is how to "do it all." Indeed, it can be overwhelming to think about how much there is to think about—how to balance strong antibias education and the academic skills kids also need to succeed. But as I mentioned earlier, this is not a case of either-or but *both-and*. **The most rigorous and challenging academic work students can do necessitates a close and careful examination of the biases they bring to their literacy experiences.**

As educator Johnson (2020) points out,

> Teaching children the skills of reading—decoding and comprehension—is critical. Reading skills are, after all, thinking skills. If they master the strategies we teach them, children will indeed be readers who get it—inferences and so much more—"right" much of the time. But will those strategies lead them to be the kind of citizens [who] are galvanized by their reading lives if we fail to teach them to dig deeper and see beyond themselves to other possibilities and move beyond empathy to compassion?

In the following section, we'll look at how we can embed antibias instruction—and the active, intentional perspective-taking that's

integral to developing an antibias mindset—into our literature units. By digging deeper into multiple perspectives, we can help students move toward a compassion that helps students not just be good *at* something—but good *for* something (or *someones*) beyond themselves.

Beyond the Capital-T Text

One of the most critical changes I made in recent years was shifting from teaching a novel to teaching *ideas*, from teaching a *text* to teaching students to wrestle with the *questions* and tensions a text *and other texts* raise.

While this might seem an obvious point, consider the ways in which our language reveals our intentions. When we talk about what we're teaching, we often name a particular *text*: "I'm teaching *Gatsby*" or "We're doing *Scarlet Letter* right now" or "We're doing Shakespeare." While this might be a small point, language matters. Language shapes the way we approach our teaching. When we consistently focus on specific texts, we reduce our discipline to content to be delivered, tested, and regurgitated.

Reading and writing are about the imagination. **We are stewards of stories and of the imaginative possibilities these stories offer.** What we read with students can not only shrink or broaden the individual imaginations of each student but also the collective imagination of a new generation. We need to think beyond the individual texts we teach—even those we might love to teach—and instead wrestle with the **themes and tensions** that can "push against and beyond the boundaries" (hooks) of what we know.

Once I understood this simple fact—**that texts we teach are a *means*, not an ends, to engage the imagination**—how I framed my teaching came into sharp relief.

Suppose an outsider came into your classroom to observe and asked students what they were doing in class. One student responds, "We're reading *1984* right now," and goes back to their book. A second student, however, responds, "We're in the middle of a unit on truth, how we know what's true and not true, and right now, we're reading *1984* to see Orwell's perspective on truth." Which framing would you want your students to have?

Finding the Tension

The wonderful thing about the language arts is that curricula doesn't have to be prescribed in the same way that other disciplines are. While I have many mixed feelings about the College Board, *neither* AP English Literature & Composition nor AP Language & Composition requires students to have read any specific texts or authors. The College Board makes recommendations, but there is *no prescribed text list*. Likewise, for all its shortcomings, even the Common Core does not require any specific text list. This, of course, doesn't mean that teachers don't have limits regarding the texts they teach. After all, text selection is often driven by book closets (and lately, school board) as much as anything else.

For me, the power and purpose of reading has never been about a specific text. No, the **power and purpose of reading lies in the invitation to wrestle with deep tensions in the human experience: to better understand ourselves, others, and the world around us.** When we organize instruction around these tensions, and do so with care and intention, we invite students to participate in a tradition of discourse that is as old as humankind.

Teaching with an antibias lens requires that we set aside the bias our society tends to place on the Text and instead put our students at the center of instruction and plan around the *tensions* (the "big ideas") that can engage their imagination. In Figure 5.3 are examples of tensions that we can invite our students to examine when they read, whether it's fiction, poetry, or nonfiction.

FIGURE 5.3   TENSIONS IN LITERARY STUDY

Acceptance	Failure	Integrity	Power
Achievement	Fairness	Intelligence	Prejudice
Adventure	Faith	Justice	Pride
Anger	Family	Kindness	Privilege
Apprenticeship	Fate	Knowledge	Progress
Beauty	Fear	Language	Protest
Belief	Feminism	Leadership	Purpose
Belonging	Forgiveness	Leisure	Race
Chaos	Fortune	Loss	Reason
Childhood	Freedom	Love	Rebellion
Choice	Friendship	Loyalty	Resistance
Community	Future	Masculinity	Respect
Control	Gender	Memory	Responsibility
Courage	Generosity	Mercy	Sacrifice
Culture	Goodness	Monsters	Safety
Death	Grief	Motivation	Scholarship
Deception	Growth	Movement	Service
Defiance	Happiness	Music	Strength

(Continued)

(Continued)

Determination	Health	Opportunity	Success
Discipline	Heroism	Oppression	Talent
Doubt	Home	Optimism	Trust
Dreams	Honesty	Pain	Truth
Education	Honor	Parenthood	Unity
Empathy	Hope	Passion	Voice
Energy	Hubris	Perseverance	War
Entertainment	Humility	Pleasure	Wealth
Environment	Humor	Politics	Wisdom
Evil	Identity	Poverty	Worth

I use the word *tension* intentionally here to capture the push-and-pull of ideas that can happen when we lean into all the complexities that a text may offer us, when we resist "one size fits all"— or "one theme fits all"—literature study. For example, consider some of the most taught texts: *The Great Gatsby, Of Mice and Men, Things Fall Apart*. None of these texts is about any single theme, and to teach them as such oversimplifies them. One could study the theme of power in *Things Fall Apart*, but the novel could also be studied for the way it explores tensions around feminism, masculinity, politics, leadership, or failure. **The more that we can normalize seeking multiple perspectives—ways of seeing, interpreting—in our classrooms, the more students will seek those multiple perspectives outside the classroom walls.**

To determine what tension to use to organize a unit of study, I consider the following:

1. **Students (Who).** Which tensions will most engage students at this particular time? Knowing our students is critical here: What are their interests? What funds of knowledge (Moll et al., 2006) do they bring from outside school? What topics and tensions have they already studied this year and prior years? Based on your experiences with students in this age or social group, are there particular tensions that would be especially engaging for them?

2. **Context (Where/When).** Because teaching is always personal, local, and contextual, consider the most pressing local, national, and even international issues in the news recently. What issues and related tensions might be in students' social media and news feeds? Our classrooms can be brave spaces where students unpack these issues with the guidance of a skilled teacher as facilitator. The

more that students can see a direct connection between the classroom and their lived experiences outside the classroom, the more authentic and engaging their learning has the potential to be.

3. **Texts (What)**. Are you required to teach particular texts? What tensions or themes do these texts examine? What other texts do you have available to you in your book room or on your district's approved book list? How can you put this text in conversation with other texts with diverse perspectives? What texts can I choose to build students' knowledge base around key issues related to both their own experiences and the most pressing issues we face in society? What texts might provide effective counter-narratives to the dominant narratives or biases students may have?

4. **Skills (How)**. What skills have students been working on and what are the skills they need *next*? What skills will they need to pursue this unit successfully, to study this tension with the complexity and nuance it requires? How can students practice these skills each day or each week during this unit?

Engaging the Questions

After identifying a tension for inquiry, I then turn to Learning for Justice's Antibias Framework and Social Justice Standards. Although I had been developing my own approach to antibias teaching for years, Learning for Justice's framework crystallized my approach, and I draw from their work for instructional planning through an antibias lens. Their complete framework with supporting materials

Learn more about the Social Justice Standards (Southern Poverty Law Center, 2014–2022).

can be found on their website. The Framework for Antibias Education is rooted in the work of educators Derman-Sparks and Edwards (2010) in *Anti-Bias Education for Young Children and Ourselves*. The four domains of the framework are:

- **Identity**: Each child will demonstrate self-awareness, confidence, family pride, and positive social identities.

- **Diversity**: Each child will express comfort and joy with human diversity; accurate language for human differences; and deep, caring human connections.

- **Justice**: Each child will increasingly recognize unfairness, have language to describe unfairness, and understand that unfairness hurts.

- **Action**: Each child will demonstrate empowerment and the skills to act, with others or alone, against prejudice and/or discriminatory actions.

With these domains in mind, I create essential questions around the tension we'll be studying. In Figure 5.4 are the guidelines I've developed to help me craft these essential questions in each domain.

FIGURE 5.4   PLANNING FRAMEWORK FOR CREATING ESSENTIAL QUESTIONS USING SOCIAL JUSTICE STANDARDS

DOMAIN	ESSENTIAL QUESTION	ADDITIONAL QUESTIONS TO EXPLORE
Identity	How does this tension apply to the *self*?	• What do I know about this tension? • What perspectives do I have about this tension? • What experiences in my life have shaped this perspective and how?
Diversity	How does this tension apply or relate to *others*?	• What do others know about or view this tension or theme? • What are others' varied perspectives about this tension? • How have their experiences shaped their perspectives and how?
Justice	How does this tension exist in *society and systems*?	• In what ways do we see this tension reflected in society? • In what ways does this tension manifest itself in larger societal norms, which may be fair or unfair?
Action	How can we *act* to address this tension?	• What would action look like that addresses this tension? • What can we do to make a difference?

In Figure 5.5, you can see some examples of essential questions I've created around three different tensions: *home, storytelling,* and *truth.* Consider the strategies I shared in chapter 3 around helping students unpack their identities. I use many of those strategies in a unit of study on storytelling, using the essential questions below. Figure 5.6 provides a summary of how to put this framework together. As you read on, consider how you might frame these tensions and questions in the context of specific strategies I share.

FIGURE 5.5   ESSENTIAL QUESTIONS AROUND A TENSION

Storytelling	Identity	What stories make up our identity?
	Diversity	What stories make up the identities of others?
	Justice	How can stories be used to amplify and marginalize? Who gets to tell their own stories and those of others? What stories are often centered and what are left out?
	Action	How can we use stories to tell our or "The" Truth?

Home	Identity	What is home to me? Where do I feel most at home? Where do I locate my home?
	Diversity	How do others define home? How do our shared and differing ideas of home reveal cultural and social identities?
	Justice	In what ways have homes—physical, cultural, social—been passed down and protected or threatened and erased?
	Action	How can we ensure that all people have opportunities to build and sustain homes or a sense of home for themselves?
Truth	Identity	How do I know something is true?
	Diversity	How do others perceive truth? How does truth vary, person to person, group to group?
	Justice	How can language clarify and obfuscate the truth in ways that are both fair and unfair?
	Action	How can we use language in ways to tell the truth in socially responsible ways?

FIGURE 5.6   FRAMEWORK FOR PLANNING AROUND A TENSION

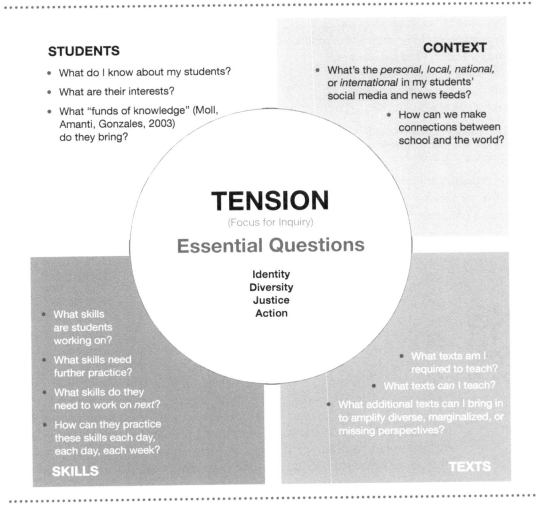

STUDENTS

- What do I know about my students?
- What are their interests?
- What "funds of knowledge" (Moll, Amanti, Gonzales, 2003) do they bring?

CONTEXT

- What's the *personal, local, national,* or *international* in my students' social media and news feeds?
- How can we make connections between school and the world?

TENSION
(Focus for Inquiry)
Essential Questions

Identity
Diversity
Justice
Action

SKILLS

- What skills are students working on?
- What skills need further practice?
- What skills do they need to work on *next*?
- How can they practice these skills each day, each day, each week?

TEXTS

- What texts am I required to teach?
- What texts *can* I teach?
- What additional texts can I bring in to amplify diverse, marginalized, or missing perspectives?

While this framework has helped me to move from focusing on texts to tensions to questions—and thus, inquiry—it might be helpful to familiarize yourself with other frameworks for thinking about how to plan a unit through an antibias lens. Consider, for example, three additional options in Figure 5.7: How might you adapt and integrate elements of these frameworks for your own classroom instruction?

FIGURE 5.7 ADDITIONAL FRAMEWORKS FOR PLANNING A UNIT

In *Cultivating Genius*, Dr. Muhammad (2019) outlines "an equity framework for culturally and historically responsive literacy." Dr. Muhammad recommends framing instruction in a four-tiered approach:

1. Identity development; defining self; making sense of one's values and beliefs
2. Skill development; developing proficiencies through reading and writing meaningful content
3. Intellectual development; gaining knowledge and becoming smarter
4. Criticality; developing the ability to read texts to understand power, authority, and oppression

Likewise, in *Case Studies on Diversity and Social Justice Education*, Gorski and Pothini (2013) propose an Equity Literacy Process that includes the following steps:

1. Identify biases or inequities
2. Take stock of various perspectives
3. Consider possible challenges and opportunities
4. Imagine equitable and just outcomes
5. Brainstorm immediate-term solutions
6. Brainstorm long-term solutions
7. Craft a plan of action

In 2018, educators Dr. Kim Parker, Lorena Germán, Julia Torres, and I outlined an approach to teaching as part of our #DisruptTexts framework. In this framework, we outline four key principles to consider when teaching any unit of study:

1. Continuously interrogate your biases.
2. Center the voices of Black, Indigenous, and People of Color in text selection.
3. Apply a critical literacy lens to your teaching practices.
4. Work in communities with other antibias, anti-racist educators.

Read this primer about the #DisruptTexts framework.

The Role of Texts in an Antibias Framework

As antibias teachers seeking to build students' capacity for perspective-taking, we can better capture the full breadth and depth of human diversity through more equitable text choices. I spend some time discussing this need later in this chapter, but here I want to briefly point out the need to *plan for diverse and inclusive text selection from the beginning of a unit of study* rather than treat diversity and inclusion as an "add-on" to an already existing unit.

This might seem at odds with my previous argument that the texts we teach are a *means*, not an end, to engage the imagination. But as a *means*, texts play a critical role. Note that I refer to texts in the *plural* here. Once we've identified the tension and questions for a unit of study, we can and must bring in representative and inclusive texts that can offer diverse perspectives. And because antibias education is about addressing inequities, we must work to *center and amplify* the voices of historically marginalized groups—the counternarratives—when building rich text sets for our students.

Figure 5.8 outlines how text selection plays an important role in planning a unit around the tension *home*, for example, and the essential questions that form the basis of our inquiry. As you can see, many of the text selections focus specifically on Native and Indigenous writers. This is intentional. Too often, when a work by a Native or Indigenous writer is included—or of any cultural or racial group—it is the only one that students might read that year, or even their entire school experience. Unfortunately, when students only encounter one or two stories from a particular cultural or racial group, those one or two stories end up doing the work of becoming representative of that entire group.

For example, consider how even great works like *Beloved* may inadvertently become representative of the entire Black and African American experience. Or how a novel by Amy Tan might represent all Asian American experiences. In the unit outline in Figure 5.8, I intentionally included diverse Native voices to make sure that students do not see any single text as being representative or definitive. Societal biases tend to "flatten" and make the same all members who belong to a cultural racial group, erasing the rich diversity within them. Any time we can disrupt this bias is critical work.

FIGURE 5.8   UNIT OF STUDY FOCUSING ON HOME

SOCIAL JUSTICE DOMAIN	ESSENTIAL QUESTIONS	TEXTS*	STUDENT LEARNING
Identity	What is home to me? Where do I feel most at home? Where do I locate my home? (*focus on self*)	"A House Called Tomorrow" by Alberto Rios (poem) "Those Winter Sundays" by Robert Hayden (poem) "Perhaps the World Ends Here" by Joy Harjo (poem) "Where I'm From" by Renee Watson (poem) "This I Believe" essays on the theme of *home*.	Read poems and journal about what home means to them. Create home maps in their writer's notebooks (p. 103) Write their own "This I Believe" essay or poem about what home means to them.

(Continued)

(Continued)

SOCIAL JUSTICE DOMAIN	ESSENTIAL QUESTIONS	TEXTS*	STUDENT LEARNING
Diversity	How do others define home? How do our shared and differing ideas of home reveal cultural and social identities? (*focus on others*)	*Away from Home: American Indian Boarding School Experiences, 1879–2000* edited by K. Tsianina Lomawaima, Brenda J. Child, Margaret L. Archuleta (book)	Compare and contrast how home is defined by different individuals, cultures, and contexts.
Justice	In what ways have homes—physical, cultural, social—been passed down and protected or threatened and erased? (*focus on systems*)	*Unspoken: America's Native American Boarding Schools*, PBS (Video) *#NotYourPrincess* edited by Charleyboy and Leatherdale (book) *American Indian Stories* by Zitkala-Sa (memoir)	Trace and analyze the ways in which homes and land rights are intertwined. Identify patterns of systemic oppression *and* examples of collective healing, resilience, and joy.
Action	How can we ensure that all people have opportunities to build and sustain homes or a sense of home for themselves? (*focus on action*)	Literature circles with children's books centered on the theme of home (Examples: *Going Home, Coming Home* by Truong Tran, *Where Three Oceans Meet* by Rajani Larocca, *When I was Eight* by Christy Jordan-Fenton and Margaret Pokiak-Fenton, *Forever Cousins* by Laurel Goodluck) Excerpt from *There, There* by Tommy Orange *The Marrow Thieves* by Cherie Dimaline (novel) Literature circles with novels (Examples: *Hearts Unbroken* by Cynthia Leitich-Smith, *How I Became a Ghost* by Tim Tingle, *My Name is Not Easy* by Debby Dahl Edwardson, *If I Ever Get Out of Here* by Eric Gansworth)	Learn about Native tribes and nations and their efforts at decolonization and fights for their sovereign rights. Discuss the issue of racism of Native mascots on professional and school athletic teams. Learn about the Indian Child Welfare Act and recent efforts to dismantle the law (Season 2 of the podcast *This Land*). Outcomes may include letter-writing, awareness campaigns, opinion-editorials, and other projects. Students collaborate in groups to research and determine a potential action step(s).

SOCIAL JUSTICE DOMAIN	ESSENTIAL QUESTIONS	TEXTS*	STUDENT LEARNING
		Conversations with Native Americans About Race (*NY Times* opinion documentary)	
		Dawnland (documentary)	
		"Thoughts on Resistance" by Rebecca Roanhorse (essay)	
		Select episodes from TV series, *Reservation Dogs* ("Decolonativization") and/ or from *Rutherford Falls* ("Land Back")	
		Online exhibits from the Smithsonian National Museum of the American Indian	

*Please note that this is a small selection of possible texts that are widely available and would enhance students' learning in this unit.

Framing a Unit for Perspective-Taking

The old adage that success is 90 percent preparation and 10 percent perspiration holds true as much in teaching as it does in any other area.

Because of the **framing effect,** how we choose to introduce a text to students is perhaps one of the most critical decisions we make as teachers.

The **framing effect** is a simple but powerful cognitive bias: how we introduce an issue or topic affects the way we interpret all subsequent information and make

▶ I learned to think from a new perspective. Even though I've always had my own opinions I learned in our class discussions that I should stay open-minded to new perspectives and opinions that I may not have bothered to consider or had thought about.

—11th-grade student

decisions. This seems so obvious that it almost seems not worth mentioning, but it's precisely because the framing effect *is* so ubiquitous that we need to pay more careful attention. In marketing, an example of the framing effect occurs when customers are introduced to two of the exact same product but are only framed differently: a drink that is 20 percent fat versus 80 percent fat free can be perceived very differently. While such contrasts aren't always as clear in our classrooms, consider how the following two approaches to introducing *The Great Gatsby* frame the text for students:

Approach 1

After asking students to brainstorm a list of prior knowledge they have about the 1920s, the teacher then presents a brief overview of the time period. Most of the information is conveyed through a slide deck that includes the following information:

- Post-war 1920s economic prosperity in the lead-up to the Great Depression

- Cultural shifts, including the changing role of women, prohibition, and popular music such as jazz

- Facts about F. Scott Fitzgerald, including themes common in his work and the relationships he had with other writers as part of the "Lost Generation"

- Basic overview of setting, characters, and plot

- Images of flappers, speakeasies, Al Capone, and New York City sprinkled throughout various slides

Approach 2

Students enter the classroom to see stations set up around the room that include various texts to be studied in small groups. As students work their way through the stations, they are asked to consider how they describe the 1920s in the United States, citing evidence from the various texts as support. Texts may include:

- A variety of cover art for the novel throughout its publication history

- A sampling of music from prominent artists such as Duke Ellington and Louis Armstrong

- A collection of images of fashion for men and women from the 1920s

- A newspaper headline and image of Italian immigrants in New York city in 1923

- An opinion piece titled, "A Century Ago America Built Another Kind of Wall," which chronicles restriction in immigration laws

- A news article titled, "The Untold Story of Asian Americans in Early Hollywood," with images of Asian American actors from the early 1900s

- A sampling of poems from writers of the Harlem Renaissance

- An article about "Black Wall Street" in Tulsa, OK, during the early 1900s

- A news podcast summarizing the harmful impact of American Indian boarding schools at the turn of the twentieth century

- Movie trailers for the two major film adaptations for *The Great Gatsby*: the 1974 film directed by Jack Clayton, featuring Robert Redford as Gatsby, and the 2013 film directed by Baz Luhrmann, featuring Leonardo DiCaprio as Gatsby

As you reflect on these two approaches, consider what implicit and explicit messages these two approaches send and how they differ.

1. **Students as Creators of Knowledge**

   At first glance, one major difference between the two approaches is in how students are positioned as learners. In the first approach, students are generally passive, taking notes and receiving information predetermined by the teacher. The information shared in the second approach is also predetermined by the teacher, but students are clearly positioned in a more active inquiry stance as they construct knowledge together.

2. **Multiple Perspectives including Intentional Counternarratives**

   But aside from the difference in learning stance, notice how many more perspectives about the 1920s are offered in the second approach. In the first approach—an approach which I admit I used for many years—the information shared with students might be like what you learned when you read *The Great Gatsby* in school. One could argue that the information presented in the first approach represents a **dominant narrative** about the 1920s (even a quick glance at teaching materials for *Gatsby* on Teachers Pay Teachers confirms this dominant narrative). The perspectives in the second approach are more varied and while certainly not definitive, they represent more voices and experiences from the 1920s time period.

Thus, the *first* thing we should consider when we approach teaching any piece of literature is how we can use the **framing effect** to our advantage. Rather than frame the 1920s in one way—*as a set of facts to learn*—the second approach offers multiple and varied **counternarratives** about the 1920s. Students will still build essential background knowledge, but such knowledge will be rich and varied and nuanced. These counternarratives extend beyond the particular world and setting created by Fitzgerald's text. After all, if *Gatsby* is considered the "Great American Novel," it's incumbent upon us to ask, *whose America?*

Prepare for Tensions That May Challenge Students

Finally, when teaching a text that deals with issues that you know could be challenging for your students, one reflection strategy to prepare is to

ask two clarifying questions: (1) **What's the best-case scenario in teaching this text?** (2) **What's the worst-case scenario in teaching this text?**

When my colleagues and I taught Octavia Butler's *Kindred*, we talked through our best- and worst-case scenarios. Published in 1979, *Kindred* is the story of a Black woman named Dana who is transported back in time from her California home in 1976 to a Maryland plantation in 1815. In the tradition of speculative fiction and Afrofuturism, Butler's novel asks readers to consider questions about the ongoing impact of the past generally, and slavery specifically, on who we are in the present.

> ▶ "The notion that a curriculum writer's or teacher's intention matters misses the point: Intentionality is not a prerequisite for harmful teaching. Intentionality is also not a prerequisite for racism. As I define it in my work, curriculum violence occurs when educators and curriculum writers have constructed a set of lessons that damage or otherwise adversely affect students intellectually and emotionally."
>
> – Stephanie P. Jones, "Ending Curriculum Violence"

In the case of teaching *Kindred*, my best-case scenarios include the following:

- That Black students feel validated, valued, and affirmed in whatever way they can.

- That White students' understanding of racism and slavery is made more complicated, nuanced, deepened—and that this knowledge helps them to unpack their own racial identities in ways that help them think and act in more just and antiracist ways.

- That nonBlack students of color can deepen their own understanding of race and become invested in the dismantling of racism along the false Black-White binary.

In my best-case scenario, reading *Kindred* is empowering for all my students—not necessarily in the same way, but in the ways each student needs.

On the other hand, my worst-case scenarios were multiple and varied, not least among them were the following:

- That students walk away from the novel with a simplistic understanding of racism ("Slavery was terrible; I'm glad that's over!")

- That students of color, particularly Black students, are harmed either through my own words and actions or those of their peers', regardless of our intentions

By naming my worst-case scenarios—but also keeping the best-case scenario in my line of vision—I can be more intentional in my instructional choices and hopefully stay true to my cardinal rule as a teacher: first, do no harm.

READING AGAINST OUR BIASES

For the first few years of my teaching career, I taught books. On good days, you could even say I taught literature, sometimes even capital-L Literature (notice my bias). I thought I was doing good work—and it was work I knew how to do well. After all, my love for books was one of the primary reasons I went into teaching.

But in the second half of my teaching career, I came to this realization: as much as I believe that literature and the imaginative possibilities that it offers are numerous and rich and limitless, I see my role as a *literacy* teacher. A literature teacher teaches books and everything that they have to offer. A *literacy* teacher, on the other hand, teaches not what, but *how*: how to read, think, wonder, critique, evaluate, interrogate, compose, deconstruct, unpack, analyze, question, compare, contrast, synthesize, recommend, and act.

> *A literacy teacher . . . teaches not what, but how: how to read, think, wonder, critique, evaluate, interrogate, compose, deconstruct, unpack, analyze, question, compare, contrast, synthesize, recommend, and act.*

Thus, no matter the text or context, perhaps the most important skill we can and must teach students to do is to *reason*, and to *reason well*. **And to do that, students need to identify and engage with the biases that too often impede our ability to reason.**

Some might argue that teaching cognitive biases is more suited to a psychology or social science course rather than an English class. But every time we've studied biases in class, students often share that it's one of the most powerful (and engaging) things they've learned. While there are any number of ways to teach students about different biases, here's what has worked for me and my students.

First, I assign each student a different cognitive bias to research. I typically use the list curated by The School of Thought, which is available online. My directions are simple:

24 Cognitive Biases (The School of Thought)

1. Research your bias: What is it? Who discovered it? When? How?

2. Provide examples: Where does this bias most often occur in our lives? Why? If you have committed this bias, when and how?

3. Share solutions: How can we fight against this bias? What works?

Each student then teaches the class about their bias. Presentations usually consist of a few slides and last about five minutes each. Students in the audience take notes and ask questions. Because it can be overwhelming to learn about twenty-four or more biases at once, I pause after every four to five students and have students discuss in groups:

- Which of these biases so far feel most relatable to you? How?

- What makes this bias particularly challenging or potentially negative? In other words, what are the implications or consequences?

After we finish all the presentations, we review. Sometimes our review is as straightforward as a class Kahoot or other game, and sometimes students perform skits illustrating the biases. Other times, students go on a bias scavenger hunt, bringing in examples of the biases they start to notice in their daily lives (including their social media feeds, where they tend to be, unfortunately, abundant).

In the next chapter, we'll look at how students can also apply their knowledge of biases to their reading. In the meantime, Figure 5.9 lists some resources to teach about bias.

FIGURE 5.9   RESOURCES FOR TEACHING ABOUT BIAS

- "How Alexandra Bell is Disrupting Racism in Journalism" by Doreen St. Félix in *The New Yorker*

- "Immaculate perception" by Jerry Kang at TEDxSanDiego (2013)

- "26 Mini-Films for Exploring Race, Bias and Identity With Students" from *The New York Times*

- "Your Lying Mind" by Ben Yagoda in *The Atlantic*

- "The Mind of the Village: Understanding Our Implicit Biases" by Shankar Vedantam, Hidden Brain podcast

- The Decision Lab (glossary of biases available online)

- Cognitive Bias: How to Make Objective Decisions from Mind Tools

How can we get free through intentional, practiced **perspective-taking?**

Over the years, I've come to the realization that one of the most important goals of education is to help move kids to complex thinking. That might seem an obvious point, but I think it's precisely because it is that we also take it for granted.

Whenever I taught argument writing, I began by asking students what their reasoning skills were like when they were younger. While they're puzzled by my question, there's a general murmur of agreement: "Not very good." We laugh a little about some of the faulty thinking they used to have when they were younger. When I ask students what the biggest difference is between how they used to think as five- or six-year-olds and how they think now as teenagers, they generally agree that when they were younger, they saw the world as "black and white." (I think the fact that so many students over the years cite the specific binary of "black and white" is . . . notable.) As they get older, students share, they learn to see beyond "good versus evil" or "right versus wrong." As they grow, they become capable of and exercise more complex thinking. Again, this might seem obvious, something that just happens in terms of cognitive development as students' brains mature.

Yet, again, I don't think we can take this for granted. After all, even as adults, it's easy for us to fall into either-or traps of thinking or to accept, as given, many dominant (and harmful) narratives we have about the most important issues of our time. Every day, in our news and social media feeds, we can see the way that fear and bias are used to manipulate the public, and our kids are not immune to this.

But as Eberhardt reminds us, "Neither our evolutionary path nor our present culture dooms us to be held hostage by bias. Change requires a kind of open-minded attention that is well within our reach" (7). Every day in our classrooms, we can engage in an "open-minded attention" that not only protects kids against biased thinking traps but also empowers them to seek perspectives beyond their own and beyond those loudest in the room or on their devices.

In this chapter, we'll explore strategies we can practice with our students as they read, respond, and interpret texts and the world beyond those texts. We can seek answers to questions like the following: *What other possibilities exist? Whose voice or perspective am I missing? Whose voices or perspectives have I dismissed and why? What do I have to learn here? How can I know better, think expansively, and see more clearly?* We can make *looking again, behind, next to* a habit of mind.

So let's get looking.

CHAPTER 6

PERSPECTIVE-TAKING
AND PERSPECTIVE-
BENDING

Strategies for Reading Instruction

> *Reading always requires critical perception, interpretation, and "rewriting" what is read. Its task is to unveil what is hidden in the text. I always say to the students with whom I work, "Reading is not walking on the words; it's grasping the soul of them."*
>
> —Paolo Freire

I used to think that we are what we read, that what we choose to read is a direct or indirect reflection of who we are as people. But I realize now that it's not just what, but how—*in other words, we are* how *we read.*

In Chapter 3, we examined some of the ways we can help students unpack their identities. When students understand themselves—can see themselves more clearly—they can also begin to understand those around them. Like all things, however, to do this well also requires practice—intentional, consistent practice in perspective-taking.

▶ When students are practiced in **perspective-taking,** they exercise the flexibility and empathy required to understand issues and ideas from multiple points of view. In fact, I'd argue that given the problems we face in the world today, we need more young people who are practiced in seeing issues from varying, even contradictory perspectives.

This work of perspective-taking is, of course, perfectly suited to our work in the language arts. After all, consider how much of our work is about helping students to develop empathy with and for other experiences through their reading. But what I've realized over the years is that while it's true that students can develop empathy for characters and experiences through reading, it's also true that without a thoughtful and intentional examination of the biases they hold (as well as the ones we hold as teachers), our reading experiences can fall woefully short. In fact, reading might only confirm our preexisting biases further. Understanding the *facts* of a text in the context of our classrooms is one thing—but understanding *what we and others respond to in that text and why that matters*—those are the critical literacy skills that our students need to exercise in the world.

By taking an antibias approach, as teachers, we can reframe our literacy instruction to take advantage of the powerful opportunities for perspective-taking that literature provides. Just as teachers need to be aware of the perspectives and biases they bring into the classroom, we can also help students become more mindful of the ones that they too carry. Students are not blank vessels, waiting to be filled with the knowledge that we provide to them. We can help students become more aware of how their biases, identities, and experiences (or lack thereof) affect the way they respond to texts at every stage of their reading process: before, during, and after.

BEFORE READING: ANALYZING THE PERSPECTIVES WE BRING TO READING

In chapter 3, recall the "identity inventory" reflection I adapted from Learning for Justice to help students unpack who they are. This inventory asked students to consider several dimensions of their identity:

- Gender
- Race
- Sexual Orientation
- National origin or immigration status
- Socioeconomic status
- Home Language(s)
- Religion/Spiritual practice
- Ability
- Age

Rather than using this inventory as something to do as a get-to-know-you activity at the beginning of the year (and then forgotten), I use it as a touchstone that we return to repeatedly in our notebooks throughout the year. Some of the most pressing issues we face as a society—and that are most difficult to talk about are reflected in this inventory (in fact, they're also reflected in most of the great literature we teach!). Sexism, transphobia, racism, homophobia, xenophobia, classism, religious discrimination, ableism, ageism—these are problems that need to be addressed, disrupted, and dismantled, but as I have said here and elsewhere, **we cannot disrupt systems of oppression if we don't first understand how systems of oppression work; and we can't understand how systems of oppression work until we understand how they have worked on us.**

This internal work matters . . . really matters.

To read, write, and *reason* well, we must have a full awareness of the ways in which our personal identities and biases play a role. Recall, for example, the "Writing Through Identity Lenses" exercise in chapter 3 (p. 142). Later in this chapter, you'll see a similar exercise, "Responding Through Our Identity" (p. 185) that asks students to consider how their identities both implicitly and explicitly informs their reading—and more importantly, how to think critically about this.

In this section, we'll review some strategies—some familiar and some new—that help students consider what identities, experiences, and background knowledge they're bringing to a text.

Anticipating and Planning for What Students *Don't* Know

While the strategies on the following pages ask students to consider what identities, experiences, and background knowledge they bring to their reading experiences, sometimes students' lack of background knowledge about a topic becomes not just a challenge but also a barrier.

(Continued)

(Continued)

A few years ago, I asked my students to read Valentine's (2018) *New York Times* opinion piece, "P.C. Languages Saved My Life" In it, Valentine argues that gender-neutral language was a "lifeline" that allowed him to feel fully comfortable as someone who didn't conform to gender binaries when he was growing up. It was the type of argument that I believed could serve at least three distinct purposes:

- Provide a well-written mentor text for argument that students could analyze for its rhetoric and craft.

- Provide a mirror text for students in the room who may have gender nonbinary identities.

- Provide a window text for cisgender students into experiences different from their own.

While Valentine's essay did accomplish these purposes, I had a student in the class who shut down and argued that it made them uncomfortable to read the essay—much less analyze it, as they had been assigned to do. When I heard this, I couldn't help wonder how much of their resistance to the essay was because of the topic of gender identity. I was ready to defend the topic's inclusion in class.

Read "P.C. Languages Saved My Life" by Gioncarlo Valetine

But when I spoke with the student, I realized that the barrier wasn't really the content (or at least, not only the content). Yes, the student was uncomfortable, but as we talked, I realized it wasn't the content as much as it was their lack of background knowledge about the topic. Because this was the only text that they had ever read regarding gender-neutral pronouns and nonconforming gender identities, this student lacked the schema necessary to access the text. This lack of schema frustrated them. Furthermore, for students who might be academically high achieving, the lack of schema might not only be frustrating but also threaten their sense of being "good" students.

Our students come to us with varying levels of schema for any number of issues. While that's an obvious point, it's one we need to remember as teachers, especially when it comes to helping them analyze and write complex arguments. While students bring their *misconceptions* when responding to arguments, their *lack of schema is also a form of bias.* When schools fail to provide students with a curriculum that captures the rich diversity and breadth of human experiences, especially those of Black, Brown, and LGBTQ+ communities, students will not have the background knowledge they need to be able to make meaning of the issues they see, hear, and read about as they continue through school.

So, what can teachers do? After all, we can spend our entire lifetime trying to learn the histories and experiences of those different from ourselves (or even our own history and experiences as people of color)—and it would still not be enough. I've found the following helpful:

- **Know your students.** What background do you think they will have about this topic? Survey students ahead of time to get a sense of what they both know and don't know about the topic. Do not assume what students know or don't know. They might (and often do) surprise us (for better or worse).

- **Identify the dominant narrative.** Even if it seems like your students have very little background knowledge, note that this could be itself a *dominant narrative.* In other words, *not knowing* about a particular topic may convey a dominant narrative that that topic is not *worth* knowing. The *lack* of background knowledge about a topic is important to point out. For example, many students may know nothing about Claudette Colvin, who was another young Black woman who refused to give her seat on the bus during the 1960s Civil Rights movement. Asking students why that might be the case is critical. Colvin refused to give up her seat *before* Rosa Parks did, yet Parks is the name almost all students know. Why is that?

- **Teach the counternarrative.** Once you determine what students know and don't know—especially what potentially harmful or incomplete dominant narratives they have—decide what essential background information they will need to *counter* this lack of

Learn more: "Before Rosa Parks, there was Claudette Colvin."

schema. What information do they need to engage with this upcoming text or unit in a more responsible, thoughtful way? How can you teach what's needed in a way that is *constructive* versus didactic?

(Continued)

(Continued)

- **Plan for different starting points.** There will be times when some students may have rich background knowledge, while some students have very little, and still others have biased or misinformation about the topic. As you plan, consider how you might make sure that whatever students' schema may be, that you ensure a *common starting point* or set of *shared assumptions* on the onset.

- **Remember to do your own work, continuously.** Of course, being able to do any of the above well means that we, as teachers, must do our own work so that we can plan for what misinformation (or disinformation) constitutes students' schema. We will need to understand the complicated and subtle ways that oppressive ideas are sometimes used to justify or explain racially inequitable outcomes or realities. For example, in a discussion about an issue such as college admissions, some students may argue that one reason affirmative action was wrong is because Black and Brown students had a difficult time at college because they were admitted to colleges that they were unqualified to attend. However, this "mismatch theory" has been debunked by legal scholars (Chingos, 2015; Lempert, 2016; Turetsky & Purdie-Vaughns, 2015). Although the Supreme Court banned racial preferences in college admissions in 2023, some students may point out that legacy admission, which was not banned, disproportionately favors White students. Because issues such as college admissions are topics that students are interested in, we must make sure that we do our own due diligence in understanding the way that bias or misinformation can manifest in class discussions. (Chingos, 2015; Lempert, 2016; Turetsky & Purdie-Vaughns, 2015)

Modified K-W-L Chart

One of the first strategies I remember learning as a student teacher was the K-W-L chart (What I Know, What I Want to Know, and What I Want to Learn). When students assess their own current understanding of a topic, they are in a better position to be able to take an informed approach to the text or topic of study.

And as teachers, we also know how important it is to know what knowledge students are bringing with them into the classroom. More than once, I've found myself teaching a concept only to discover that some, if not all, of my teaching was redundant as students already had sufficient working knowledge from a previous English teacher or from their Social Studies classes. Or I might have assumed students to have sufficient working knowledge that they did not. Thus, by accessing student's prior knowledge, we can build new knowledge more effectively. For example, before studying *The Crucible*, I survey students about what they know about the Salem Witch Trials and McCarthyism, and likewise, before we read *Things Fall Apart*, I ask students what they know about Africa and imperialism.

All that said, I think we inadvertently do a disservice to our students when we ask only about what *facts* they know. Taking a critical literacy lens means that all knowledge is a social construction, that learning is not just about the acquisition of new knowledge but also about the meaning that we ascribe to that knowledge (Sensoy & DiAngelo, 2017). Therefore, we need to help students unpack not just *what* they know, but *how* they know what they know, and then to assess the *attitudes, feelings, beliefs,* and *biases* that inform or result from this knowledge.

One way we can do this is by tweaking the traditional K-W-L chart as fifth-grade teacher Jess Lifshitz does with her own students whenever they begin an inquiry (Figure 5.8). As you can see, Lifshitz (2020b) asks students to consider not what they *know* but what they have *heard.* Notice too her choice of the words: *probably, skeptical, uncertain.* This is a critical distinction to make because students enter the conversation from a stance of humility rather than certainty. Moreover, Lifshitz asks students to also consider the biases they have as they begin their research.

Figure 6.1 offers a sample chart completed just before students begin a unit focusing on Native and Indigenous writers. Although the information here isn't verbatim, it's typical of the responses students have shared. As you can see, asking students to name what they already (and "probably") think or heard is true can be very helpful in understanding what knowledge, or lack thereof, students have—*and most importantly,* it gives me an opportunity to correct any misconceptions and provide accurate information up front. I can't emphasize how important this is. How many times have you found yourself partway teaching a unit or novel and a student makes a comment that makes it clear that they were either missing critical background information or had been making false assumptions? For example, in Figure 6.1, here are the handful of things I know I would need to address, either immediately or in the course of our study:

- While it's true that European colonizers did oppress and kill many Native and Indigenous peoples, I would also need to make sure that students understand that there are many strong Native and Indigenous peoples, communities, and nations present *today.* *Teacher action*: will be important to focus away from oppression-only and toward strengths and resilience-based narratives.

- The idea of "special rights" granted to Native and Indigenous peoples is one that will need clarification, beginning with what "rights" students are referring to. Here, students could be referring to the rights Native individuals have in accordance to their enrollment in a specific Native or tribal nation. But students could also be referring to harmful narratives they may have heard about special preferences Native students get when applying to colleges. *Teacher action*: Knowing what misinformation students might be carrying and needs correcting is critical.

- Referring to "what happened in the past," which is often how students describe atrocities committed against Native peoples, perpetuates the idea that these were isolated incidents that have passed rather than part of an ongoing pattern of injustice against Native peoples that continues today. *Teacher action*: Be sure to include examples of current day forms of discrimination.

FIGURE 6.1 IDENTIFYING PRIOR KNOWLEDGE, POTENTIAL MISCONCEPTIONS, OPINIONS, AND BIASES

What have you ALREADY heard about this topic that you believe is probably true?	What have you ALREADY heard about this topic that you are skeptical or uncertain of?	What are your personal opinions of this topic? What biases might you already have?	What questions do you hope to find answers to through your reading or research?
European colonizers oppressed and killed Native and Indigenous populations.	Native people get special rights that give them advantages.	I think it's wrong what happened in the past. I don't know.	Learn more about different ways Native people told stories.

K–T–D Chart

Before students can take on and deeply appreciate the perspectives of others, it's important that they first take time to consider their own perspectives—to take an inventory of what they know and don't know. After identifying a key topic in the literature to be studied—perhaps a theme or time period, such as "The Roaring 20s"—I ask students to open their notebook and take a moment to assess what they know, what they think they know, and what they don't know.

WHAT I KNOW	WHAT I THINK I KNOW	WHAT I DON'T KNOW

The value of this exercise, like in Lifshitz's modified K-W-L chart, is that it asks students to consider their *actual* knowledge versus the knowledge they *think* they have. In fact, every time I have used this quickwrite with students, they almost always comment that writing down what they *know* in the first column is very difficult for them. The mere presence of the middle column—what they *think* they know— forces students to pause and question their confidence in what they know. They begin, therefore, from a stance of humility. It is this stance of humility which allows students to be, as Wheatley reminds us, more open to be "willing to be disturbed" (p. 75).

Beyond Prior Knowledge With an Open-Ended Survey

Depending on the literature we're about to study, sometimes the most powerful way for me to understand what perspectives and biases students potentially bring to our learning is to design a simple, open-ended reflection survey. This is especially critical if the literature deals with issues that may be difficult for students to discuss. When it comes to these potentially difficult issues, as a teacher, I need to not only understand what *cognitive* schema they have, but also what *emotional* or *moral* schema they carry with them as well. **In other words, it's not just what they *know* but how they *feel* and what they *believe*.**

When my students and I read Octavia Butler's *Kindred*, I knew that because the novel centers on issues related to slavery and racism, many students had difficulty during class discussion. We also know that as a whole, schools are not doing a particularly good job in teaching a full and accurate history of American slavery (Stewart, 2019). This difficulty is compounded by the fact that I taught the novel in a predominantly White school where discussions about race and racism are sometimes harder to develop—not because race is *inherently* harder to talk about for White students, but because they are often *unpracticed* in doing so. Depending on the racial makeup or culture of your school, the level of comfort or discomfort students have in talking about race and racism may differ.

No matter what the context, however, the less we assume and the more we know what students are bringing to the conversation, we can put ourselves in the best position to predict moments that could be difficult or even traumatic for the students entrusted to our care. Asking students, confidentially, to share their concerns is one way we can set the tone for the honesty and vulnerability necessary for conversations about race and to understand *what perspectives students are bringing with them into the room.*

Figure 6.2 shows the questions that I used before teaching *Kindred.* Depending on how students respond to these questions, I adjust my instruction accordingly. For example, teaching a class with a majority of students who do *not* believe talking about race or racism is important (question 5) will need a different approach than a class in which the majority of students believe it is. And of course, giving students space in this survey to give voice to those concerns, directly and confidentially to me, can also help alleviate some anxiety they might be feeling while also helping me to meet students where they are in their understanding.

FIGURE 6.2   OPEN-ENDED REFLECTION SURVEY FOR *KINDRED*

1. In discussions about race and racism, I generally feel . . .

   a. angry
   b. annoyed
   c. comfortable
   d. confident
   e. curious
   f. excited
   g. fearful
   h. hopeful
   i. motivated
   j. nervous
   k. passionate
   l. shy
   m. thoughtful
   n. tired
   o. understanding
   p. unsure
   q. other: _____

2. Choose TWO of the words above that you feel most strongly about and briefly explain: why do you feel this way? under what circumstances? for what reasons?

3. Choose ONE of the words above that you DID NOT choose and briefly explain: why does this NOT apply to you?

4. I talk about race or racism . . .
   Never   1   2   3   4   5   Always

5. I believe it is important to talk about race or racism . . .

Not at all 1 2 3 4 5 Very Important

6. It is hard for most people to talk about race or racism.

Disagree 1 2 3 4 5 Agree

7. If you would like to explain any of your ratings in statements 4-6, please feel free to use the space below.

8. Complete and explain in a few brief sentences: The first time I learned about slavery, I . . .

9. Complete and explain in a few brief sentences: More recently regarding slavery, I learned . . .

10. Complete and explain in a few brief sentences: Knowing that *Kindred* centers around issues of race, racism, and slavery, some concerns or questions I have are . . .

Beyond Anticipation Guides: Four Corners, Spectrum, Meet in the Middle

Anticipation guides may not be new, but they can sometimes be overlooked. Comprising several statements that have a thematic connection to a text, anticipation guides activate prior knowledge and ask students to take some time to consider their own perspectives before starting a text. Setting aside even a few minutes for students to reflect can help to continue to build a habit of self-reflection as students ask themselves, what do I think and why?

In Figure 6.3, for example, are a few anticipation guide statements I have asked students to consider before our study of Chinua Achebe's *Things Fall Apart*.

FIGURE 6.3 ANTICIPATION GUIDE FOR *THINGS FALL APART*

	DISAGREE			AGREE	
Masculinity is defined by physical strength.	1	2	3	4	5
Hard work is necessary for self-respect.	1	2	3	4	5
Success can be judged by material wealth.	1	2	3	4	5
Keeping traditions is more important than change.	1	2	3	4	5
As a man dances, the drums beat for him. (proverb from the novel)	1	2	3	4	5

As you create your own anticipation guide statements, some considerations:

- Can these statements be used across multiple texts or units? Using an anticipation guide at the beginning of a unit of study can be a way to frame a more expansive line of inquiry. See Figure 6.4 for an anticipation guide for a unit of study exploring resilience.

- What is the tension you're exploring with this text or unit? How might you frame your statements to reflect the various aspects of this tension?

FIGURE 6.4 ANTICIPATION GUIDE FOR *RESILIENCE*

	DISAGREE			AGREE	
Overcoming obstacles is necessary for a person to grow.	1	2	3	4	5
There are some challenges that are impossible to overcome.	1	2	3	4	5
It's easier to overcome a challenge when working with others.	1	2	3	4	5
To be resilient, you have to accept that life is not always fair.	1	2	3	4	5
Having a positive outlook is the best way to deal with challenges.	1	2	3	4	5

After students have rated each of these statements, I often ask students to reflect on a select few from across the spectrum of their responses: one they agree with, one they disagree with, and one they might feel more neutral about. Students reflect by journaling in their writer's notebooks. From there, they might then turn and talk to a neighbor.

While it's helpful for students to reflect privately or in small groups—and there are situations where this more private reflection is sufficient—the power of anticipation guides can be amplified when students can see and hear the perspectives of others. To do this, I project some of the statements and ask students to move to the area in the room that best reflects their point-of-view.

- In **Four Corners**, students move to one of the corners labeled: strongly agree, agree, disagree, and strongly disagree. Once in their corner, students turn to talk to one to explain why they chose that corner.

- In **Spectrum**, students stand in a line, choosing a position along the spectrum from strongly disagree to strongly agree. They then turn to a person next to share their rating.

After students move around the room, I often ask students in each area to share so that students can also hear from those who disagree with them. Another way to encourage students to hear alternative perspectives is an extension I call *Meet in the Middle*.

- In **Meet in the Middle**, students begin in one of the four corners of the room. I ask them to make eye contact with someone in an opposite corner (students who strongly disagree meet with those who strongly agree; students who disagree meet with those who agree). This works best when there are generally equal numbers of students in each corner, but students can also meet in groups of three. If working in pairs, this is also an excellent opportunity for students to practice *constructivist listening dyads* (see Chapter 4).

- Depending on the size of the class and the distribution of the corners, I've also had students form groups of four in which groups are comprised of one student from each corner so that the entire spectrum of opinions is represented.

> ▶ I learned through class discussion that every person carries their own unique life story, experiences, and values that others may not even be able to comprehend. The collective experiences also in large shape one's view on many concepts such as truth and justice. I realized that one person's definition of truth may vary vastly from another person's and even so, both of their perspectives on truth may be correct. This fact taught me to be a more open-minded and humble human being because many times I fall victim to assuming and judging others for the things visible on the surface.
>
> —*10th-grade student*

As they share their perspectives, I make sure to remind students that the point here is not to try to convince others to change their mind, but simply to share their own opinion and to listen thoughtfully to the perspectives of others. After sharing, students move back into the corners, but now they can move to a new area if they've found their thinking has changed. This type of movement can encourage flexible thinking.

Journaling Tensions and Essential Questions

Although a simple move, journaling in their writer's notebooks can help students document their thinking-in-progress. I often ask students to do two types of journal entries at the start of any unit of study.

- *Defining the tension.* For this, I ask students to define a tension or big idea that we're exploring in the text. For example, at the start of our study of *The Crucible*, I ask students to define terms like *conformity* and *rebellion*. We can then revisit these definitions as we make our way through the play.

- *Exploring essential questions.* At the start of each unit, I ask students to answer the essential questions that are guiding our inquiry, such as those listed on the previous pages for units on *home, storytelling,* and *truth* (p. 218). Sometimes I'll ask students to answer all the questions or, more often, we work on one question at a time.

To make sure that this journaling activity helps students practice intentional perspective-taking, I make sure to give students opportunities to share, choosing a conversation strategy from chapter 4 that best suits the situation.

Concept Mapping Definitions and Essential Questions

As an extension of the previous journaling activity, students then form small groups to create concept maps. Students might create a concept map to define the tension, adding ideas from their own individual journaling as they build out their concept map. Or instead of a term, students build a concept map around an essential question.

If I have students journal multiple essential questions, I assign each group a different essential question. For example, one group might build a concept map around the question, "What does truth mean to me?" Another group might work on "How do others know what is true?" This group concept mapping activity can then be followed up with:

- *Gallery Walk:* Concept maps are posted around the room and students add their thoughts to each one, either directly writing on the poster or using sticky notes.

- *Silent Discussion:* Concept maps are passed from group to group and students add to their thoughts *but* do so silently. Silent discussions honor and allow for individual student perspectives to be shared in a different way than when their responses are socially constructed in group discussion.

Now that students have taken stock of the perspectives they're bringing into a text, we can invite students to continue the habit of perspective-taking by embedding experiences that ask students to pause throughout their reading to think flexibly and intentionally.

Rethinking Characters and Characterization

When I first started teaching, and still today, I ask students to keep track of characters, often through a simple list. We stop and revisit our character list throughout our reading, and students keep track of significant quotes: things the narrator says about the characters, things characters say or do, and things other characters say about them.

▶ I learned that it is important to understand many different perspectives even if they are different than yours, and that your ideas will be strengthened if you are a good listener. If you are a good listener, you will be able to interpret the ideas of others and compare them to your own either learning something new and changing your perspective or strengthening the idea that you already have. Either way, it is important to be open-minded and thoughtful when listening to the ideas of classmates. I have learned how to use the ideas of others to strengthen my own ideas.

—12th-grade student

But to help students develop critical literacy skills, we can ask them to consider not just *who or what* the characters are, *but how they are*. In other words, *how* are characters represented and what can we infer from this representation?

For example, one of the major criticisms of *To Kill a Mockingbird* is about *how* Harper Lee treats the Black characters in her novel. While many of the White characters—such as Scout (as the narrator), Atticus, and Jem—are developed and nuanced, the Black characters in the novel are not. In fact, Professor Randall (2017) argues that the novel "should be taught by asking questions about why there are no black characters with agency in the novel." As an example, Randall asks readers to:

> think of Calpurnia, the older black maid who cooks and serves without seeing much: she isn't developed as a character as much as written as a set piece, suggesting the worst to young readers about the role of black women and black female intelligence.

Tom Robinson's character, too, is no more than a device to move the plot forward, a Black character whose function is to develop the White

character's coming-of-age journey. Some might argue that there is nothing inherently wrong with this. After all, that's what minor characters do: they serve to develop the main character. But the subordination of Black characters in service of White characters fits a broader and consistent pattern in storytelling, whether those stories are found in literature, television, or film. For example, when looking at Oscar-nominated films featuring Black characters, critic George (2013) asks,

> Are black characters given a real back story and real-world motivations? Are they agents of their own destiny or just foils for white characters? Are they too noble to be real? Are they too ghetto to be flesh and blood? Do any of these characters point to a way forward?

I share the criticisms of *To Kill a Mockingbird* here not necessarily to single this novel out, because the truth is that many texts have similar problems, particularly if you, like me, teach any traditionally canonical texts. And because of the biases that we have as readers, we may fail to notice these problematic tropes. I have not been immune to this either.

For years, I taught Tim O'Brien's *The Things They Carried* to my eleventh- and twelfth-grade students. We unpacked the beauty of O'Brien's language and all the ways in which he explored the nuances of "story-truth" versus "happening-truth." And of course, we examined O'Brien's novel as a "Vietnam War" novel, one that captured the moral complexities associated with being a soldier.

It wasn't until I read T. A. Nguyen's (2018) essay, "The Things They Made Me Carry: Inheriting a White Curriculum," that I realized how I had failed to see how O'Brien had written an entire novel about the Vietnam War without any real Vietnamese characters. Nguyen, a Vietnamese American teacher, writes:

> How could I teach Tim O'Brien's version of the Vietnam War that actually has no Vietnamese people in it? When I've said this to people in the past, they were always shocked: How can a book about the Vietnam War have no Vietnamese people in it? The main scene that describes Vietnamese people has them symbolized as water buffalo (my white colleagues had a whole lesson built around this water buffalo metaphor as if it was the most exciting thing in the world to discover that the animal represented my people).

> Like the water buffalo, Vietnamese people are shot and killed. They have no personalities. No families. They are just the backdrop for American bravery and grief.

I continued to teach *The Things They Carried* but not only did I include Nguyen's perspective, but together, students ask themselves, with this text and others we read, Which characters and perspectives are represented? Who is centered? Who is marginalized? Who is missing?

Who Is Centered? Who Is Marginalized? Who Is Missing? (C-M-M)

In addition to a simple character list, students can also consider the *positionality* of those characters. I remind students of the "Circles of Self" (p. 116) writing prompt they did earlier in the year. Recall that for this writing prompt, students drew concentric circles, placing themselves in the middle and then filling in the names of people in their life in the other circles, closer or farther away from themselves, depending on how significant a role those people have in their lives.

For a C-M-M analysis for literature, I ask students to do the same for the characters in the novel we're reading. Students place the protagonist and other main characters at the center and then fill in the outer circles with other characters, placing them at a distance from the center relative to how significant they are. Perspectives that are missing from the novel are placed outside the outermost circle (see example in Figure 6.5).

▶ "[The margins are] also the site of radical possibility, a space of resistance. It was this marginality that I was naming as a central location for the production of a counter-hegemonic discourse that is not just found in words but in habits of being and the way one lives. As such, I was not speaking of a marginality one wishes to lose—to give up or surrender as part of moving into the center—but rather of a site one stays in, clings to even, because it nourishes one's capacity to resist. It offers one the possibility of a radical perspective from which to see and create, to imagine alternatives, new worlds."

—bell hooks, "Choosing the Margin as a Space of Radical Openness" (1989)

When I ask students to consider the significance of a character, I always frame this question as to what the *author* is doing. Whom does *Miller* center? Whom does *O'Brien* center? Whom does *Fitzgerald* center? I use this framing to remind students that whether a character or perspective is centered, marginalized, or missing *is a choice that the author has deliberately made*. Whose voices are valued (and how) is always under an author's creative control. Knowing this, then, we can interrogate the implications and consequences of this positioning. What does it mean, for example, that O'Brien relegates the Vietnamese to the margins in a novel about the Vietnam War? What does it mean that Miller positions the only Black character in *The Crucible* as a scapegoat in Act 1 and then effectively writes that character out of the play?

Note that **we can also apply a C-M-M analysis when students are reading nonfiction or analyzing arguments.** For many years, I had students complete a Weekly Annotated Reading (WAR, for short) in which they chose any long-form or feature essay from a list of

FIGURE 6.5 C-M-M ANALYSIS

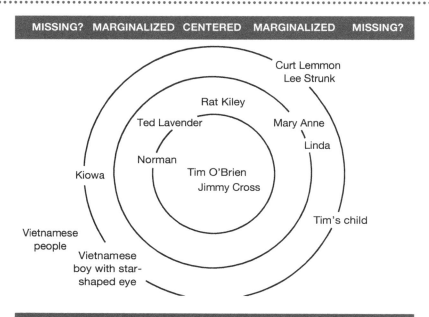

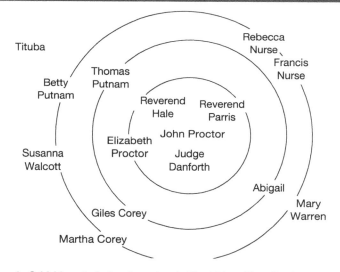

Top: Sample C-M-M analysis for characters in *The Things They Carried. Below*: C-M-M analysis for the characters in *The Crucible*.

suggested publications. They had to annotate the text as well as summarize and analyze the strategies the author used. If I was doing this assignment again, I would also ask students to consider what voices or stakeholders were *centered, marginalized (or minimized),* and *missing* in the author's argument. Or I might curate a collection of essays that cover the same topic, divide students into groups, give each group one of the essays, and then ask them to apply a C-M-M analysis. Students could then share out, comparing and contrasting the choices each author makes about which voices were present and to what degree.

Reframing Character Analysis

Another way to support students in thinking about how some characters and perspectives are centered, marginalized, or missing is to revisit literary terms related to characterization.

> *Whether a character or perspective is centered, marginalized, or missing is a choice that the author has deliberately made.*

Consider the various types of characters that might exist in a text. Applying a critical literacy lens, we can ask students to determine if there is any pattern as to what types of characters are written as round or flat, dynamic or static, and so on. See Figure 6.6 for details.

FIGURE 6.6 TYPES OF CHARACTERS

TYPE OF CHARACTER	DEFINITION
Major	Characters who make major decisions or take significant actions over the course of the entire narrative; generally given more "space" in the story and pages
Minor	Characters who do not make major decisions on their own but rather support major characters in their development; generally, lack agency
Round	Characters who feel like "real" people as they are well developed and many sided
Flat	Characters who are one sided with little to no development
Dynamic	Characters who undergo a major change, internally; their opinions, beliefs, or attitudes may change
Static	Characters who remain relatively the same throughout the story
Foil	Character who serves as a contrast to another
Stock	Character that serves as a recognizable "type" of character rather than a unique one for this story (Ex. sidekick, mentor figure, magical helper, etc.)

This exercise is particularly useful for texts that have many characters, but even texts with relatively few characters can also work. I ask students to list all the characters in the story and begin grouping them according to the types of characters mentioned in Figure 6.6. As students do this, I ask them to notice and name which characters the author determines are major versus minor, round versus flat, dynamic versus static. What patterns do they notice? Or I might ask students to rank characters along a spectrum of major versus minor, round versus

flat, dynamic versus static. This too can be clarifying for students as they may notice, as is the case in *The Things They Carried*, in which characters and perspectives are often at the least developed end of each of those spectrum, similar to the C-M-M analysis (p. 247).

Step In, Step Out, Step Back

This is one of my favorite thinking routines from Harvard University's Project Zero because of how it encourages students to think empathetically *and* metacognitively about character perspectives in any given story. (If you are not already familiar with Project Zero, I highly recommend browsing and trying the thinking routines they have developed to help students become more critical thinkers across a wide variety of tasks and contexts.)

I find that this thinking routine works best after a major development in a text we're reading, the crisis points that put characters in moments of decision, action, and reaction. Students select a character (or a character may be assigned) and then follow this protocol, which I have tweaked slightly from Project Zero's description:

- *Step In:* Step into the story and reflect: What might this character be feeling, thinking, feeling? How are they acting? What does this character know (or not know)?

- *Step Out:* Take a step outside the story: What additional information do you need or want to know to better understand this character or this character's perspective?

- *Step Back:* Take a step further outside the story and look at yourself as a reader: What was it like for you to step into this character's perspective? What did this make you think, feel, experience? What elements of your own identity do you think informs the way you are able to relate to this character?

Above and Below the Line

Just as students can use this activity as a writing prompt to inspire personal narrative writing (chapter 3), students can also consider what information about a character is obvious (above the line) and perhaps hidden (below the line) in a text. After drawing a horizontal line in their notebook, students place what they see as the **dominant narrative** about the character above the line, and lesser-known **insider** information about the character below the line.

Distinguishing between the above-the-line information from the below-the-line information can be challenging for students as it requires that they understand how *other characters in the novel perceive that character*. For example, what is above the line for Jay Gatsby requires that students understand how he is perceived by other characters in the novel. On the other hand, through the character of Nick, the reader is able to get additional below the line information about Gatsby.

In addition to applying this framework to characters in novels, we can use it for studying current events and issues. For example, students might use this framework when researching topics, issues such as affirmative action, gun control, or sustainable farming. What are the dominant narratives and what counternarratives or insider perspectives might they learn about these issues?

If students struggle with the concept of what might be below-the-line information, students could also include questions they have about the character: What additional information would they like to know about this character in order to better understand them?

This above- and below-the-line exercise works particularly well for novels with strong characters, especially many young adult and coming-of-age novels in which the protagonist struggles with revealing their whole selves to others. This exercise would be well suited for texts like *Speak* by Laurie Halse Anderson, *After the Shot Drops* by Randy Ribay, *The Hate U Give* by Angie Thomas, *Internment* by Samira Ahmed, *Frankly in Love* by David Yoon, and *The Marrow Thieves* by Cherie Dimaline.

Character Spectrum

Students can have complex and rich reactions to the characters they encounter in literature, but sometimes they may struggle with naming how to describe what they're noticing. Recall the spectrum exercise earlier in this chapter (p. 243) in which students responded to statements related to the reading and positioned themselves from strongly disagree to strongly agree to reflect their opinion. Here, students will instead position *characters* across a spectrum of character traits.

For example, in Figure 6.7, students worked in groups to place the characters from *The Great Gatsby* across a spectrum of three different character traits. First, as a class, we brainstormed a list of character traits that we observed in the novel, not necessarily specific to any character. From there, we considered what the "opposite" of that character trait would be (for example, *loyal* versus *disloyal*). Then, in groups, students chose three to four traits and placed each character along this spectrum. Students then walked around to see how other students viewed the characters.

This exercise reinforces perspective-taking in at least two different ways: not only do they get to see how their perspectives differ from their classmates, placing characters along a *spectrum* encourages them to again

practice seeing beyond binary character traits (not to mention the critical thinking that happens when reasoning through their decisions).

FIGURE 6.7   CHARACTER SPECTRUM

Identity Inventory: Character Analysis

In chapter 3 (pp. 93–100), we looked at how students could consider which different elements of their identities play a role in how they navigate their own world. We can also apply this same analysis to the characters that students encounter in the texts that they read. For example, when my students read Octavia Butler's science fiction/fantasy novel *Kindred*, we considered how the characters' various identities informed their thoughts, feelings, and actions. In *Kindred*, Dana is a Black woman in the 1970s who is mysteriously transported back in time to the 1800s, a time period in which she is considered an enslaved person. Through this time-travel mechanism, Butler explores how Dana's consciousness as a modern Black woman is impacted by the horrors of enslavement and her resilience in fighting against it both physically and psychologically. An identity inventory for Dana might look like this:

Gender - female

Race - Black

Sexual Orientation - straight

National origin or immigration status - US citizen in 1970s, but enslaved person in 1800s

Socioeconomic status - Middle class in the 1970s, but enslaved person in the 1800s

Home Language(s) - fluent reader and writer of English

Religion/Spiritual practice - unclear in book

Ability - fully able-bodied

Age - 26 years old

To do this inventory, students must be able to draw on evidence from the text to determine directly or to infer what identities the character embodies. When examining Dana's various identities, I ask students to consider which of these have the least and most impact on how she is able to navigate the various conflicts she experiences. Students notice that some of her identities are advantageous in certain situations while also dangerous in others. For example, Dana's ability to read and write is certainly an advantage to her when she is in the 1800s as an enslaved person trying to escape, but that same ability also puts her in danger because the ability to read and write as a Black person was threatening to White enslavers. Students also complete identity inventories for other characters in the novel and compare and contrast how each character's positionality and power is impacted by their various identities. For example, Kevin, Dana's White husband, hold more social power because of his racial identity, and he is able to use that power to help Dana at various points in the novel.

Rethinking Conflict

In his essay, "25 Essential Notes on Craft," Salesses (2021) writes, "Craft tells us how to see the world" and that "[c]raft is support for a certain world view." Salesses argues that definitions of concepts like plot, conflict, setting—all of the literary devices many of us learned in sixth-grade English class—are not *objective,* but *subjective.*

Read "25 Essential Notes on Craft" by Matthew Salesses.

For example, Salesses points out that many Western conceptions of plot focus on how an individual has a goal and then something that gets in the way of that goal. Notice that this conception of plot is "inherently conflict-based" (p. 28). Typically, the "something that gets in the way" is conflict, which is usually broken down into six types:

- Man v. Self
- Man v. Man
- Man v. Society
- Man v. Technology

- Man v. Nature
- Man v. Fate

However, Salesses points out that in Eastern storytelling, plot is less focused on confrontation. Instead, the plot unfolds through a series of encounters and coincidences rather than obstacles or challenges to be overcome.

When I read Salesses' description, I finally understood why some colleagues and friends, who were White, would be less engaged, even bored, with some of the books we read that were written by non-Western authors. As someone whose immigrant parents often expressed an "it is what it is" worldview, and as a member of the Asian diaspora, I wasn't bothered by the lack of explicit confrontation in the plot; instead, I was drawn to the nuances in the characters' development.

What does this have to do with our students? I often think about how the stories students tend to gravitate toward are those that are *plot-centric*. And by that, I mean *conflict-centered*. Stories that are more *character-driven*, without an explicit or concrete *obstacle to be overcome* are often a harder sell. Maybe you've noticed the same pattern. In the past, I attributed this bias to students' age and immaturity. But the truth is, our literary tastes and expectations of stories are just as *socially constructed* as many parts of our identities. This raises the question: **What do we teach students to *value* in the stories we choose to read in class?**

White Supremacy culture tends to have a bias for individual success and achievement. It's no surprise, then, that this bias appears in our reading preferences. One shift I've made is to turn students' attention away from whether an individual character succeeds or fails, and instead ask how the *society or community* is able to *support or not support* the protagonist in their growth. This is a subtle but significant difference in framing. This framing turns students' attention to the *systemic* or *cultural factors* that facilitate or impede how an individual navigates their world.

Notice the connection to the fundamental attribution error (p. 31). Rather than hold a character solely responsible for whether they succeed or fail in achieving their goals, we can turn our attention to the context around them and its impact.

Furthermore, rather than focus on the growth of an individual character, I also ask students to consider how the society or community has grown (changes or fails to change). Students reflect on this dynamic considering four different possible outcomes for any story:

1. Character changes; Society changes

2. Character does not change; Society changes

3. Character changes; Society does not change

4. Character does not change; Society does not change

These four different outcomes are also represented in the chart below. First, I ask students to identify which outcome most applies to the story we're reading. For example, *Things Fall Apart* would be an example of a story in which a character (Okonkwo) does not change, but his community (Ibo tribe) does. On the other hand, Jay Gatsby is an example of a character who changes who he is, but the old-money society he longs desperately to be part of does not change. After students identify which scenario applies to the story, they are then invited to consider the other three outcomes: *How might the story have turned out differently? What would it take for the character or society to change (or not change) and what are the implications?*

	CHARACTER CHANGES	CHARACTER DOES *NOT* CHANGE
Society or Community Changes		
Society or Community Does *Not* Change		

Tracking Their Perspective-Taking Over Time

Keeping track of evolving perspectives about characters can help students exercise consistent flexibility in their thinking, which is required when practicing perspective-taking. The key here is to make sure that their evolving perspectives about the characters are both rooted in the text *and* honor what the perspective they're bringing with them to that text. Here, students can keep a log similar to the one found in Figure 6.8. When we make time for students to reflect on how *new information* can confirm, challenge, or change their thinking, they practice and normalize the flexibility that comes with intentional perspective-taking.

FIGURE 6.8 TRACKING PERSPECTIVES OVER TIME

PAGES: ACT 2 SCENE 2	CHARACTER NAME: MAMA
What the Character Said or Did	After Mama buys a house in Clybourne Park, she also tells Walter she'll give him money for his store.
Supporting Evidence (quoted passage) from text	"Listen to me, now. I say I been wrong, son. That I been doing to you what the rest of the world been doing to you."

(Continued)

(Continued)

PAGES: ACT 2 SCENE 2	CHARACTER NAME: MAMA
Before this happened, I used to think . . .	Mama would never give Walter any of the money.
Now, my perspective of this character has been confirmed/challenged/ changed because . . .	I think it's risky for Mama to give Walter the money, but it seems like she understands how much this really means to Walter now, so she's willing to do it.
As I continue to read, regarding this character, I want to find out . . .	If Mama was right to trust Walter with the money and if she was right about buying the house in the neighborhood.
This could be important because . . .	It could determine if the play will have a happy ending.

▶ The most important thing I learned is how to write down my thoughts. This sounds stupid because it's not a huge crazy new idea or anything, but I really appreciated when you would give us a few minutes for free write or when we were forced to answer prompts about the lesson. I also liked when there would be a series of prompts where I would have to continue to build up my ideas. That's a nice lesson/skill that I learned because I can use it for the rest of my life. I want to write things down more because then I can come back and read over how I felt about something or find an idea I once had.

—*11th-grade student*

Second (and Third) Draft Thinking

If initial journaling and activities around the anticipation guide statement, tension exploration, and essential questions for the unit were a way to capture students' "first draft thinking," making time for students to revisit, reflect, and revise represents their "second (and third) draft" thinking. We know that we don't always do our best thinking when something is new to us. We often need multiple iterations before we can start to truly understand an idea.

Thus, throughout the reading of the text, students should revisit their ratings from their anticipation guide statements. Through brief journaling and then discussion opportunities, students might explore the following:

• Which anticipation guide statement seems especially relevant at this point in the text?

• How has my initial rating of and thinking about this statement changed? What was the cause of this change? Or if it hasn't changed, what would need to happen in the text to change my mind?

- How did I define the tension earlier and how has my thinking deepened around this? Or if it hasn't, why and what else do I need to know or learn?

- How has my thinking around the essential questions evolved? Why?

Naming Beliefs That Impact Interpretation

The beliefs we have and the experiences that have informed them can deeply affect the way we respond to texts. This is especially true when we read texts that reflect cultures, communities, and experiences that are different from our own. We can encourage students to identify their beliefs but not allow those to limit their ability to seek other complexities within the text.

For example, whenever I taught Chinua Achebe's *Things Fall Apart*, students often feel angry when the protagonist, Okonkwo, abuses and beats his wife. Because they believe, strongly, that Okonkwo's actions are wrong, they often conclude that Igbo society was sexist. And because of **negativity bias**, which occurs when we allow negative events to overshadow all others, I encourage students to *also* analyze the many ways in which Igbo society was organized around female power.

Students might journal using the following questions as a starting point for reflection and discussion:

- What do I **think** about this character's actions?

- How does my reaction to this character's actions align with or challenge something I **believe** or assume?

- How might my own **belief** or **assumption** limit my understanding of this character?

- What *alternative* **beliefs** or **assumptions** might result in a *different* interpretation of this character?

Applying these questions to *The Great Gatsby*,

- I think it was wrong for Daisy to allow Gatsby to take the blame for her actions.

- Daisy's actions confirm my belief that we should take responsibility for our actions and accept the consequences of those actions.

- However, I need to also consider the power, or lack of power, that Daisy had as a woman in her particular situation to fully understand her choice.

- If I believe that there can sometimes be circumstances that limit our choices, then I might interpret Daisy's choice as practical, even if it is unethical.

This reflection works particularly well when students might have a difficult time empathizing with a character. Note that this reflection is not constructed to *excuse* characters' actions that are wrong or harmful, but to better understand how our beliefs affect how we interpret those actions. This reflection works particularly well when paired with a listening dyad (p. 174) so that students can share their "thinking in progress."

Bias Check-in

In the previous chapter, we looked at the way we can explicitly teach students about different biases, examples of these biases in their lives, and then what to do when they notice them. Unfortunately, however, we can't depend on students noticing these biases on their own; after all, biases happen so naturally, frequently, and often subconsciously, that we need to be intentional about making time to stop and ask, *what bias might be informing my thinking right now?*

The more emotional, contentious, or charged the topic or text we're studying may be, the more critical it is to stop and reflect on the role of bias in our thinking. After teaching students about different biases (see chapter 5), we can revisit in a few different ways. For example:

- When studying arguments, such as opinion pieces, ask students to identify any biases that an author may be making and how.

- When writing arguments, make a "bias check" part of the peer response and feedback process.

- When reading a novel, ask students to check if any of the character's thoughts or actions may reflect a bias (see Figure 6.9).

- When reading and studying any text, fiction or nonfiction, ask students to consider how the text may lead readers to use biased thinking or how the author might be relying on a bias they believe their audience has. This can be especially useful when analyzing opinion/editorial pieces.

FIGURE 6.9   APPLYING BIASES IN ANALYZING LITERATURE

Students reviewed the definitions of various biases and then applied them to their study of The Crucible. *Students identified which biases were reflected in characters' thoughts and actions and matched these biases to a quote or passage in the play.*

Making and Remaking Claims

Often, we think of claims and evidence when we teach students how to write arguments. For many years, I believed in the false dichotomy between teaching *argument* and teaching *literature*. These seemed like two completely different tasks: After all, when I taught *argument*, we

read and studied nonfiction, and when I taught *literature*, we focused on novels and poetry. Yet arguments are everywhere. In fact, in literary analysis, themes are claims. Themes answer the question: What does the writer want us to think, believe, feel, or how to act? In novels, short stories, and poetry, writers make claims, as do essayists, journalists, scientists, historians, and even mathematicians.

First, just as we can teach students about different biases, we can also teach students about different types of claims they might encounter. The more we can teach students the complexities of the types of claim they hear, see, and question, the better able they are to think critically, to exercise nuance and depth in their reasoning. Figure 6.10 provides a brief overview and some examples of how we can expand students' perspectives about different types of claims they might see in both fiction and nonfiction.

FIGURE 6.10 TYPES OF CLAIMS (IN LITERATURE AND LIFE)

TYPE	DESCRIPTION	EXAMPLES
Fact	Claims of *fact* argue whether something exists, is true, or happens.*	Racism exists in our school. Gender discrimination still happens in the workplace. In *The Great Gatsby*, Nick is a gay man struggling with his feelings for Gatsby. The Black characters in *To Kill a Mockingbird* are underdeveloped in the story.
Definition	Claims of *definition* argue about the characteristics or qualities of something, what it consists of or made of.	Upper Dublin High School is a high-performing, successful school in the state of Pennsylvania. Racism is both individual and structural. With its focus on the impact of race in the protagonist's life, Richard Wright's *Native Son* is the preeminent American novel of the 20th century.
Value	Claims of *value* argue whether something is good or bad, desirable or undesirable.	A college degree is the most important goal for young people. The Marvel Cinematic Universe films are better than the *Star Wars* franchise. Because of its depiction of motherhood, *Beloved* is one of the greatest American novels written. Perhaps the strongest element of Hansberry's work is her interrogation of gender.
Cause	Claims of *cause* argue that something causes another.	Because she exercised every day, she hardly ever got sick. By studying hard, he was able to get good grades. Although there are several reasons justice was not served, the primary causes of the tragedy in *The Crucible* were rooted in Puritan fundamentalism. Okonkwo's death in *Things Fall Apart* can be best understood through the lens of imperialism.
Policy	Claims of *policy* argue about what should be done, what actions should be taken.	School should start later so that students can get more sleep. Grades should be eliminated to reduce student stress. Need literature examples

*Note: *Claims of fact, like other claims, must be arguable. Not every fact is a claim of fact. Some facts are just that: facts.*

Regardless of whether we were reading fiction or nonfiction (and truthfully, a good text set would include both!), we can encourage students to think about what *claims* are being made in a particular text. By making claims explicit, we can invite students to consider how their own perspectives may align (or not) with those claims—and why.

As you can see in Figure 6.11, students consider which characters from *A Raisin in the Sun* might agree or disagree with the claim presented.

FIGURE 6.11 CHARACTER CLAIMS

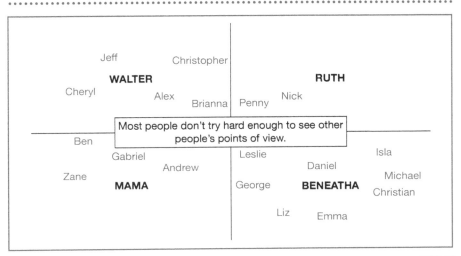

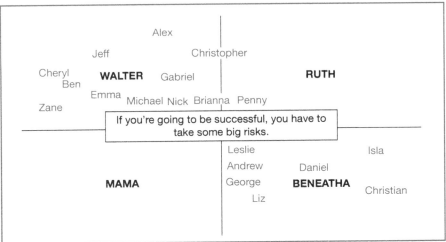

As students examine where authors or characters stand regarding a specific claim, they can deepen their thinking and perspective about this claim by asking themselves:

- Where does the author's (or character's) claim come from?

- What is my own perspective on this?

- Where does my perspective come from?

- What are my peers' perspectives on this? What can I learn from their perspective on this?

Also, note that these claims are similar to ones that can be used in traditional anticipation guides. In this way, claims can be revisited in at least three different ways.

- Before reading, students consider to what extent *they* might agree or disagree with a claim.

- During reading, students can consider how *characters* might agree or disagree with a claim.

- After reading, students can determine where the *author* might stand.

- And finally, students can revisit their initial perspective about the claim to see if their perspective has now changed.

If . . . Then . . .

How we interpret the thoughts and actions of one character can inform the way we interpret the thoughts and actions of others. When I taught *The Crucible*, students generally came to two competing interpretations of Abigail's character. Some students see her as the "villain" of the play for having an affair with the married John Proctor, while other students explain her actions as the "victim" of a Puritan society that generally afforded her little power.

While competing interpretations are a central part of literary analysis, we can extend this line of thinking to focus on how these competing interpretations then affect our perspectives of other characters. For example, if Abigail is a "villain," then students will see John Proctor and Elizabeth in a more sympathetic light. However, if Abigail is a "victim," then they will be more inclined to hold John Proctor responsible for the affair he has with Abigail (especially as he was the married one).

Likewise, *if* students identify Abigail's lies as the central cause of the Salem tragedy, *then* they may see individual actions as being more powerful than the social norms in Puritan society that might explain why Abigail would lie in the first place. Or *if* students identify Danforth's pride as the central cause, *then* they may see his refusal to admit his possible mistakes as either an individual character flaw *or* as a function of social norms that prioritize a person's reputation above all else. See Figure 6.12 for an example of this analysis.

FIGURE 6.12 IF . . . THEN . . . ANALYSIS FOR *THE CRUCIBLE*

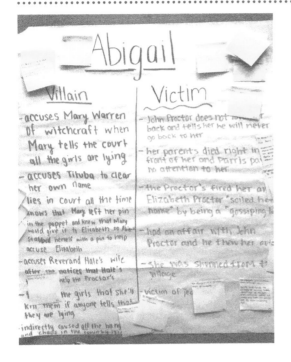
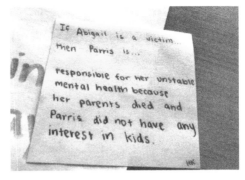
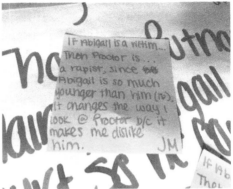

Students work in groups to list evidence for two possible interpretations of Abigail's character in The Crucible: *villain or victim. Then students apply an "If . . . then . . ." annotation using sticky notes, writing down how their interpretation of other characters in the play would change depending on their assumptions of Abigail.*

Consider the texts that you teach and look for opportunities where you might help students to engage in this *if . . . then . . .* thinking.

- If I see a character as ___, then how does that affect how I see other characters?

- If I think the author's message (theme) is ___, then does that change the way I interpret specific events or characters?

As you'll see in the next section, this *if . . . then . . .* exercise complements and prepares students for engaging in critical theory.

Using Literary Theory as Lenses for Perspective-Taking

As you have already noticed, the strategies I've shared throughout this book are rooted in examining *who is the I who reads*. Too often,

however, we reduce reader-response theory to platitudes about how we *felt* about a text and how we can *relate* to text rather than serious interrogation of the self at the center of this meaning-making. In other words, we ask students to make a connection with a text that starts and ends with the reader.

I was a senior in college when I first encountered *Literature as Exploration* by Louise Rosenblatt. Her theory of reader response, or the transactional nature of reading, spoke to me on so many levels. After all, it was the personal responses I had as a reader that drew me to books, hiding under the covers late at night reading my Babysitter's Club books. But what stood out to me most was Rosenblatt's deep, abiding respect for the reader and all the things that a reader brings with themselves to a text. It lined up with my own still-forming beliefs about student-centered instruction.

Yet despite the power of personal response, we see over and over again today the way that instructional strategies espoused by reading programs, corporations, and standardized tests ignore the value of personal response when it comes to reading and interpreting texts, as if you could divorce the person reading from the act of reading. Text-dependent analysis, too often, has become reader-erasing analysis.

Again, we cannot separate what we read from *who is the I who reads*. But rather than focus solely on the singular experience of an individual person, or even a single interpretation, we can help students broaden and deepen the varied ways they engage with a text.

Enter the power of literary theory.

Literary theory is inherently perspective-taking. When we ask students to consider not only the various voices and perspectives represented in a text, but also what *perspective they're using as readers to interpret a text*, we help students become more active and responsible readers of texts. After all, *all* readers bring an interpretive lens to texts:

- When readers make personal connections to a text, they may be using a reader-response lens.

- When readers ask questions about why characters make the decisions that they do, they may be using a psychological lens.

- When readers ask about how the author's personal experiences might be showing up in the text, they may be using a biographical lens.

By teaching students literary theory more explicitly, we can support students with the language and framework for understanding texts more deeply. For example, as a woman of color, I had very few characters

The Problem of Universal "Truths"

When we study literature, one of the biggest barriers to developing a habit of intentional perspective-taking—and the seeking of multiple perspectives—is universalism. Universalism happens anytime we claim that a text *is* about the X (or Y or Z) in humanity, human nature, or, if you're in an AP class or college, the "human condition." For example, when we say that *Lord of the Flies is* about the exploration of the darkness in human nature, or that John Proctor is the "Everyman" hero of *The Crucible*, or that *The Great Gatsby* is about the "American Dream," or that Shakespeare's plays are about the "invention of human," as critic Harold Bloom argues, we impose a singular interpretation, **one that is often rooted in dominant culture**.

In each of these interpretations, we must ask ourselves, for *whom* is this interpretation "universal"? Under what circumstances and conditions? After all, the darkness that Golding saw emerge on the island in *Lord of the Flies* isn't so much universal as it is particular to *White, British masculinity* during a specific time in history after World War II and the Holocaust. And of course, it's also just as possible to imagine that cultures and communities whose values are rooted in collectivism might have had a different outcome on Golding's island.

who represented, even vaguely, my racial or cultural experiences in the books that I read when I was growing up. Recall the experience I shared reading *Jane Eyre* in the introduction to this book. In connecting with Jane's character, I employed a reader-response lens. But when I read Rhys's *Wide Sargasso Sea,* I realized that there were other ways of interpreting—of *talking back to*—*Jane Eyre*. As I unpacked the way that Bertha was treated in the novel, I began to read with a postcolonial lens. As I reflected on the relationship between Jane and Rochester, I read through a feminist lens. As I examined the ways that Jane's choices were limited by her economic position, I used a Marxist lens.

With our increasing polarization and echo chambers of confirmation bias—I believe that teaching students to read literature through the multiple and varied lenses that literary theory offers us is not only still possible but an urgent need.

We can do this intentional perspective-taking with any text, and in doing so, we can also help students surface the ways in which their biases might inform what lenses they use to interpret a text. Consider:

- As a person of color navigating predominantly White spaces my entire life, I tend to lean into literary theories that help me to

better understand the role that power plays in a text—whether that power is related to race, gender, or class. I naturally lean into this type of perspective-taking because of my lived experiences.

- For readers who are part of dominant social groups, this type of perspective-taking might feel less natural, and thus more challenging. Readers from dominant social groups might instead show a preference for literary theories like formalist approaches that focus on the text alone.

As teachers, we can pay attention to how these social identities in our students might surface in their reading responses—and ask our students to reflect on this as well.

Figure 6.13 summarizes a list of the literary theories that may be most accessible to high school students. Please note that what I offer here is more of an introduction to these theories and that the questions, in particular, are only a starting point for students to begin practicing these lenses. For a more detailed understanding, I highly recommend reading Dr. Appleman's book, *Critical Encounters in Secondary English: Teaching Literary Theory to Adolescents*, which is now in its third edition.

Bias Alert: While I wasn't aware of it at the time, I was taught to read primarily using a formalist lens, with a focus on close reading that assumed that meaning was limited to what could be found on the page (and the page alone). This **bias** for the authority of the written word over other forms of meaning-making is one characteristic of White Supremacy culture (Okun, 2021a). Consider how much of our English language arts instruction is focused on "text dependent analysis" or TDAs. There is nothing wrong with asking students to provide textual evidence for their thinking (in fact, it's a necessary skill). However, when we only focus on what's in the text to the exclusion of other resources of knowledge that can and do inform analysis (i.e. historical context, biographical information, social and political theory), we not only miss opportunities to expand students' thinking but we reinforce White mainstream ways of knowing.

FIGURE 6.13 LITERARY THEORIES

LITERARY THEORY	STUDENT-FRIENDLY LANGUAGE	SOME QUESTIONS TO ASK WHEN PRACTICING THIS PERSPECTIVE-TAKING LENS
Reader-Response Theory	This lens looks at the way that the experiences and identities of individual readers	• How are you responding to this text? • What connections between the text and your experiences exist? • How do your experiences affect the way you're responding to the text?

LITERARY THEORY	STUDENT-FRIENDLY LANGUAGE	SOME QUESTIONS TO ASK WHEN PRACTICING THIS PERSPECTIVE-TAKING LENS
Historical Criticism	This lens examines the historical context in which the text was written may inform the themes found in the text.	• What were the major historical and social events, ideologies, and movements at the time the text was written? • How are these historical and social contexts reflected in the characters' thoughts and actions? • In what other ways does the author incorporate historical and social events of the time?
Biographical Criticism	This lens looks at how the author's personal experiences might be reflected in the text.	• What do you know about the author's biography: their personal experiences, especially noteworthy life events and people? • How might these experiences, people, or events inform the choices the author made in the text regarding characters, conflicts, and themes?
Feminist Criticism	This lens looks at the role of—and the relationships between—women and men and their positioning relative to each other and in society.	• What patterns do you notice between male and female (or male- and female-presenting) characters? • How are male and female roles (or male- and female-presenting) defined and how do you know? • How do these roles reflect who has power and in what ways? • How do the male and female (or male- and female-presenting) relationships reflect or challenge gender dynamics, historical or contemporary?
Marxist Criticism	This lens examines how socioeconomics and class affect who has power in a story.	• What social classes do the characters belong to or represent? • In what ways do the interactions of characters from different social classes reflect larger patterns in society? • How do the social classes the characters belong to affect their thoughts and actions?
Psychoanalytic Criticism	This lens uses psychological theories to better understand why characters act the way they do.	• How can you use psychology to better understand the characters' thoughts, feelings, and actions? • How might characters' thoughts, feelings, and actions represent a particular psychological theory or framework?
Critical Race Theory	This lens examines the way race and racism are reflected in the narrative and affect the characters.	• How do the racial identities of the characters affect their thoughts, feelings, and actions? • How do the experiences of the characters reflect racialized historical and contemporary events and people? • How are the conflicts in the text related to race and racism?

(Continued)

(Continued)

LITERARY THEORY	STUDENT-FRIENDLY LANGUAGE	SOME QUESTIONS TO ASK WHEN PRACTICING THIS PERSPECTIVE-TAKING LENS
Gender Studies and Queer Theory	This lens examines the way in which nonbinary gender identities and experiences are reflected in the text.	• How are traditional gender roles reinforced or challenged in the text? • How do characters adhere to or challenge binary gender roles? What happens as a result? • How might the relationships between characters reflect (or be coded for) queer, gay, or lesbian histories and experiences?
Postcolonial Criticism	This lens asks us to examine the effect of colonialism and imperialism through the characters.	• How are colonizer-colonized relationships or history revealed in the characters' relationships? • How do the events of the story mirror historical or contemporary examples of colonialism or imperialism—or their effects? • How do the characters' thoughts, feelings, or actions reflect mindsets or behaviors associated with colonialism or imperialism?

To see how we might use literary theory to deepen students' reading and analysis skills, let's consider Randy Ribay's keynote at the 2019 ALAN meeting (Assembly on Literature for Adolescents of the National Council of Teachers of English). Ribay is the author of several novels for young adults, including the National Book Award nominated, *Patron Saints of Nothing*. During his keynote, Ribay, who is also a high school English teacher, shared how his literary theory could be used to unpack his novel. To begin, he proposed looking at a story and asking these questions:

Read Randy Ribay's ALAN Keynote in its entirety.

1. Does the character reinforce ideas about male, white, and/or wealth supremacy, are they challenging those ideas, or are they doing a mix of both? How so?

2. Where does that seem to come from?

3. How does that impact their life and the lives of those around them?

4. Does the character change in this regard throughout the story? Why or why not?

In *Patron Saints of Nothing*, Filipino American teenager Jay Regeuro travels to the Philippines in order to find out what happened when his cousin dies mysteriously. The novel is a coming-of-age story about the intersections of family and identity, grief and culture, and Jay's character, in particular, can be read through three lenses, which are summarized from Ribay's keynote as follows:

> *Feminist lens:* Students can analyze the extent to which Jay's uncle, Tito Maning, and his ingrained patriarchal thinking alienates everyone in his family and plays an enormous role in Jun's death. From this lens, students can also see how ideas about stoic masculinity negatively impacted Jay by causing him to repress his sensitivity and empathy.

> *Postcolonial lens:* Students can find much to analyze in Jay's biracial immigrant identity: the confusion of self he experiences daily, the loss of language and culture he's suffered through the pressure immigrants feel to assimilate. In addition, students can also see the contradictory nature of Tito Maning's pride in Filipino culture juxtaposed with his colorism.

> *Marxist lens:* Students can understand how Jay's economic privilege isolates him from injustices and can also make him complicit in those injustices. Students can also see how his cousin Jun, on the other hand, completely rejects the individualistic call to pursue economic success by caring more about the well-being of others, how he rejects the deeply capitalist impulse to ignore and devalue the lives of those lacking material means.

In the rest of his keynote, Ribay described the ways in which these same lenses also can be applied more broadly in the novel to interrogate not just individual characters, but also the *systems* they're in. (Ribey's complete keynote can be found on his website, randyribay.com.)

Likewise, educator Cody Miller also advocates for the use of literary theory in the classroom. Miller (2016) notes that students engage in active perspective-taking as they "reassess their original interpretation of a text." For example, in Miller's class, "students noted how femininity was punished in *Lord of the Flies*, whether it be through the absence of women or the tragic fate of Simon." Furthermore, Miller argues:

> We know that knowledge is not objective; what is considered "right" and "common sense" are often manifestations of dominant cultural values and norms. Using literary theory with fiction and nonfiction alike helps students articulate and

confront their own belief system in analyzing the world around them. When literary theory is taught to students as a framework for understanding the broader sociocultural realities students experience, then theory is not a form of academic esoteria. Rather, literary theory becomes a vehicle for students to adopt and implement new perspectives on a similar topic.

When introducing reading through a critical lens with students, fairy tales are familiar stories that students can reimagine through literary theory. For example, students might examine the Cinderella story through reader-response, feminist, and Marxist lenses. To extend this, students could also read several Cinderella folktales from around the world and analyze how these lenses might reveal differences based on country or culture of origin.

Engaging and Tracking Perspective-Rich Text Sets

Finally, perhaps one of the most powerful ways we can help students practice intentional perspective-taking is to build rich text sets that address the essential questions in the unit of study and *put those texts in conversation with one another.* In other words, how might a text confirm, challenge, or change our thinking based on the perspectives it presents? As Pitts (2021, p. 83) reminds us, as literature teachers, "Literature is about discussion, awareness, and critical thinking. Writers throughout history have used their pens and pencils to challenge the very structures that still harm our students today. They have done the work for us. Create units around James Baldwin, Richard Wright, Toni Morrison, Alice Walker, Michelle Alexander, and Ta-Nehisi Coates . . ."

▶ It was really interesting to think about how everyone has a different idea of what the truth is to them. This idea of everyone having their own truth is the basis for another interesting idea that we talked about in class, and that is how history is written by the victors, the losers' truth is never told since they are never given a chance to. I had never thought about this before and it made me realize that we only really know about one side of every story.

—*11th-grade student*

This part is critical: in building a text set in literature study, it's important to **consider what the dominant narratives might be and then to carefully choose texts that can complicate and offer nuanced perspectives to those narratives.** And by *texts,* we should consider what poetry, podcasts, articles, essays, songs, music, visuals, and other genres can be included. Figure 6.14 provides a small sampling of texts that could be used to provide multiple perspectives around a particular tension and essential questions.

Some questions students can consider as they interact with these multiple texts and perspectives:

- How does this text answer the essential question?

- What perspectives—people and experiences—are represented in the text? What voices are centered and marginalized?

- How do the texts "talk back" to one another? How do they complement each other?

- How does each text deepen or complicate our understanding of the essential question?

The questions above can be organized in an analysis chart such as Figure 6.15 and completed collaboratively by students.

FIGURE 6.14 BUILDING PERSPECTIVE-RICH TEXT SETS

UNIT: ESSENTIAL QUESTION	TEXT	GENRE	PERSPECTIVES OFFERED
Truth: How do I know what is true? What factors determine whether stories become accepted as historically true?	*1984*	novel	Orwell's text serves as an allegory for how authoritarian governments manipulate the truth to control its citizens
	"Your Lying Mind" by Ben Yagoda	essay	Yagoda's long-form essay in *The Atlantic* provides an overview of common cognitive biases that affect the way we think (and thus perceive the truth). Students can see the connection, for example, between confirmation bias and what becomes "historical truth."
	"Visible Means of Support" by Kerry James Marshall	painting	At first glance, these murals seem to simply depict Monticello and Mount Vernon, but upon a closer look, viewers see how Marshall also included every enslaved person on these plantations in the paintings.
	Polling Data from 1960s	survey data	This data reveal low public support for Civil Rights legislation and particularly toward Dr. Martin Luther King, Jr. The data provide an alternative point-of-view to the dominant narrative of Dr. King as a popular historical figure.
	"Two States. Eight Textbooks. Two Americas."	news article	This *New York Times* article reveals discrepancies between the history textbooks of California and Texas.

(Continued)

(Continued)

UNIT: ESSENTIAL QUESTION	TEXT	GENRE	PERSPECTIVES OFFERED
Resistance: How do we define resistance? In what ways can individuals and communities resist forces that threaten to destroy them?	*The Marrow Thieves* by Cherie Dimaline	novel	In Dimaline's post-apocalyptic novel, a climate change disaster leaves the majority of the population unable to dream. Only Indigenous peoples still retain the ability to dream and are thus hunted for their bone marrow, where the power to dream resides. Together, the Indigenous characters work together to resist capture, search for their families, and find a new home.
	Away from Home: American Indian Boarding School Experiences, edited by Margaret Archuleta, Brenda J. Child, and Tsianina Lomawaima	essays, photographs, artwork, first-hand accounts	This collection includes historical accounts from Indigenous peoples who were forced to attend American Indian boarding schools and provide a perspective of what happens when individuals and communities are torn from their families and homes.
	"A Conversation with Native Americans on Race" from the *New York Times*	video documentaries	In this opinion-documentary, Native Americans share their experiences and illuminate the ways in which the government and government policies threaten their connection to their families and their tribes.
	Fry Bread: A Native American Family Story by Kevin Noble Maillard	children's picture book	In this picture book, students can appreciate the ways in which maintaining traditions around food can be an act of resistance.
	"Thoughts on Resistance" by Rebecca Roanhorse	essay	In this brief, poetic essay, Roanhorse defines what resistance is in the context of the Native peoples and identities.
	"Once the World was Perfect" by Joy Harjo	poetry	In this poem, Joy Harjo meditates on the way communities have worked together throughout generations

FIGURE 6.15   TRACKING PERSPECTIVES

RESISTANCE: HOW DO WE DEFINE RESISTANCE? IN WHAT WAYS CAN INDIVIDUALS AND COMMUNITIES RESIST FORCES THAT THREATEN TO DESTROY THEM?				
TEXT	*THE MARROW THIEVES* BY CHERIE DIMALINE	*FRY BREAD: A NATIVE AMERICAN FAMILY STORY* BY KEVIN NOBLE MAILLARD	"THOUGHTS ON RESISTANCE" BY REBECCA ROANHORSE	"ONCE THE WORLD WAS PERFECT" BY JOY HARJO
How it Answers the Essential Question				
Perspectives this Text Includes / Centers				
How it compares / contrasts with another text				
Additional thinking / question that this text leads us to consider				

AFTER READING: REFLECTING AND RECONSIDERING OUR PERSPECTIVES

Supporting students' capacity to exercise perspective-taking as a *habit* is crucial to engaging in antibias reading and critical literacy. By practicing intentional perspective-taking skills as they read, students build these skills as a habit. This habit continues when they're finished reading, too. Here, I share a few strategies that encourage students to look back on their reading with a little distance and assess their takeaways.

▶ One thing that I learned is that everyone has a different level of interpretation of the texts that we read. In this way, no one person comes away having read the same book. It was interesting to hear what other people focused on, or interpreted, compared to me. I like seeing that some people approached it emotionally, some logically, or some from an action standpoint.

—11th-grade student

Reading Through Identity Lenses

After students have read several texts, we take time individually and as a class to think explicitly about the ways in which our identities may have informed our reading and response to these texts. (Note that this is the same process in chapter 3 (p. 93) when students reflect on the identities they brought to their writing, except now applied to reading.) I ask students first to consider all the texts we've read—whether those texts are full-length books, longform essays, or brief excerpts of mentor texts—and choose five that can be grouped into the following categories: texts they loved, others they liked, and those they didn't like.

Next, we brainstorm a list of elements of identity that are central to who we might be as readers and people. We review our initial identity inventory to generate this list, and as a class, we agree on five to seven elements that we feel are most important to consider. Then I invite students to complete their list of elements with choices of their own. We write these elements across the top of the table (Figure 6.16).

I then ask students to think back to their reading of these texts and to consider which elements of their identity were active during their reading. For example, in reading Jesmyn Ward's "Raising a Black Son," was their own awareness of their own racial identity heightened or "activated" during their reading? Students consider each of these aspects of their identity and indicate the extent to which they might have been active as they read:

- Checkmark: Definitely activated this element of my identity as I read; I was conscious and aware of doing so

- Horizontal line: May have activated this element of my identity a little; I wasn't necessarily conscious or aware of doing so

- Zero: Definitely did not resonate with any element of my identity

Students then look at the data, and I prompt them to look for any patterns in their reading: Is there any relationship between their perceived enjoyment of a text and the connections they make to their own identity when they are reading? If so, which elements? (A blank version of this chart can be downloaded from the online companion, resources .corwin.com/getfree.)

Responding Through Identity Lenses: Identity-Conscious Reader Response

Noticing patterns of how our identities surface in our reading is one thing. But taking the time to consider how these elements of their identity actively inform their reading is where students can elevate their critical consciousness. Figure 6.17 outlines a structure to help students

FIGURE 6.16 READER-IDENTITY STANCE

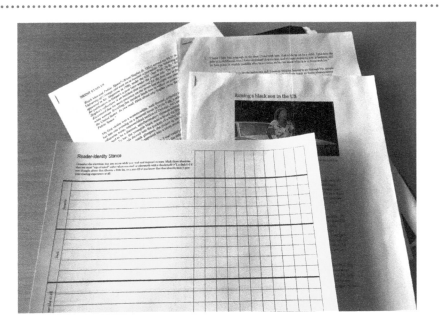

Reader-Identity Stance

Decide which pieces you've read that you've loved, liked, or thought were just okay. Then consider the identities that you accessed while you read and responded to those texts. Mark those identities that are most "top of mind" either when you read or afterwards with a checkmark (✔), a dash (—) if you thought about that identity a little bit, or a zero (0) if you know that that identity wasn't part of your reading experience at all.

		race	gender	nationality	language	socioeconomics	daughter	wife	mother	teacher	ability	friend
L O V E D	"The Future Needs Us" - Rebecca Solnit	✓	✓	✓	✓	✓	—	—	✓	✓	—	✓
	"Raising a Black Son" - Jesmyn Ward	✓	✓	✓	—	✓	—	—	✓	✓		
	"What We Hunger For" - Roxane Gay	✓	✓	—	—	—	—	—	✓	✓	—	✓
	Patron Saints of Nothing - Randy Ribay	✓	✓	✓	✓	✓	✓	—	✓	✓	✓	✓
	"To be of Use" - Marge Piercy	—	✓	—	—	—	✓	—	✓	✓	—	—
L I K E D	"Allowables" - Nikki Giovanni	✓	✓	✓	—	✓	—	—	✓	✓	—	—
	Writings on the Wall - K.A.Jabbar	✓	✓	✓	—	—	—	—	✓	✓	—	—
	"Reading Jane Eyre while Black" - T.Coleman	✓	✓	—	✓	✓	✓	—	✓	✓	—	—
	The New Plant Parent - D. Cheng	✓	✓	—	—	—	—	—	✓	—	—	✓
	Starfish - A.D Bowman	✓	✓	—	—	✓	—	—	—	—	—	✓
O K A Y	Klara and The Sun - K. Ishiguro	✓	✓	—	—	✓	✓	—	✓	✓	—	—
	Turtles All The Way Down	—	✓	—	—	—	—	—	—	✓	✓	✓
	The Memory of Things - G. Polisner	—	—	—	—	—	—	—	—	—	—	✓
	Girls Burn Brighter - S.Rao	✓	✓	✓	—	—	—	—	—	—	—	—
	Heart of Darkness - Conrad	✓	✓	✓	—	0	0	0	0	0	0	0

take a step back and reflect on how their reading has been informed by their various identities. Note that structures can be used both during and after reading a text to help students make meaning and deepen their understanding.

FIGURE 6.17 IDENTITY CONSCIOUS READER RESPONSE

Scaffold for reading and responding to arguments:

As a person who _____ (identity/experience), I see _____ (issue or perspective) with/as _____ (opinion or reaction) because in my experience,_____ (possible reasoning or support).

I recognize that my view may be limited or challenging to me because . . .

In order to deepen my understanding, here are some questionings or wonderings I can explore . . .

Scaffold for reading and responding to fiction:

As a person who _____ (identity/experience), I see _____ (moment, character, or conflict in the story) with/as _____ (opinion or reaction) because in my experience,_____ (possible reasoning or support).

I recognize that my view may be limited or challenging to me because . . .

In order to deepen my understanding, here are some questionings or wonderings I can explore . . .

Scaffold for reading and responding to poetry:

As a person who _____ (identity/experience), I see _____ (moment, word, or line in the poem) with/as _____ (opinion or reaction) because in my experience,_____ (possible reasoning or support).

I recognize that my view may be limited or challenging to me because . . .

In order to deepen my understanding, here are some questionings or wonderings I can explore . . .

This structure provides just enough scaffolding to encourage students to connect how their response—to a specific issue, perspective, text, or an element of fiction (character, plot, conflict, theme)—may be informed by an identity or experience they have. For example, here is how I might model this for students with my own response to the immigration and border challenges:

> As a person who *is Catholic and the child of immigrants,* I see *the current immigration and border crises with sympathy for those who may be fleeing danger in search of safety for their families,* because in my experience, *it is the responsibility of those with the means to help those who seek help.*
>
> I recognize that my view may be limited because I don't live in a border state and the practical realities of what communities in those areas face is not something I encounter on a daily basis.
>
> In order to deepen my understanding, I would want to read more first-hand accounts of people in those communities to learn about the impact of these issues on them.

Or here's another example related to the issue of school choice:

> As a person who is a *public school teacher*, I see *the school choice debate and charter schools* as a *distraction from addressing deeper issues of poverty and systemic inequality,* because in my experience, *student academic success depends on environmental factors as much as it does on the quality of the school.*
>
> I recognize that my view may be limited because I have had access to go to well-funded and resourced schools and haven't had to worry about not having a good public school option.
>
> In order to deepen my understanding, I want to learn more about the challenges that under-resourced communities face and why a school choice program would have its advantages.

Below is an example of how I might use this scaffold to model responding to a moment in the novel *A Nectar in a Sieve* by Kamala Markandaya, in which a young character dies.

> As someone who is a mother, I read the scene where Kuti dies with intense sorrow and sense of helplessness, because in my experience, I would do anything for my own children and would be devasted if I could not help them.
>
> I recognize that my reaction is challenging for me because I am also a daughter of immigrant parents who sacrificed so much in their own lives to ensure that I had every opportunity possible. I know my parents would do everything for me and therefore, I would do everything for my own children.
>
> In order to deepen my understanding, I may want to learn more about how issues of poverty or colonialism in the novel can have lasting impacts on generations of families.

▶ When using this scaffold for responding to elements of a novel or poem, I often ask students to first mark in the text or list specific moments, characters, conflicts, or lines that both resonated with them as well as challenged them. They can then choose from their annotations or lists of what resonates and what challenges them to complete the scaffold.

And finally, here is how I might use this scaffold to respond to Ariana Brown's spoken word poem, "Ode to Thrift Stores."

> As someone whose immigrant mother was a bargain hunter shopper, I resonated with the lines "Mom had rules when I was young. Pants should be under $10, shirts less than

twenty, a good jacket maybe 15 or 20," because in my experience, my mom had similar rules and never considered something "on sale" unless it was at least 50 percent off.

In order to deepen my understanding, I may want to learn more about how thrift stores came to be and what role they play in different communities.

As you can see, this scaffold is versatile enough to use when responding to characters in a novel or to an issue in an argument. If we can identify not just how we feel or think about an issue but also where those feelings or thoughts come from, we can see the issue with the complexity it warrants. Furthermore, we can and should push our students to dig deeper. As much as our identities inform our feelings and thoughts, they can also limit us. Even our strongest opinions need to be approached with humility, and we need to name the lenses that we bring to a text. That said, notice that in the last example, I did not include how the poem limited or challenged how I responded. In this case, that part of the scaffold didn't apply—and that's okay. While scaffolds can support understanding, we also should encourage students to consider how some scaffolds may not be the right tool they need. We can adapt them as needed for our purposes.

Watch and listen to Ariana Brown perform her poem, "Ode to Thrift Stores."

To see this type of self-reflection at work in an authentic mentor text, consider what writer Tyrese L. Coleman has written about reading *Jane Eyre* as a Black woman. Because Coleman is Black, and because the "dark skin" of the Bertha Mason in the novel is repeatedly referenced and vilified, Coleman (2017) does not have the "privilege of escapism, which is a fundamental reason that people read fiction." She continues:

> Even if I wanted to, I would be barred from ever seeing any part of myself in Jane—because to be Jane would mean to be in direct opposition to myself.
>
> Much has been written about *Jane Eyre* and its revolutionary feminism. But many of these readings are not intersectional. Instead, they promote a particular understanding of white feminism, one that erases women of color and fails to consider the demeaning ways Brontë draws any woman who isn't white. Any present-day analysis of *Jane Eyre* that does not address the racial complexities of this book is being deliberately dismissive of readers like me. Brontë's intentions do not trump the effects of the text. To call this book

feminist is to forget about me, that I am a reader too, that I am a woman too. That according to Brontë, I am a savage.

Identity-Conscious Character Analysis

Just as we can use an Identity-Conscious Reader Response approach to help students better understand how their own identities inform their response, students can also apply this approach for the characters in texts that they read (or even the authors of those texts). How might characters' various, complex, and nuanced identities inform how they navigate the worlds in the texts they inhabit? To begin, students create an identity inventory for a character (pp. 93–100), and then adapt the scaffold from the previous section to that character. Figure 6.18 provides an adapted version of this scaffold to help students process and analyze characters.

FIGURE 6.18   IDENTITY-CONSCIOUS CHARACTER ANALYSIS

As someone who _____ [character's identity/experience], _____
[character] responded to _____ [moment/other character/conflict] with
_____ [reaction] because _____ [possible reasoning/support].

As a reader, I understand / am challenged by _____'s [character's] response because . . .

In order to deepen my understanding, here are some questions or wonderings I can explore . . .

Why Identity-Conscious Reader Response Matters

Asking students to consider how their *multiple* identities affect how they read the world is more important now than ever. We live in an increasingly divided society; more often than not, people seem to interpret the same news in drastically different ways. We're talking over, around, and at each other. Perhaps with a better understanding of the ways our identities can give us insight but also blind us, we can engage in more critical, reflective inquiry. We can approach reading knowing that each of us contains multitudes. As you can see in Figure 6.19, there is *so much* that informs how we read and respond. The better we can understand how this process works in ourselves, the better we can engage with others knowing that they, too, bring multitudes.

FIGURE 6.19   COMPLEXITIES OF READER RESPONSE

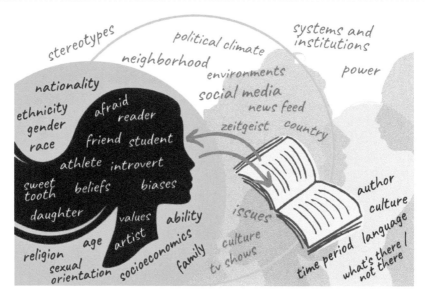

Figure 6.19 captures some of the incredibly complex and simultaneous forces at work whenever we engage in reading.

This structure I've outlined here is a *starting point* for reflection, not the end goal. I ask students to dig deeper and continue writing and reflecting on this, first in their notebook (and during class when I know that they can have quiet time to reflect deeply) and then in a typed response that they share with me. I then use both the chart and the reflection during teacher-student conferences. Figure 6.20 provides an overview of the process of how we can support students in making the connections between their identities to their reading of themselves, texts, and the world.

From Reading (themselves and the world) to Writing (themselves and the world)

When I confer with students about the identity stances they're using when they're reading, it also serves as an opportunity to think about what they might want to write about when the time comes. "Writing floats on a sea of talk" (Britton, 1970, p. 164), and as students become more comfortable talking about their identities, the possibilities for their writing expand. Students might, for example, feel challenged to think about issues about themselves and/or others they had not yet considered. My hope is that students walk away from these conversations grappling a little with their responses to texts, whether those responses are positive or negative, and how they might lean into these responses in their writing about their identities through personal narratives or other types of essays.

FIGURE 6.20 SYNTHESIZING AN IDENTITY-CONSCIOUS READER RESPONSE AND CHARACTER/TEXT ANALYSIS

1. READER	2. TEXT	3. IDENTITY-CONSCIOUS READER RESPONSE	4. IDENTITY-CONSCIOUS CHARACTER/TEXT ANALYSIS	5. CRITICAL CONSCIOUSNESS
• What identities do I have? • What identities and experiences do I bring when I read?	• What moments resonate? What moments challenge? • What characters resonate? What characters challenge? • What questions do I have?	• How do my identites impact how I read this text? How I respond to characters? • How do my identites enrich and deepen my response to this text? • How do my identites limit my response to this text?	• How do the character's identites impact how they navigate their world? • What questions are raised? • What do I need to learn or understand better?	How do systems and institutions of **power** or privilege play a role in these dynamics between readers, texts, and the world?

Not surprisingly, when I've done this exercise with students, one key finding is clear: **Students of color are more likely to keep race or culture in mind no matter what text they read than White students, who typically only consider these aspects of identity if the text is explicitly about race or culture.** While this seems an obvious point, we can't underestimate its power. If we want students to grapple with issues of race, culture, and identity—and grapple in a way that is nuanced and complex—we need to give them the opportunities to do so through all of the texts we read and study in class.

You'll find a blank, downloadable reader identity stance chart on the online companion, resources.corwin.com/getfree. But before using this tool with students, I encourage you to use the tool for yourself. Think about the last dozen or so things you've read recently: Which facets of identity were active as you read and why? What might this reveal about your own reading processes? Which elements of identity do you consider most often, and why? And how might these processes affect the choices you make as a teacher?

When you do this exercise with students, ask yourself: What patterns do you notice? What might these reveal about how students are reading and responding to texts? In what way could these charts provide data to guide instruction?

This is a simple but potentially powerful reflection that echoes a K-W-L but at the end of a reading rather than the beginning. Students think about the essential questions and consider the ways in which their thinking has changed as a result of a text or text set.

- I used to think . . .

- Now I think . . .

- But I still want to know . . .

After identifying what they still want to know, students then research and identify an additional source for the text set that not only helps to answer what they still want to know but also offers an additional perspective that can make the original text set richer and more nuanced. Along with the source, students may offer a written explanation of their rationale for including this in the text set.

Personal Perspective-Taking Through Writing

Finally, extended writing responses are opportunities for students to marry their own perspective with the text in ways that can be equally authentic and powerful.

Rumination Essays

A few years ago, I came across the concept of a rumination essay from English teachers at Stuyvesant High School. Put simply, in a rumination essay, a student selects a key passage or scene from a text, analyzes it, and then uses it as a starting point for reflection for the rest of the essay.

A rumination is a hybrid: it begins as an analytical essay but develops into a personal narrative. For example, below is the opening of a rumination essay I wrote to share with students. This rumination essay uses Alberto Rios's poem, "A House Called Tomorrow" as the starting point—

> In Alberto Rios's poem, "A House Called Tomorrow," the speaker reflects:
>
> > When you as a child learned to speak,
> >
> > It's not that you didn't know words—
> >
> > It's that, from the centuries, you knew so many,
> >
> > And it's hard to choose the words that will be your own.
>
> Rios subverts the reader's expectations in these lines as he reframes a child's inability to speak not as a deficit but as *abundance*. A *blessing of abundance*. It's not that the child

doesn't have the words, but that he has too many—and not just too many but "centuries" worth of words.

My parents emigrated from the Philippines in the 1970s, and although I grew up knowing I was proud of my cultural roots, there was so much I didn't know. The Tagalog words that rolled off my parents' tongues, the *kumustas!* and *pares!* and *oys!* that danced in the air and announced my relatives' arrival before their feet stepped through the doorway—these words are the only ones I have. Whenever I read these lines from Rios's poem, I think about all the words that I didn't know as a child—and that I still don't know even now, decades later. Unlike the speaker in Rios's poem, it's not because I couldn't choose the ones to be my own, but because there were the only ones I had left. Of the centuries of words that came before remain but a few.

How does a rumination essay help students practice perspective-taking? To write a rumination essay, students need to consider a small passage in its original context, but by linking it to a personal experience, students must think about *their own positionality compared to the text*: how the passage might function differently in the text than it does for them as readers.

Learn more about rumination essays from Dr. Dana Huff.

Letter-Essays

Similarly, a letter-essay (Atwell, 2014) invites students to respond to text from the reader's personal stance. Figure 6.21 shows a sample letter-essay that my colleague, Ben Smith, uses with his own students after they finish reading *October Mourning*. As you can see, it includes the assignment details, but it also invites students to take a personal perspective to the literature. I also often encourage and even ask students to include, as part of their reflection, how their thinking has changed over time as a result of this text.

FIGURE 6.21 PERSONALIZING PERSPECTIVE-TAKING THROUGH LETTER WRITING

Hey, Writer's Craft Folks!

Thanks for your time and thoughtfulness in reading Leslea Newman's *October Mourning*.

When I start the poetry unit, I'm always aware that there are students in the room who haven't read much poetry at all. For the reasons we talked about with Billy Collins' poem "Introduction to Poetry," we often feel like we need to "figure out" a poem, as opposed to looking at one, feeling one, skimming across one. In a collection like *October Mourning*, where all the poems fit together to tell a single story, I've noticed that students find it easier to follow the abstract nature of the poems, as each page builds off the last. Did you find that to be true?

(Continued)

(Continued)

I also appreciate the seriousness you brought to the text and our discussions. Matthew's story is tragic and upsetting. Newman's poems are very emotional, and it can be exhausting to make your way through those details and images. I'm aware that it may have been more difficult for some readers.

I'm also aware that members and allies of the LGBTQ+ community likely have a more personal and visceral reaction, as they see echoes of themselves or their friends and family in Matthew's story, and may carry that extra weight of *closeness*.

I'm glad we can share Matthew's story with you. If you consider every book you've ever read in school, it won't be a surprise to realize there have been few (if any) about gay characters. It's also probably not a surprise when the stories we *do* have access to are painful ones. When your story isn't part of the dominant narrative, it can be filled with challenges and trauma many of us can't see. We're seeing some change now in this representation, but we still have a lot of work to do.

But like all good art, stories like Matthew's, no matter your background or experience, remind us what it means to be human—in this case, how we experience pain and loss and, importantly, how we find ways to heal and carry on.

Losing my dad last year has me reading this collection a little differently. In rereading the poems, I'm thinking about how often Newman personifies objects to help tell Matthew's story. In past years, I've appreciated the cleverness of this poetic strategy. It made sense to me intellectually—as an English teacher. But this past year, as I wander around in the fog of my dad's death, I know how powerfully objects can take on meaning. I spend more time looking at his ring that I wear; before I leave for school, I touch the laminated portrait and prayer card from the funeral; I reread a quote he left in his desk at work; I keep trying to find the best place for two of his ties I kept.

My biggest takeaway from *October Mourning* is how desperately we need love to guide our words and actions, how that love can smite hate, and how it's our job to amplify the stories of the lost and the lonely, the depressed and oppressed.

Instead of an essay or a quiz, here's what you can do: write me a letter in response. Your response should/can:

- Be a personal and specific reaction to *October Mourning*.
- Feel free to address any idea or question I bring up in my letter.
- Ask questions—rhetorically or to me.
- Comment on the experience of reading the book; on poetry or other readings.
- Divide it up into smaller paragraphs; use your voice.
- Refer to the text.
- Around 250 words would be good. A little more or less is fine.
- Bring a printed copy to class.

Thanks again. I look forward to hearing from you,

Mr. Smith

PERSPECTIVE-TAKING IN INDEPENDENT CHOICE READING

If active and intentional perspective-taking is a key element of antibias education and critical literacy, then we cannot limit students to the perspectives that we include in our curricular choices, no matter how rich, diverse, and inclusive those are. Students need to be able to *choose* perspectives that can be "window, mirrors, and sliding glass doors" (Bishop, 1990). So although I focus on strategies throughout this chapter for whole-class, shared literature study, **we must also remember to provide support—access, time, and space—for students to develop a rich, independent reading life and identity through choice reading.**

Students need *access* to diverse and inclusive texts from which they can choose, to explore the issues that matter to them outside the choices we make for them in our curriculum. Students need *time* dedicated during the school day to read, because we know that students are more likely to

▶ "Immerse yourself in literature that matters and that sharpens your zeal for human rights, social justice, and teaching. Connect yourself with others who are doing this work."

—Jamilah Pitts (2021, p. 84)

choose to read outside our classrooms if we build a habit of choice reading within our classrooms. My students, for example, begin each class with ten minutes of independent reading, during which time I can confer with a few students at a time. Finally, students need *space* to share their reading, to talk with their peers, to recommend books to each other, and to write about what they're learning about themselves and others.

At the same time, however, we must also remember **the role that bias can play in students' independent reading selections**. I firmly believe in not judging students on the choices they make about what to read; students *read what they need, whatever that may be* (recall my affection for *Sweet Valley High* books). That said, as teachers, we can guide students to be aware of the biases they bring to their choices and encourage them to enact a "liberatory consciousness" in their independent reading. How can we help students find those critical mirrors but also seek windows and sliding glass doors?

In addition to active and intentional book-talking of diverse and inclusive literature, here are some other considerations:

- Ask students to keep track of their reading *and* to notice what patterns emerge: do they tend to choose the same thing (and same perspectives)? How might you nudge students toward expanding their choices? Because of **confirmation bias**, students may only be seeking mirrors: how can we help them notice, name, and change this?

- Likewise, as teachers, we often recommend books to students based on our own biases. Because of the **availability heuristic**, we recall titles based on what's readily available in our working memory, and

because of the **recency effect,** we also tend to recall what was more recently in time. As teachers, we can address this by taking the extra time to consider titles, keeping a running list, or simply intentionally forcing ourselves to dig back in our memory for another title we may not have thought about in a while but may be the next "right" book for the students in front of us.

- Create connections between texts that might not be readily apparent to students. If a student loves reading dystopian literature, in addition to encouraging them to read outside the genre, encourage them to diversify their experiences *within* the genre, particularly by recommending authors of color they might not yet know. For example, while students may have read Suzanne Collins and Neal Shusterman, have they read Tomi Ayedemi or Nnedi Okorafor? Or if a student loved a fantasy like *Children of Blood and Bone*, suggest a realistic fiction title *Nigeria Jones* that connects thematically as a coming-of-age story.

- Provide students with a checklist or menu of options that encourage them to read more broadly. Next to my classroom library, for example, I display a poster with such options and that I can easily reference when conferring with students while we're looking through the shelves for their next independent reading selection. (include photo)

- Remember, too, that any of the strategies I've shared here with whole-class, shared texts may be adapted for independent, choice reading as well. The more we ask students to apply the skills and habits of thinking they employ in whole-class texts with their independent reading, the better able they will be to *transfer* their skills across a variety of contexts and tasks.

These suggestions are a good starting point, and I encourage you to read Dr. Sonja Cherry-Paul and Dana Johansen's wonderful book, *Breathing New Life into Book Clubs*. In it, they provide wisdom and countless practical strategies for how to expand students' reading lives.

FIGURE 6.22   SUMMARY OF PERSPECTIVE-TAKING AND PERSPECTIVE-BENDING READING STRATEGIES

Before Reading: Analyzing the Perspectives We Bring to Reading	Modified K-W-L Chart	p. 236
	K–T–D Chart	p. 238
	Beyond Prior Knowledge With an Open-Ended Survey	p. 239
	Beyond Anticipation Guides: Four Corners, Spectrum, Meet in the Middle	p. 241
	Journaling Tensions and Essential Questions	p. 244
	Concept Mapping Definitions and Essential Questions	p. 244
During Reading: Practicing Perspective-Taking and Perspective-Bending	Rethinking Characters and Characterization	p. 245
	Who Is Centered? Who Is Marginalized? Who Is Missing? (C-M-M)	p. 247
	Reframing Character Analysis	p. 249
	Step In, Step Out, Step Back	p. 250
	Above and Below the Line	p. 250
	Character Spectrum	p. 251
	Tracking Their Perspective-Taking Over Time	p. 255
	Second (and Third) Draft Thinking	p. 256
	Naming Beliefs That Impact Interpretation	p. 257
	Bias Check-in	p. 258
	Making and Remaking Claims	p. 259
	If . . . Then . . .	p. 262
	Using Literary Theory as Lenses for Perspective-Taking	p. 263
	Engaging and Tracking Perspective-Rich Text Sets	p. 270
After Reading: Reflecting and Reconsidering Our Perspectives	Reading Through Identity Lenses	p. 274
	Responding Through Identity Lenses: Identity Conscious Reader Response	p. 274
	What I Used to Think, What I Think Now, What I Still Want to Know	p. 282
	Personal Perspective-taking Through Writing	p. 282
	Rumination Essays	p. 282
	Letter-Essays	p. 283

EPILOGUE

Raising a child requires profound strength and hope. You must believe in your ability to forge a future that is better than the one we currently inhabit, even if you never live to see it.

—Angela Garbes, *Essential Labor: Mothering as Social Change*

I don't know what's coming. I do know that, whatever it is, some of it will be terrible, but some of it will be miraculous, that term we reserve for the utterly unanticipated, the seeds we didn't know the soil held. And I know that we don't know what we do does. As Shane Bauer points out, the doing is the crucial thing.

—Rebecca Solnit, "The Arc of Justice and the Long Run"

What is grief, if not love persevering?

—Vision, from Marvel's *WandaVision*

This book is a love story.

It's also a grief story.

. . .

Here's the love story.

I started this book in 2018. I never thought I'd write a book, or wanted to, even though I've always been a writer. I'd been intensely shy in school, so what I couldn't say aloud, I wrote down. I was lucky enough to have teachers who noticed and encouraged me to write more. It's partly because of those teachers that I became a teacher: they saw something in me and created a space where that something could be heard and known.

I didn't consider teaching as a career until I was more than halfway through college. I loved reading and writing, I enjoyed being around people, and I believed in the powerful role that schools had in a democracy. Teaching seemed a good fit.

Sometime during those early years in the classroom, I fell in love. I loved being a high school English teacher. I didn't always love everything I taught, or decisions that were out of my control, and I definitely did not love all that came with having to navigate a predominantly White profession—but I loved teaching, and I loved being with young people. I loved seeing the ways students were challenged and challenged each other, I loved the way they asked the best questions and were funny when they didn't mean to be. I loved how smart and wise they were, even when they didn't always make the smartest or wisest decisions. I loved that I had things I could teach them, and I loved how there was always something new they taught me. I loved the way we built community in the classroom together, day in and day out. I loved it all—even on the hardest of hard days.

Perhaps especially on those days.

I also loved working side by side with colleagues who were as smitten with kids as I was. Over the years, I found community with fellow teachers—both in and out of school, in the classrooms next door and in classrooms across the country—who pushed me to be a better version of myself. I loved their creativity, and I was continuously awed by their talent for finding ways to make learning relevant and meaningful for the kids sitting in front of them. I loved nerding out with people who laughed at the same teacher puns I did but who also cried with me on those heart-wrenching days after. Days like the ones after Parkland, where a shooter gunned down seventeen people at Marjorie

Stoneman Douglas High School in 2018 in Florida. And the many days after March 2020, when the world declared the global COVID-19 a pandemic and the world turned upside down.

. . .

And now here's the grief story.

I started this book in 2018. As I began closing in on my second decade of teaching, and with the encouragement of some friends and mentors, I realized that some of the things I did in the classroom might be helpful for others. This book could be a humble contribution, an offering, to our collective conversations about teaching and learning.

This book was set to be published in late 2020—and then the pandemic hit.

I stopped writing.

As frightening images of the pandemic filled our screens, essential workers and frontline nurses and doctors in head-to-toe protective gear, the rest of us retreated into our homes and held our collective breath. Then the entire world bore witness to the murder of George Floyd and images of the largest civil rights protests in the nation's history filled our news feeds. Violent acts of anti-Asian hate, particularly against Asian elders, added another level of worry for my own elderly parents' health and safety. And amidst all of this, I had students to teach.

Like many educators across the country, I spent every spare minute trying to adjust curriculum, figure out how to screen-share, create breakout groups, teach kids at home and in-person simultaneously, to keep learning going, sometimes, it seemed, at all costs. And like many parents, I also had my own children at home. Looking back, the stack of N95 masks and hand sanitizer were woefully insufficient, but it felt like the least I could do to keep my family safe.

I was about 75-80 percent finished with the manuscript for this book, but I couldn't write a single word. How could *anything* I wrote matter when we were all just trying to survive?

. . .

Much has been written about how the pandemic revealed the weaknesses in many of our systems—from healthcare and social welfare, economics and education. When each of these systems was challenged by the pandemic, the weakest parts of each of them were strained and exposed. When the news began reporting that the pandemic was having a disproportionately negative impact on Black and Brown communities

and calls to "open" schools and businesses soon followed, it became clear whose lives were considered essential and disposable. Of course, this wasn't news to anyone with an understanding of history, but that didn't mean it hurt any less.

Teaching had always been demanding work. Yet even before the pandemic, I could feel the work I was doing—teaching full time and facilitating much of the equity work in my department and school—was becoming unsustainable. But I was sustaining it. I was doing what many women, and especially women of color, do—I was figuring it out. The work was too important.

A few days after six Asian women were killed at an Atlanta spa in March 2021, I found myself sitting alone, behind my plexiglassed desk, and just. . . sobbing. Everything that I had been so skilled at holding in—every racial trauma and hurt I'd experienced and that I'd compartmentalized—now refused to stay quiet. My insides screamed. I could no longer explain away or unsee the way people and systems showed up during the pandemic, after George Floyd, after those six women were killed. I couldn't understand how reimagining education really meant keeping the status quo. And so even though there was so much and so many to love where I was, there was also too much to bear.

In June 2021, and after twenty years, I made the decision to leave the school where I had fallen in love with teaching and kids.

I've been grieving every day since.

. . .

That grief has nothing to do with regret, however.

Though my work looks different now in my current school and in this new leadership role, I still get to teach and spend time with young people. Not a day goes by that I'm not reminded of how important social justice, antibias education is. It didn't take very long for me to fall in love with sitting in a circle with four-year-olds, as they learn to appreciate that what makes us different—whether it's the people in our families, the melanin in our skin, or the foods we love to eat—also makes us stronger. Every day, I'm humbled and honored to be sitting with middle schoolers who are vulnerable and brave enough to share their truths in ways that take my breath away.

Life—for me and I suspect for many others—is often marked by a before and after, an indelible moment that changes forever how we move in the world. My teaching life has a before and after, marked by a pandemic whose effects none of us have even begun to understand. Fights about mask mandates have been replaced by book banning crusades and anti-LGBTQ laws that put kids' lives in danger. The list of things to fight against is relentless.

. . .

When I put this manuscript down and stopped writing three years ago, I struggled because I wasn't sure that anything I had to say mattered. When I picked it back up again, however, I struggled because I realized that everything I'd written *did* matter. It was painful to reread words I'd written before the pandemic, before I left the only school I'd ever known as a teacher. Revising and revisiting this "before" time made all the old griefs fresh again.

But then I was reminded that you can only experience grief after experiencing love. Like I said, this book is a grief story, but it's also a love story.

Teachers know about love. When we teach with love, we see each of our kids with the respect and compassion, complexity and messiness that makes them human. When we teach with love, we lead with grace and openness and hope. When we teach with love, we know that our liberation is bound in each other. If you're reading this book, I hope that it may encourage you to love fiercely even on days when our grief about the world, when people or systems let us down, seems unbearable.

Perhaps especially on those days. Because the list of things to fight *for* is everlasting.

ACKNOWLEDGMENTS

> *The only way to survive is by taking care of one another.*
>
> —Grace Lee Boggs

There are too many people to thank, but I will try.

I owe so much of who I am to my first teachers, my mom and dad. Mom and Dad, from you I learned what it means to be generous, kind, and a good person in the world. You taught me the value of integrity, of working hard, and most of all, of loving unconditionally. I am a better parent and human being because of you.

To my brother, Jay. Growing up together and having you as a brother helped me become a better person. Our shared love of X-Men and pop culture helped me see things from new perspectives I always appreciated.

Writing this book was a labor of love that wouldn't be possible without the women who picked me up, cheered me on, and insisted I had something important to say. We are each other's harvest, magnitude, and bond.

To Anna Osborn: I admire the way you fight for kids' literacy lives, day in and day out, and your infinite capacity for care (and iced tea). To Aeriale Johnson: you are an expert in all things tiny humans, and I only wish you could be every child's first teacher. To Tiana Silvas: I am in awe of the way you show such deep respect for every student's voice and the way you show fearless loyalty for all those you love. To Dr. Sonja Cherry-Paul: you challenge me to be the best version of myself. You are relentless in your pursuit of justice and building a better world. I can't wait for the day we get to open that ice cream shop. To Dr. Kim Parker: I will never forget the way you pulled me aside on our first day in NH together and said, *Tricia, come here, you're one of us.* Since then, we have bonded in friendship, built community, and gotten into shenanigans I will forever be grateful for. May we all dazzle and bedazzle for decades to come. To my fellow disruptors, Julia Torres and Lorena Germán: I am endlessly awed by your power as educators, as mothers, as women who know themselves, give of themselves, and stand unabated in the fight for justice. And to Dr. Valeria Brown: one of the only people in this world who could get my introverted self to go all-in on ice-breakers. Thank you for being a role model for how to lead with curiosity, humility, and a steadfast commitment to justice.

I'm not the teacher I am today without those who loved me through these many years of ups and downs. To Karen Gately: I don't think there are words to express how grateful I am that you were there when I started teaching. Thank you for being my first teacher friend, and then for being my person through all the hard, messy, and heartaching tears and laughter. And to Ben Smith, my friend and next-door neighbor, thank you. It's been one of my greatest joys getting to teach with you and lesson-plan together on the way to our cars, in the hallway, over text message, and in the five minutes in between bells. Your creativity is only outmatched by your heart. To Judith Shepherd and Bridget McGuinn: I'm so grateful that yours were voices who guided me through those first formative years I was learning to be a teacher. To Katie Wilson: thank you for being someone who always stands clearly on the side of doing right by kids. To Keri Phillips and Brooke Hauer: thank you for being people who fight for kids' reading lives and who enrich my own. Thank you to Christopher Brown, Steph Matula, and Dr. Chandra Singh, whose friendships remind me how teaching well means teaching in community. To Leashia Lewis, my friend, my sister: I'm so grateful how we were there for each other at all the right times in the most important ways and will be for the rest of our lives.

To all those part of the IREL family, #31DaysIBPOC communities, and all the people who I'm honored to count among my people: Sara Ahmed, Scott Bayer, Dr. Sarah-Soonling Blackburn, M. Colleen Cruz, Dulce-Marie Flecha, Shana Frazin, Joel Garza, Chris Hall, Amanda Hartman, Jess Lifshitz, shea martin, Jessyca Mathews, Dr. Cody Miller, Christie Nold,

Minjung Pai, Kate Roberts, Maggie Roberts, Keisha Smith-Carrington, Josh Thompson, LaMar Timmons-Long, and Michelle Yang-Kaczmarek. I am grateful for your trust, wisdom, and immense talents.

To the "PAWLP" Writing Project family: you were there in my early days of writing, thinking, and learning. This book is because of you.

To Tobey Antao, who stewarded me through this writing journey with grace, respect, compassion, and care, thank you. You pushed me to think deeply about my work and this book is better because of you. To Tori Bachman, who helped me get over the finish line, whose encouragement and faith meant so much exactly when I needed it, thank you. And thank you to Sharon Wu, Scott Van Atta, Sarah Ross, Amy Schroller, Margaret O'Connor, Lynne Curry, and the entire team at Corwin and Sage who helped bring this book to its final stages. To Gian Wong, whose beautiful artwork graces these pages—maraming salamat.

To all the students I've ever taught and who have taught me—thank you.

And finally, to my husband, Brian, and our three boys, Matthew, Toby, and Colin. To Brian: you have been a patient and supportive partner who always helps me be my best self. You encourage me, you encourage the boys, and you hold our family together and make all our dreams possible. To Matthew, Toby, and Colin: so much of who I am and why I want to make the world better is borne out of my love for you. No matter what else I do in my life, being your mother is the work that I am most proud of. I love you, no matter what, deeply and always.

Publisher's Acknowledgments

Corwin gratefully acknowledges the contributions of the following reviewers:

Jessyca Mathews
Language Arts Educator and Public Speaker
Michigan Teacher of the Year Network
Burton, MI

Theresa Walter
English Department Chair and English Teacher
Great Neck Public Schools
Greenlawn, NY

REFERENCES

Abdul-Jabbar, K. (2016). *Writings on the wall: Searching for a new equality between black and white*. Time Inc.

Acevedo, E., Matam, P., & Yamazawa, G. (2014). *Unforgettable. Button poetry*. [Video] https://youtu.be/Xvah3E1fP20

Aguilar, E. (2013). *The art of coaching*. Jossey-Bass.

Aguilar, E. (2013, October 21). A coaching framework for thinking before acting. *Education Week Teacher*. http://blogs.edweek.org/teachers/coaching_teachers/2013/10/a_coaching_framework_for_think.html

Aguilar, E. (2014, January 14). Spheres of control. *Education Week Teacher*. http://blogs.edweek.org/teachers/coaching_teachers/2014/01/spheres_of_control.html

Ahmed, S. (2018, September 12). On identity and experience. *Heinemann*. https://blog.heinemann.com/sara-ahmed-on-identity-and-experience

Alexander, K. (2016, August 8). Kwame Alexander on Children's Books and the Color of Characters. *The New York Times*. https://www.nytimes.com/2016/08/28/books/review/kwame-alexander-on-childrens-books-and-the-color-of-characters.html

Andrew, Mari. (2018, March 18). *Am I there yet?* Clarkson Potter.

Andrew, Mari. (2019, April 16). *Little gestures: Postcards for any occasion*. Clarkson Potter.

Anzaldua, G. (1987). *Borderlands / La Frontera: The new mestiza*. Aunt Lute Book Company. p. 87.

Appleman, D. (2000). *Critical encounters in high school English*. Teacher's College Press.

Armstrong, A. (2021, December 1). *The representation of social groups in U.S. educational materials and why it matters*. New America. https://www.newamerica.org/education-policy/reports/the-representation-of-social-groups-in-u-s-educational-materials-and-why-it-matter/

Atwell, Nancy. (2002). *Lessons that change writers*. Heinemann.

Atwell, Nancy. (2014). *In the middle, third edition: A lifetime of learning about writing, reading, and adolescents*. Heinemann.

Azalia, C., et al. (2021). *The state of America's children: 2021* [Report]. Children's Defense Fund. https://www.childrensdefense.org/wp-content/uploads/2021/04/The-State-of-Americas-Children-2021.pdf

Beers, K., & Probst, B. (2015). *Reading nonfiction: Notice & note stances, signposts, and strategies*. Heinemann.

Birch, S., & Bloom, P. (2006, October 30). The curse of knowledge in reasoning about false beliefs. *Psychological Science*, *18*(5), 382–386.

Bishop, R. S. (1990). Windows, mirrors, and sliding glass doors. *Perspectives*, *6*(3), ix–xi.

Black, D., & Crolley, A. (2022, April 19). *Legacy of Jim Crow still affects funding of public schools*. University of South Carolina. https://www.sc.edu/uofsc/posts/2022/04/conversation-jim-crow.php#.Y1vzHezMK3I

Boggs, G. L., & Kurishige, S. (2012, May 31). *The next American revolution: Sustainable activism for the twenty-first century*. University of California Press. p. 47.

Britton, J. (1970). *Language and learning*. University of Miami Press.

Brookfield, Stephen. (2012). *Teaching for critical thinking*. Jossey-Bass.

brown, a. (2017). *Emergent strategy: Shaping change, changing worlds*. AK Press.

Brown, Ariana. (2017, December 7). *Ode to thrift stores. Button poetry*. [Video] https://www.youtube.com/watch?v=PFZJoU44uOo&t=1s&ab_channel=Button Poetry

Brown, V., & Keels, C. L. (2021). *What it means to be an anti-racist teacher*. Learning for Justice. https://www.learningforjustice.org/magazine/spring-2021/what-it-means-to-be-an-antiracist-teacher

Bunn, C. (2022, March 3). *Report: Black people are still killed by police at a higher rate than other groups.* NBC News. https://www.nbcnews.com/news/nbcblk/report-black-people-are-still-killed-police-higher-rate-groups-rcna17169

Burkeman, O. (2015, February 3). Believing that life is fair might make you a terrible person. *The Guardian.* https://www.theguardian.com/commentisfree/oliver-burkeman-column/2015/feb/03/believing-that-life-is-fair-might-make-you-a-terrible-person

Burton, N. (2014, November 27). The meaning of nostalgia: The psychology and philosophy of nostalgia. *Psychology Today.* https://www.psychologytoday.com/us/blog/hide-and-seek/201411/the-meaning-nostalgia

Campbell, Edith. (2019, December 4). The problem with picture book monkeys: Racist imagery associating simians with Black people has a long history. *School Library Journal.* https://www.slj.com/story/The-problem-with-picture-book-monkeys-racist-imagery-libraries.

Center for Teaching and Learning. (n.d.). *Reducing Stereotype Threat: A Resource Overview.* Washington University in St. Louis. https://ctl.wustl.edu/resources/reducing-stereotype-threat/.

Chang, A. (host). (2019, March 28). *Can we overcome racial bias? 'Biased' author says to start by acknowledging it.* [radio broadcast episode]. https://www.npr.org/2019/03/28/705113639/can-we-overcome-racial-bias-biased-author-says-to-start-by-acknowledging-it

Cherry-Paul, S., & Johansen, D. (2019). *Breathing new life into book clubs: A practical guide for teachers.* Heinemann.

Cherry-Paul, S., & Ebarvia, T. (2023, March 29). Diversifying classroom texts. [Webinar]. Learning for Justice. https://www.learningforjustice.org/professional-development/webinars/diversifying-classroom-texts

Chen, G. (2022, May 21). Students of color disproportionately disciplined in schools. *Public School Review.* https://www.publicschoolreview.com/blog/students-of-color-disproportionately-disciplined-in-schools

Cherry-Paul, S. (2018, January 28). Teacher voice: It's time to shatter the silence about race. *Hechinger Report.* https://hechingerreport.org/teacher-voice-time-shatter-silence-race/

Chingos, M. (2015, December 10). *Affirmative action 'mismatch' theory isn't supported by credible evidence.* Urban Institute. https://www.urban.org/urban-wire/affirmative-action-mismatch-theory-isnt-supported-credible-evidence

Chung, N. (2018). *All you can ever know.* Catapult.

Cisneros, S. (1991). *The house on Mango Street.* Vintage.

Coleman, T. (2017, August 28). *Reading Jane Eyre while Black.* Literary Hub. Retrieved from https://lithub.com/reading-jane-eyre-while-black/

Corcione, A. (2018, August 2). How transgender people choose their names. *Teen Vogue.* https://www.teenvogue.com/story/how-transgender-people-choose-their-names

Crenshaw, K. (2018, June 22). *Kimberlé Crenshaw: What is intersectionality?* [Video]. National Association of Independent Schools. https://youtu.be/ViDtnfQ9FHc

Dahlen, S., & Hyuck, D. (2019). *Diversity in children's literature 2018.* [Image]. Cooperative Children's Book Center, School of Education, University of Wisconsin-Madison. https://readingspark.wordpress.com/2019/06/19/picture-this-diversity-in-childrens-books-2018-infographic/

Derman-Sparks, L., & Edwards, J. (2010, July 31). *Anti-bias education for young children and ourselves. 2nd edition.* National Association for the Education of Young Children.

Devine, P., Forscher, P., Austin, A., Cox, W. (2012, November). Long-term reduction in implicit bias: A prejudice breaking intervention. *Journal of Experimental Social Psychology.* 48(6), pp. 1267–1278. https://www.ncbi.nlm.nih.gov/pmc/articles/PMC3603687/pdf/nihms396358.pdf

Donny, L. et al. (Writer), & Shakman, M (Director). (2021, February 26). Previously On (Season 1, Episode 8). In K. Fiege, et al. (Executive Producer), *WandaVision.* Disney.

Eberhardt, J. (2019) *Biased: Uncovering the hidden prejudice that shapes what we see, think, and do.* Penguin Group.

Edlagan, C., & Vaghul, K. (2016, December 16). *How data disaggregation matters for Asian Americans and Pacific Islanders.* Washington Center for Equitable Growth. https://equitablegrowth.org/how-data-disaggregation-matters-for-asian-americans-and-pacific-islanders/

Everett, C. (2017, November 17). There is no diverse book. *Imagine Lit.* http://www.imaginelit.com/news/2017/11/21/there-is-no-diverse-book

Facing History and Ourselves. (2021, January 17). *Universe of Obligation.* https://www.facinghistory.org/resource-library/universe-obligation

Flecha, D. (2018, June 18). *Trauma-informed teaching practices: Personal narratives.* [Tweet] [Image attached]. https://twitter.com/DulceFlecha/status/1008884615409487873/photo/1

Flecha, D. *How teachers rob students of ownership over their writing.* https://medium.com/@dulcemarie.flecha/how-teachers-rob-students-of-ownership-over-their-writing-c0ad39802225

Gaither, S., Remedios, J., Sanchez, D., & Sommers, S. (2015). Thinking outside the box: Multiple mind-sets affect creative problem solving. *Social Psychological and Personality Science*, 1–8.

Gallagher, K. (2009). *Readicide: How schools are killing reading and what schools can do about Iit.* Stenhouse.

Garbes, A. (2022). *Essential labor: Mothering as social change.* Harper Collins.

Garcia, B., & Van Soest, D. (2003) *Social work practice for social justice: From cultural competence to anti-oppression.* Council on Social Education Press.

George, N. (2013, February 15). Still too good, too bad, or invisible. *New York Times.* https://www.nytimes.com/2013/02/17/movies/awardsseason/black-characters-are-still-too-good-too-bad-or-invisible.html

Germán, L. (2021). *Textured teaching: A framework for culturally sustaining practices.* Heinemann.

Gonzales, J. (2016, June 12). *The danger of teacher nostalgia.* Cult of Pedagogy. https://www.cultofpedagogy.com/teacher-nostalgia/.

Gorski, P., & Pothini, S. (2013). *Case studies on diversity and social justice.* Routledge.

Graff, G., & Birkenstein, C. (2021). *They say I say: Moves that matter in academic writing.* W. W. Norton.

Grim, R. (Host). (2023, February 3). Tema Okun on her Mythical Paper on White Supremacy. (Season 10, Episode 5). In *Deconstructed.* The Intercept. https://theintercept.com/2023/02/03/deconstructed-tema-okun-white-supremacy/.

Harro, B. (2018). The cycle of socialization. In M. Adams, W. J. Blumenfeld, D. C. J. Catalano, K. DeJong, H. W. Hackman, L. E. Hopkins, B. J. Love, M. L. Peters, D. Shlasko, & X. Zúñiga (Eds.), *Readings for Diversity and Social Justice.* (4th Ed., pp. 28). Routledge.

Harro, B. (2018). The cycle of liberation. In M. Adams, W. J. Blumenfeld, D. C. J. Catalano, K. DeJong, H. W. Hackman, L. E. Hopkins, B. J. Love, M. L. Peters, D. Shlasko, & X. Zúñiga (Eds.), *Readings for Diversity and Social Justice.* (4th Ed., pp. 629). Routledge.

Headlee, C. (2016, March 8). *10 Ways to have a better conversation.* TED Talks. [Video] https://www.youtube.com/watch?v=R1vskiVDwl4&ab_channel=TED

hooks, bell. (1989). Choosing the margin as a space of radical openness.

hooks, b. (1994). *Teaching to transgress: Education as the practice of freedom.* Routledge.

hooks, b. (2010). *Teaching critical thinking: Practical wisdom.* Routledge.

Hudson, B. (2023, February 15). *Flint is not fixed: Activists demand change years after water crisis started.* Fox 2 Detroit. https://www.fox2detroit.com/news/flint-is-not-fixed-activists-demand-change-years-after-water-crisis

Hune-Brown, N. (2015, January 22). The monstrous cruelty of a just world. *Hazlitt.* https://hazlitt.net/blog/monstrous-cruelty-just-world

Institute for Democratic Renewal and Project Change Anti-Racism Initiative. (2000). *Project change's: 'The power of words' A community builder's dictionary.* [Appendix]. p. 32. https://

drive.google.com/file/d/1mM2ATbM9aUwBRFxuk7O1hgIjzYYV5IKl/view

Johnson, A. (2020, February 20). *Inference, empathy, and erasure, or overthinking?* Kinderbender. https://kinderbender.com/2020/02/20/inference-empathy-erasure-or-overthinking/

Johnson, A. (2018, July/August). Teaching in the gap: improving academic achievement by centering our students. *Literacy Today*, *36*(1), pp. 19–20.

Jones, S. (2020). Ending curriculum violence. *Learning for Justice*. [Issue 24]. https://www.learningforjustice.org/magazine/spring-2020/ending-curriculum-violence

Kahneman, D. (2013). *Thinking, fast and slow.* New York, NY: Farrar, Straus and Giroux.

Kendi, I. X. (2019). *How to be an antiracist.* One World.

Kent, L. (2015, August 5). *5 facts about America's students.* Pew Research Center. http://www.pewresearch.org/fact-tank/2015/08/10/5-facts-about-americas-students/

King, M. https://kinginstitute.stanford.edu/king-papers/documents/i-have-dream-address-delivered-march-washington-jobs-and-freedom

Learning for Justice. (2014–2022). *Social justice standards: The learning for justice anti-bias framework.* (2nd Ed.) Southern Poverty Law Center. https://www.learningforjustice.org/sites/default/files/2022-09/LFJ-Social-Justice-Standards-September-2022-09292022.pdf

Lempert, R. (2016, June 12). Mismatch and science desistance: Failed arguments against affirmative action. *UCLA Law Review.* https://www.uclalawreview.org/mismatch-science-desistance-failed-arguments-affirmative-action/

Li, W., & Lartey, J. (2023, March 25). *New FBI data shows more hate crimes. These groups saw the sharpest rise.* Marshall Project. https://www.themarshallproject.org/2023/03/25/asian-hate-crime-fbi-black-lgbtq.

Lifshitz, J. (2017, November 20). *Storytellers presentations from NCTE.* https://crawlingoutoftheclassroom.wordpress.com/2017/11/20/storytellers-presentations-from-ncte/

Lifshitz, J. [@jess5th]. (2020a, January 31). *This is the revised KWL we will use in order to help us determine potential misinformation, misconceptions, and biases.* [Tweet]. Twitter.

https://twitter.com/Jess5th/status/1223366278980808704

Lifshitz, J. [@jess5th]. (2020b, February 11). *And second of all, the language we use becomes a habit. And we owe it to our students to use the most inclusive language possible.* [Tweet]. https://twitter.com/Jess5th/status/1227388157915783169?s=20

Lin, J. N. (2020, May 5). Does my child's name erase my identity? *New York Times.* https://www.nytimes.com/2020/05/05/parenting/baby-name-family-history.html

Love, B. J. (2018). Developing a liberatory consciousness. In M. Adams, W. J. Blumenfeld, D. C. J. Catalano, K. DeJong, H. W. Hackman, L. E. Hopkins, B. J. Love, M. L. Peters, D. Shlasko, & X. Zúñiga. (Eds.) *Readings for Diversity and Social Justice.* (4th ed.) Routledge.

Lyiscott, J. (2017, May 19). *If you think you're giving students of color a voice, get over yourself.* Heinemann Publishing. Medium. https://medium.com/@heinemann/if-you-think-youre-giving-students-of-color-a-voice-get-over-yourself-cc8a4a684f16

Matthews, S., & Chan, S. (Hosts). (2018, April 25). The unexamined privilege of Gilmore Girls. [Audio podcast episode]. In *Represent.* Slate. https://slate.com/culture/2018/04/gilmore-girls-and-rory-gilmore-reevaluated-as-role-models-to-teenage-girls.html

Meeghan, K., & Friedman, J. (2023, April). *Banned in the USA: State laws supercharge book suppression in schools.* PEN America. https://pen.org/report/banned-in-the-usa-state-laws-supercharge-book-suppression-in-schools/

Miller, C. (2016, September 20). Literary theory's potential in secondary ELA classrooms. *NCTE.* https://ncte.org/blog/2016/09/literary-theorys-potential-secondary-ela-classrooms/

Mills, A. (2019, February 12). What do you mean when you say 'those kids don't want to learn'? *Better Lesson.* https://blog.better-lesson.com/what-do-you-mean-when-you-say-those-kids-dont-want-to-learn

Moll, L., Amanti, C., & Gonzales, N. (2006). *Funds of knowledge: Theorizing practices in households, communities, and classrooms.* Taylor and Francis.

Muhammad, G. (2019). *Cultivating genius.* Scholastic.

Murray, Don. (1991, August 27). The stranger in the photo is me. *Boston Globe.*

Murthy, V. H. (2023, April 30). Surgeon general: We have become a lonely nation. It's time to fix that. *The New York Times.* https://www.nytimes.com/2023/04/30/opinion/loneliness-epidemic-america.html

Nguyen, T. A. (2018, February 18). The things they made me carry: Inheriting a white curriculum. *Teaching While White.* https://teachingwhilewhite.org/blog/2018/2/1/the-things-they-made-me-carry-inheriting-a-white-curriculum

Nguyen, V. T. (2018, August 21). Asian-Americans need more movies, even mediocre ones. *New York Times.* https://www.nytimes.com/2018/08/21/opinion/crazy-rich-asians-movie.html.

Okun, T. (2021a). *White supremacy culture characteristics.* White Supremacy Culture. https://www.whitesupremacyculture.info/characteristics.html

Okun, T. (2021b). *White supremacy culture—still here.* White Supremacy Culture. https://drive.google.com/file/d/1XR_7M_9qa64zZ00_JyFVTAjmjVU-uSz8/view

Oluo, I. (2018). *So you want to talk about race?* Seal Press.

OWP/P Architects, VS Furniture, and Bruce Mau Design. (2010). *The third teacher: 79 ways you can use design to transform teaching & learning.* Abrams.

Palmer, P. (1997). *The courage to teach.* John Wiley and Sons.

Paris, D. (2012, April). Culturally sustaining pedagogy: A needed change in stance, terminology, and practice. *Educational Researcher, 41*(93), 93–97.

Parker, K. (2018, August 3). *An open letter to Black parents whose suns have been pushed out of preschool.* https://singlemomsofar.wordpress.com/2018/08/03/an-open-letter-to-black-parents-whose-suns-have-been-pushed-out-of-preschool/

Parogni, I. (2021, July 16). What matters in a name sign? *New York Times.* https://www.nytimes.com/interactive/2021/07/16/arts/kamala-harris-name-sign-language.html

Pierpoint, M. (2018, September 18). Was Frank Baum a racist or just the creator of Oz? *Indian Country Today.* https://ictnews.org/archive/was-frank-baum-a-racist-or-just-the-creator-of-oz

Pinkser, J. (2018, August 23). The problem with 'Hey Guys.' *The Atlantic.* https://www.theatlantic.com/family/archive/2018/08/guys-gender-neutral/568231/

Pitts, J. (2021). Don't say nothing. *Teaching When the World is on Fire.* (L. Delpit, Ed.) The New Press.

Randall, A. (2017, October 19). *Why are we still teaching* To Kill a Mockingbird *in school?* NBC News. https://www.nbcnews.com/think/opinion/why-are-we-still-teaching-kill-mockingbird-schools-ncna812281

Reese, D. (2018a, July). Critical indigenous literacies: Selecting and using children's books about indigenous peoples. *Language Arts, 95*(6), 389–393.

Reese, D. (2018b, September 24). A critical look at O'Dell's *Island of the Blue Dolphins. American Indians in Children's Literature.* https://americanindiansinchildrensliterature.blogspot.com/2016/06/a-critical-look-at-odells-island-of.html

Reese, D. [@debreese]. (2022, October 13). *Yesterday (Oct 12) on Facebook, author Kate DiCamillo wrote nostalgically of her teacher reading to her. Reading aloud is great, but.* [Image attached] [Tweet]. Twitter. https://twitter.com/debreese/status/1580687664658817024?s=20

Ribay, R. (2019, November 25). *Critical lit theory as preparation for the world.* [Speech]. 2019 ALAN Workshop Speech. Baltimore, MD. https://randyribay.wordpress.com/2019/11/26/critical-lit-theory-as-preparation-for-the-world-2019-alan-workshop-speech/

Riser-Kositsky, M. (2023, January 17). Education statistics: Facts about American schools. *Education Week.* https://www.edweek.org/leadership/education-statistics-facts-about-american-schools/2019/01

Roozen, K. (2016) Writing is linked to identity. In L. Adler-Kasner & E. Wardle (Eds.) *Naming what we know: Threshold concepts in writing* (pp. 50–51). University of Colorado Press.

Rosen, J. (2016, March 30). *Teacher expectations reflect racial biases, Johns Hopkins study suggests.* Johns Hopkins University. https://hub.jhu.edu/2016/03/30/racial-bias-teacher-expectations-black-white/

Rosenblatt, L. (1995, January 30). *Literature as exploration.* Modern Language Association.

Rowlands, C. L. (2021, September 28). *'Names have power': A reading list on names, identity, and the immigrant experience.* Longreads. https://longreads.com/2021/09/28/reading-list-names-identity-immigrant-refugee-writing/

Roy, A. (2004, November 3). *Peace & the new corporate liberation theology.* [Speech transcript]. 2004 City of Sydney Peace Prize Lecture. https://sydneypeacefoundation.org.au/wp-content/uploads/2012/02/2004-SPP_-Arundhati-Roy.pdf

Rudd, T. (2014, February). *Racial disproportionality in school discipline: Implicit bias is heavily implicated.* Kirwin Institute Issue Brief. The Ohio State University. http://kirwaninstitute.osu.edu/wp-content/uploads/2014/02/racial-disproportionality-schools-02.pdf

Salesses, M. (2021). *Craft in the real world: Rethinking fiction writing and workshopping.* Penguin Random House.

Sealey-Ruiz, Y. (2020). *The racial literacy development model.* Arch of Self. https://www.yolandasealeyruiz.com/archaeology-of-self

Sealey-Ruiz, Y. (2021, April). *Racial literacy: A policy research brief.* James R. Squire Office of the National Council of Teachers of English. https://ncte.org/wp-content/uploads/2021/04/SquireOfficePolicyBrief_RacialLiteracy_April2021.pdf

Sensoy, Ö., & DiAngelo, R. (2017). *Is everyone really equal? Introduction to social justice concepts.* Teachers College Press.

Shalaby, C. (2017). *Troublemakers: Lessons in freedom from young children in school.* New York, NY: The New Press.

Silvas, T. (2017, August 2). Fostering empathy and understanding among students. *Heinemann.* https://blog.heinemann.com/heinemann-fellow-tiana-silvas-on-fostering-empathy-and-understanding-among-students

Silvas, T. (2018, May 1). Releasing the mind of childhood trauma through writing. *International Literacy Association.* https://www.literacyworldwide.org/blog/literacy-daily/2018/05/01/releasing-childhood-trauma-through-writing

Singleton, G. (2014). *Courageous conversations about race.* [2nd Ed.]Corwin.

Smith, Clint. (2020). How culturally responsive lessons teach critical thinking. *Teaching Tolerance Magazine.*https://www.tolerance.org/magazine/spring-2020/how-culturally-responsive-lessons-teach-critical-thinking

Smith, G. (2019, March 4). *It's time to talk about Dr. Seuss.* Learning for Justice. https://www.learningforjustice.org/magazine/its-time-to-talk-about-dr-seuss

Snider, G. (2016, November 14). Choose your own memoir. *New York Times.* https://www.nytimes.com/interactive/2016/11/14/books/review/20snider.html

Snider, G. (2019, September 18). *Running.* Incidental Comics. http://www.incidental-comics.com/2018/09/running.html

Solnit, R. (2013, December 22). *The arc of justice and the long run: Hope, history, and unpredictability.* Tom Dispatch. https://tomdispatch.com/rebecca-solnit-the-future-needs-us/

Soni, P. (Hosts). (2018, May 9). Friends from India. [Audio podcast episode]. In *Represent.* Slate. https://slate.com/culture/2018/05/friends-overwhelming-popularity-in-india-makes-me-worry-about-the-shows-gender-stereotypes.html

Steele, C., & Aronson, J. (1995). Stereotype threat and the intellectual test performance of African Americans. *Journal of Personality and Social Psychology, 69*(5), 797–811.

Stevenson, B. (2014). *Just mercy: A story of justice and redemption.* One World Books.

Stewart, N. (2019, August 19). We are committing educational malpractice: Why slavery is mistaught—and worse—in American schools. *New York Times.* https://www.nytimes.com/interactive/2019/08/19/magazine/slavery-american-schools.html

Sue, D. W. (2016, February 1). *Race talk and the conspiracy of silence: Understanding and facilitating difficult dialogues on race.* Wiley.

Talusan, L. (2022). *The identity-conscious educator: Building habits and skills for a more inclusive school.* Solution Tree.

Tan, J. (2023, June 27). What Chinese calligraphy taught me about myself. *New York Times.* https://www.nytimes.com/2023/06/27/magazine/learn-chinese-calligraphy.html

Tatum, B. D. (2000). The complexity of identity: "Who am I?" In M. Adams, W. J. Blumenfeld, D. C. J. Catalano, K. DeJong, H. W. Hackman, L. E. Hopkins, B. J. Love, M. L. Peters, D. Shlasko, & X. Zúñiga. (Eds.) *Readings for Diversity and Social Justice.* (4th ed., pp. 9–14). Routledge.

Taylor, K. (2017). *How we get free: Black women and the Combahee River Collective.* Haymarket Books.

Thomas, E. (2019). *The dark fantastic.* New York University Press.

Torres, J. (2018, April 14). Literary Canon–Boom! *Julia E. Torres.* https://juliaetorres.blog/2018/04/14/literary-canon-boom/.

Truer, D. (2013). *Rez life: An Indian's journey through reservation life.* Atlantic Monthly Press.

Turetsky, K., & Purdie-Vaughns, V. (2015, December 17). What science has to say about affirmative action. *Scientific American.* https://www.scientificamerican.com/article/what-science-has-to-say-about-affirmative-action/

U.S. Department of Education Office for Civil Rights. (2014, March). *Civil rights data collection: School snapshot (school discipline).* https://ocrdata.ed.gov/downloads/crdc-school-discipline-snapshot.pdf.

Valentine, G. (2018, January 3). P.C. languages saved my life. *New York Times.* https://www.nytimes.com/2018/01/03/opinion/language-pronouns-gender-zer.html.

Van Soest, D., & Garcia, B. (2003). *Diversity education for social justice: Mastering teaching skills.* Alexandria, Va.: Council on Social Work Education.

Vanderwerf, S. (2016, August 7). Building relationships with name tents. *Sara VanDerWerf.* https://saravanderwerf.com/2016/08/07/week-1-day-1-name-tents-with-feedback/

Vedantam, S. (2010, January 25). *How the hidden brain does our thinking for us.* [Podcast]. NPR. https://www.npr.org/templates/story/story.php?storyId=122864641

Vedantam, S. (2013, April 22). *What does modern prejudice look like?* Hidden Brain. [Podcast] NPR. https://www.npr.org/sections/codeswitch/2013/04/22/177455764/What-Does-Modern-Prejudice-Look-Like

Venet. A. (2021, May 25). *How unconditional positive regard can help students feel cared for.* KQED. https://www.kqed.org/mindshift/57646/how-unconditional-positive-regard-can-help-students-feel-cared-for

Velasquez-Manoff, M. (2017, March 4). What biracial people know. *New York Times.* https://www.nytimes.com/2017/03/04/opinion/sunday/what-biracial-people-know.html

Villanueva, V. (2016) Writing provides a representation of ideologies and identities. In L. Adler-Kasner & E. Wardle. (Eds.) *Naming what we know: Threshold concepts in writing* (pp. 57–58). University of Colorado Press.

Wheatley, M. (2009). *Turning to one another: Simple conversations to restore hope in the future.* Berrett-Koehler Publishers.

White, S. (2018, June 2). Lessons in social justice. *Medium.* https://medium.com/identity-education-and-power/lessons-in-social-justice-9add44ece4ed

Winfrey, O. (2011, October 20). *The powerful lesson Maya Angelou taught Oprah.* OWN. [Video] https://youtu.be/fx447ShQLeE

Wolfe-Rocca, U. (2018, August 5). Dangerous discussions: Voice and power in my classroom. *Medium.* https://medium.com/@ursulawolfe/dangerous-discussions-voice-and-power-in-my-classroom-8e31ca2fafef

INDEX

Because...
ALL TEACHERS ARE LEADERS

AFRIKA AFENI MILLS

This guide explores why racial identity work is crucial, especially for White-identifying students and teachers, and guides educators to provide opportunities for antiracist learning.

ALLISON SKERRETT, PETER SMAGORINSKY

Engage students in critical thinking, literacy activities, and inquiry using the personal and social issues of pressing importance to today's students.

MARIA WALTHER

This resource offers a scaffolding for moving from teacher-led demonstration of read alouds to student-led discovery of literacy skills—across the bridge of shared reading.

VERA AHIYYA

Spark courageous conversations with children about race, identity, and social justice using read alouds as an entry point.

To order your copies, visit corwin.com/literacy

At Corwin Literacy we have put together a collection of just-in-time, classroom-tested, practical resources from trusted experts that allow you to quickly find the information you need when you need it.

DOUGLAS FISHER, NANCY FREY, DIANE LAPP

Like an animated encyclopedia, this book delivers the latest evidence-based practices in 13 interactive modules that will transform your instruction and reenergize your career.

JUSTIN M. STYGLES

Learn how to build relationships so shame-bound readers trust enough to risk enough to grow.

GRETCHEN BERNABEI, JAYNE HOVER

Use these lessons and concrete text structures designed to help students write self-generated commentary in response to reading.

CHRISTINA NOSEK, MELANIE MEEHAN, MATTHEW JOHNSON, MATTHEW R. KAY, DAVE STUART JR.

This series offers actionable answers to your most pressing questions about teaching reading, writing, and ELA.

Helping educators make the greatest impact

CORWIN HAS ONE MISSION: to enhance education through intentional professional learning.

We build long-term relationships with our authors, educators, clients, and associations who partner with us to develop and continuously improve the best evidence-based practices that establish and support lifelong learning.